HEROES
of the
BOB MARSHALL
WILDERNESS

JOHN FRALEY

FARCOUNTRY
PRESS

ISBN: 978-1-56037-774-0

Cover photograph: Horse and rider at Big Salmon Lake, by K. D. Swan, U.S. Forest Service. Back cover photograph: Colyne Hislop and trail crew, by Michael Reavis.

For more information about our books, write Farcountry Press, P.O. Box 5630, Helena, MT 59604; call (800) 821-3874; or visit www.farcountrypress.com.

 Produced and printed in the United States of America.

Library of Congress Cataloging-in-Publication Data

Names: Fraley, John, author.
Title: Heroes of the Bob Marshall Wilderness / by John Fraley.
Description: Helena, MT : Farcountry Press, [2020] | Includes index. |
    Summary: "Follow author John Fraley as he traces the lives and times of
    past and present heroes of the Bob Marshall Wilderness, from old-timers
    like Joe Murphy, to Smoke Elser, and on to the present. Over the past
    century, these heroes have ridden, packed, and hiked from one end of the
    Bob to the other, and they've helped make the wilderness what it is
    today. You'll ride along on horse and mule treks and wrecks, and
    discover the sport of trout wrangling. You'll meet the fluorescent
    hunter, White River Sue, and the black-clad backpacker. You'll battle
    packrats, fish-eating deer, tricky bears, and a tree-hugging criminal.
    Sit back and read about a dog rescue, smokejumper adventures, kids
    raised in the wilderness, and the first study of grizzlies in the Bob.
    Witness a tense moose-lassoing rodeo, and meet a backcountry rooster
    named Bob Marshall, the first live chicken to attempt a traverse of the
    Bob. The heroes in this book have ridden and hiked hundreds of thousands
    of miles through the Bob Marshall Wilderness Complex. Now, come along
    with them and celebrate their contributions, their challenges, and their
    fun times"-- Provided by publisher.
Identifiers: LCCN 2020030928 | ISBN 9781560377740 (paperback)
Subjects: LCSH: Bob Marshall Wilderness (Mont.)--Biography. | Bob Marshall
    Wilderness (Mont.)--History.
Classification: LCC F737.B66 F73 2020 | DDC 978.6/5--dc23
LC record available at https://lccn.loc.gov/2020030928

23 22 21 20   1 2 3 4 5

CONTENTS

THE WILDLANDS THAT BECAME THE BOB MARSHALL WILDERNESS COMPLEX

THE STORIES IN THIS BOOK take place within a vast, mountainous, roadless area along the Continental Divide in Montana known today as the Bob Marshall Wilderness Complex, or, affectionately, the Bob. The complex spans terrain administered by the Flathead, Helena, Lewis and Clark, and Lolo National Forests. In the 1930s, before they became the Bob, these wildlands were protected as the South Fork, Sun River, and Pentagon Primitive Areas, managed by the U.S. Forest Service to protect and preserve their watersheds and also their "undisturbed naturalness" for wildlife habitat, recreational use, and their "primitive allure."

In 1940, visionaries within the agency recommended that the three primitive areas, totaling 950,000 acres, be designated as the Bob Marshall Wilderness to continue the legacy of preservation, and to honor the passionate wilderness advocate, Robert "Bob" Marshall, who had passed away just the previous year at only thirty-eight years of age.

Under the Wilderness Act of 1964, the Bob gained formal wilderness designation for just over 1 million acres. The 240,000-acre Scapegoat Wilderness, adjoining the Bob's southern boundary, was designated in 1972, and the 287,000-acre Great Bear Wilderness, on the Bob's northern boundary, was added in 1978. Together the three areas total more than 1.5 million acres.

To avoid confusion over the various administrative and historical names, the stories in this book often refer to "the Bob," even when the events described occurred before this wilderness bore Bob Marshall's name.

John Fraley is a rare breed: a scientific student of the natural world and an author who takes in human stories. The living story of the Bob Marshall Wilderness is still unfolding and could not be in better hands. Three cheers for *Heroes of the Bob*.

—Ben Long, founding editor of *Backcountry Journal*

A place as big and as wild as the Bob Marshall Wilderness Complex is going to test people, and some folks ace that test and go on to become true heroes. John Fraley has captured the texture of this special place while revealing the heart of those that spend their time among the peaks and the prairies. Each page captures an experience that will call you to throw a pack over your shoulder and go live your wildest dream.

—Bill Hodge, executive director, the Bob Marshall
Wilderness Foundation

The Bob Marshall Wilderness Complex is the best of all the best places to experience and celebrate wilderness. I hope this book inspires readers to learn more about wilderness and to visit in person and make their own adventures. Enjoy these stories and then get out and create your own!

—Deb Mucklow Starling, Spotted Bear District
Ranger 1999–2017

Reading this fine book and collecting my thoughts for this review made me realize that another "Hero of the Bob Marshall Wilderness" also needs recognition. John Fraley and his books have given us a chance to experience life in the Bob no matter where we are. His chronicles preserve the histories for all time. Well done John.

—Bill Moore (Bud's son)

ACKNOWLEDGMENTS

MANY PEOPLE PASSED ALONG GUIDANCE and inspiration over the past year as I wrote *Heroes of the Bob*. Dozens of people graciously gave their time to locate information and participate in interviews.

Descendants of old-time outfitter Joe Murphy met with me many times and provided a trove of information. Through their efforts, we brought life to Joe's incredible story in the Bob. Joe's grandsons, Dennis and Ted Murphy, his granddaughter, Colleen, and his daughter Janie graciously shared their recollections, information, and photos. I visited with Janie a number of times, and I will always treasure her descriptions and fun stories about trips with her father and her brothers, the Murphy Boys. As a backcountry cook for Joe, she was a hero too. Dennis was my major communication link with the Murphy family; he shed light on details and photos dozens of times. I am so thankful that the Murphys had the foresight to preserve Joe's legacy so we can bring it forward in this book. After more than a century of outfitting, the Murphy outfit lived on through Ted's business, WTR Outfitters. Tragically, Ted passed away suddenly after he arrived back in Ovando after a long wilderness pack trip in 2019.

I'm indebted to all the heroes who shared their stories for the book: George Ostrom, Bill and Gail Workman, Greg and Deborah Schatz, the late Pat McVay, Fred Flint, George Anderson, the late Bud Moore, Colyne Hislop, Guy and Keagan Zoellner, and Smoke and Thelma Elser. Their family members also shared memories. Many of these folks and their families provided photos from their collections, and they are noted in photo credits throughout the book.

Visits with wilderness icon Smoke Elser around the woodstove in his historic barn added much to the book. Thanks Smoke.

Author and biologist Jim Williams continually encouraged me and passed along important information on some of the chapters. Dr. Harold Picton, Wildlife Professor Emeritus at Montana State University, originally transcribed biologist Bob Cooney's lost journals from the first study of grizzly bears in the Bob. Using these journals, I was able to bring this early study alive and transcribe Cooney's early wilderness travels onto the landscape. Dr. James Habeck, Plant Physiology Professor Emeritus at the University of Montana, passed along information on early plant studies in the Bob. I am proud to say that in the 1970s, Dr. Picton was my wildlife professor and Dr. Habeck was my botany professor.

Retired U.S. Forest Service ranger Dave Owen has been a keystone link between old times and new in the Bob. Thanks, Dave. Many other current and retired U.S. Forest Service folks contributed to this project as well.

Bud Moore served as a major mentor for me for decades, so I was honored to bring just a little corner of his wilderness adventures and contributions to life. I'm looking forward to writing much more. Bud's son, Bill, has given me helpful suggestions and support. Helen Dollan provided encouragement as always. Helen shared memories and photos from the Jack and Helen Dollan Collection.

Pat McVay, an important mentor for thirty years, turned 100 years of age on March 14, 2020. His memories of his trips through the Bob were as sharp as the day he experienced them. Pat lived a long life, a fair portion of it in the Bob. A member of the Montana Outdoor Hall of Fame, Pat passed away on May 18, 2020, at 100 years, two months, and five days. His story in this book, "Chapter 7: Pat McVay's Bob Marshall Secret," documents a long and eventful pack trip through the Bob with friends. We feel grateful that his story is documented, because as he noted, "I never wrote any of it down, I just kept it in my heart."

Northwest Montana History Museum director Jacob Thomas arranged for some of the photos for the George Ostrom chapter. Michael Reavis and Heather Fraley provided photographs for the book. U.S. Forest Service assistant fire management officer Mike West located historical data on the Helen Creek Fire of 1953 and the White River Fire of 1919 within the Bob. Bill Moore provided guidance on the Bud Moore chapter, and Lee Anderson did the same on the Backcountry Law chapter.

Finally, I'd like to thank my family for their support. My wife Dana, daughter Heather, and sons Kevin and Troy came along on many forays into the Bob over the years to gather inspiration and information. They've helped me now though four backcountry adventure books, and I am forever grateful.

FOREWORD

THE WILDERNESS IDEA WAS BIG. It was revolutionary for its time, and was driven by a small handful of heroes. One hero stands in the middle of that circle, and his name was Bob Marshall. Driven by his personal euphoria felt in wild places, fueled by his belief that protected public lands were the perfect manifestation of democracy, and almost singular in his focus, Bob led and funded the start of the movement. A protagonist for change within the federal government, and a financier outside those walls, he is why the wilderness idea became the National Wilderness Preservation System, even if he didn't live to see it.

Bob was legendary, and yet, as some have said, might be one of the greatest Americans that the majority of our country do not know. His impact within the Forest Service was so dramatic that in the year following his death, the Bob Marshall Wilderness would be established administratively by the agency (1940). The place, now referred to as the Bob Marshall Wilderness Complex (or simply the Bob), is as big as its namesake.

The present-day 112-million-acre National Wilderness Preservation System stands on the shoulders of people like Bob Marshall and sits on a foundation of incredible places like the Bob Marshall Wilderness Complex. Ideas like the wilderness concept, and places as big as the Bob, forge the next generation of heroes, and in the following chapters John Fraley beautifully captures the characters that have helped give the Bob its rightful place in American history.

The future of the Bob, and the future of wilderness, will rely on a new generation of heroes. It will be those not just committed to the idea of leaving places wild, but equally committed to the stewardship of the wilderness. It will be a collection of passionate people who reflect the full spectrum of the American experience. It will be a connection formed with muscle, curiosity, and passion. There will be new hurdles to overcome, and new stories forged by time spent deep in the rugged mountains. These new heroes may walk to a different rhythm from those in our history, but they will share a common bond that dates back to a time before an American nation and the western concept of preservation. We are, after all, standing on the home of the Salish-Kootenai and Blackfeet people when we travel through the Bob.

At the Bob Marshall Wilderness Foundation, we are providing the space for these new heroes to find their way and their connection. We have also had the amazing opportunity to work alongside many of the heroes in these pages. Quite simply, our history of stewardship begins with many of those profiled here and will be lived by those who create their own stories of the Bob.

A place as big and rugged as the Bob reveals character and produces characters—larger-than-life examples of folks who thrive beyond the edges of our communities. In the pages of Heroes of the Bob you will find stories of place and stories of people, and that combination has always been the story of wilderness in America.

—Bill Hodge, executive director,
the Bob Marshall Wilderness Foundation

Heroes

WE WILL PROBABLY NEVER KNOW if wilderness pioneer Bob Marshall met old-time outfitter Joe Murphy, but I'd like to think he did. Among the heroes of the Bob Marshall Wilderness, those two men rank at or near the top of the list. They came from different worlds, but both of them shared the love and inspiration of wilderness.

When Bob was fast-trekking his way up the South Fork of the Flathead River trail on August 31, 1928, he passed right through Murphy Flat, a series of extensive, level meadows scattered with stately ponderosa pines. A decade earlier, Big Prairie ranger Ray Trueman had granted Joe a special-use permit that allowed him to build a "lodge," complete with a fireplace, corrals, and other rustic structures in the center of the wilderness at the mouth of the White River. This visionary young man had great backcountry taste: he chose the best spot and went all in on it. Every year, Joe spent all summer and fall at his camp in the Bob, squiring fishing, hunting, and sightseeing trips around the Bob Marshall, sometimes using 100 stock to accommodate twenty or more guests. Over the decades, Joe, and then his three sons, introduced thousands of people to the wild country that became known as the Bob.

Bob Marshall held a master's degree in forestry from Harvard and worked at the U.S. Forest Service's Intermountain Forest Experiment Station in Missoula. He had just published a seminal paper on the value of wilderness in the agency's national bulletin. He was intensely

Joe Murphy packing in the Bob circa 1930.

PHOTOGRAPH COURTESY OF THE MURPHY FAMILY.

observant, and he aimed to know everything about the old-timers and management of this flagship swath of undesignated wilderness. Little did he know that, after his untimely death just eleven years later, this wilderness would be officially protected and bear his name.

Bob made extensive notes on each day of his 182-mile, five-day dash through the wilderness. It seems that Joe's camp would have been hard for him to miss. Was Joe there, and did they exchange greetings? In his journal, Bob didn't mention meeting him, so it's hard to say.

Across from Murphy Flat, the waters of the enigmatic White River flow over a fluvial fan of limestone rocks and into the South Fork. It seems that everyone who spends much time in the central Bob Marshall winds up at some point in the White River drainage. The White River is like a Bob Marshall vortex, and like a whirlpool, it sucks people in.

When I first saw the White River nearly a half century ago, I was captivated. Its waters are clear but look chalky at first because they flow through the shallows over the whitest bed of limestone rocks you'll ever see. The river doesn't look particularly "fishy," but boy is it. Good-sized westslope cutthroat trout stack into any area of the river that offers fish cover in the form of depth or woody debris or undercut banks. And what cutthroat they are—like chameleons, these native fish take on the pale coloration of the river and its cobbles. As a fisheries student, and then as a biologist, when I snorkeled the clear waters, I saw firsthand how many cutts and bull trout this modest-sized stream holds. For anyone interested in native fish in a remote and beautiful setting, this is the place. Joe Murphy couldn't have chosen a better spot for his home camp.

The White River is famed because it drains one of the most remote areas in the country, and it wraps around the west side of the Bob's most famous feature, the Chinese Wall. On August 30 during his 1928 trip, Bob crossed around Pagoda Mountain in the spectacular alpine zone, down through Brushy Park, and into the White River headwaters. He joyfully jogged to Salt Mountain on the Chinese Wall, then retraced his steps back to Black Bear Guard Station for a day hike of forty-two miles. The twenty-seven-year-old wilderness champion was covering ground and dunking headlong into the wilderness.

Bob Marshall in 1928, the year he dashed through the wilderness that would later bear his name.

PHOTOGRAPH COURTESY OF ARCHIVES AND SPECIAL COLLECTIONS, MANSFIELD LIBRARY, UNIVERSITY OF MONTANA.

When Bob walked past Joe's camp on the way to Big Prairie the next day, he felt the joy of a hot late summer day and the clear, chilling waters in an area he was beginning to love. He called his love of the wilderness "pure aesthetic rapture." At every ranger station and with every traveler he met, he gushed praise for wilderness; he was on a mission and acted as a wilderness evangelist. Bob reached the White River across from Joe's camp at 4:40 P.M. on that beautiful last day of August. The White River inspired Bob, and he snapped a photo of the scene. Two hours and twenty minutes later he reached Big Prairie.

Earlier that day, Bob passed Black Bear, Big Salmon Lake, and Salmon Forks on his way upriver. He was heading for a rendezvous with Big Prairie ranger Henry Thol, who had been in the South Fork almost as long as Joe Murphy and knew Joe well. Henry, maybe the best ranger ever, was a true Bob hero.

According to his journal, Bob, a student of backcountry history, talked with Henry over the next two nights while he stayed at Big Prairie Ranger Station. It's almost certain that Henry talked with Bob about Joe and explained Joe's special permit for the Murphy Flat structures in the middle of the wilderness. Henry might have told Bob about his near-fatal winter patrol the winter before, when Joe Murphy's remote cabin saved his life and the Black Bear ranger's life in forty-below temperatures and deep snow (for that story, see *Rangers, Trappers, and Trailblazers*, by John Fraley, Farcountry Press, 2018).

The Bob is a big place, but it's been populated, really, by only a small group of people over the years. And the farther back in time you go, the fewer people you find. The heroes who made the Bob what it is have formed a continuous line, from old-timers like Joe Murphy and Chick Grimsley, Joe's sons (the Murphy Boys), Tom Edwards, Howard Copenhaver, Toad Paulin, CB and Jack Rich, and Smoke Elser, right up to Gene Brash, Ray Mills, Bill Workman, and many others. These outfitters and packers devoted many years of their lives within the Bob Marshall and made it possible for countless people to enjoy, support, and treasure the wilderness. A long line of U.S. Forest Service rangers also served in the wilderness, from Tom Danaher to Henry Thol, Dave Owen, Jack Dollan, Gordon Ash, and Deb Mucklow, to Guy Zoellner and many more. All of these folks eschewed the comforts of civilization to spend much of their lives serving in the Bob. Now a younger generation of wilderness workers and outfitters are taking the reins. The heroes in these pages have carried Bob's torch and spirit in good times and in bad.

The White River near its mouth, across from Murphy Flat.
PHOTOGRAPH BY JOHN FRALEY.

Of course, I couldn't possibly feature every wilderness hero in a single book. I've unavoidably omitted many worthy people. Perhaps I'll tell their stories in another book. (Some heroes of the Bob made it into my previous book, *Rangers, Trappers, and Trailblazers*.)

In *Heroes of the Bob Marshall Wilderness*, I present a series of stories that capture the great times (and some not so great times) these heroes experienced in the Bob over the past century. I've dug deep, and it has been an absolute honor to preserve these stories for this gem of wilderness that I've spent so much time in and love so much. You will read about horse and mule wrecks, trout wrangling, the fluorescent hunter, White River Sue, the black-clad backpacker, battles with packrats, fish-eating deer, tricky bears, a tree-hugging criminal, a dog rescue, smokejumper tales, kids raised in the wilderness, the first study of grizzly bears in the Bob, moose lassoing, and a backcountry rooster named Bob Marshall.

The heroes in this book have ridden and hiked hundreds of thousands of miles through the Bob. Now, come along on their treks and celebrate their contributions, their challenges, and their fun times.

SOURCES

Marshall, Bob. "Wilderness as a Minority Right." *Forest Bulletin* (U.S. Forest Service national newsletter), August 27, 1928.

Marshall, Bob. "The Problem with the Wilderness." *Scientific Monthly* 30, no. 2 (February 1930): 141–48.

Bob Marshall journals, 1928, 30 pages. Bancroft Library, accessed via the pdf of the journals on file at Montana Fish, Wildlife & Parks, Kalispell, MT.

Joe Murphy papers collection, courtesy of Dennis and Ted Murphy and the Murphy family, Missoula, Kalispell, and Ovando, MT.

Wilderness Cowboy

A century ago, Ovando's Joe Murphy
pioneered big pack trips into the Bob.

A WILDERNESS PACKING OUTFIT earns its customers one at a time, through reputation, quality, and results. Joe Murphy, operating out of Ovando, was nationally known as a packer in the upper South Fork who treated guests to stirring backcountry adventures that reflected the Old West.

It seems that every dude who joined a Joe Murphy pack trip was profoundly affected. After a few weeks of unmatched fishing and sightseeing in the Bob country a century ago, one important guest summed up their last night in the wilderness: "It was a beautiful moonlit night," he wrote. "Up and down the valleys, the howl of the coyote echoed and re-echoed until sometimes it seemed almost continuous. It was the kind of night and the kind of setting to get into a man's blood . . ."

Back in the day, Joe's trips began at the Murphy Ranch, a perfect jumping-off point to the Bob country from the south. The ranch lay only a mile from Ovando, a tiny town with a population of "39 nice people." For clients arriving from out of state by rail, the ranch was only fifty-seven miles from the city of Missoula.

A Montana original, Joseph Blanchard Murphy was born in Great Falls, Montana, on August 23, 1890, the oldest of five children. Joe's family moved from Highwood to Ovando when he was twelve.

The Murphy family in 1910; Joe is second from right, with his little brother, Robert. PHOTOGRAPH COURTESY OF THE MURPHY FAMILY.

To reach Ovando, the family may have traveled over Marias Pass and down the Swan Valley in a wagon, perhaps pulled by oxen. They came into the valley with a cage of chickens and a milk cow. They camped their first night in Ovando near a little cabin that still stands east of the post office. The family bought a place near Ovando Mountain, which they called "in the timber." Eventually, Joe homesteaded a place near Browns Lake and planted grain. After a harvest, he would drive a team and wagon to Drummond to sell the grain. On the return trip, he supplied the few stores and bars along the route with liquor and other goods.

Joe married Mattie Viola Spencer in 1918; her parents had homesteaded in Ovando in 1884. Joe courted Mattie in the valley's first automobile. Joe's outfitting business in what is now the Bob Marshall Wilderness actually began in 1911 on a small scale, then blossomed. He packed extensively for the U.S. Forest Service, starting in 1910 after the big fires, and especially during and after the big fires of 1919. Joe also packed for family friend Dr. Gordon, who had a ranch near Holland Lake. He packed across the Bob in the early days, when the land in the upper South Fork of the Flathead was a collection of unofficial primitive areas, and the Wilderness Act was a half century into the future.

Eventually, this visionary man and his sons, Bob, Tom, and Harold, built the business into a 100-horse-and-mule outfit that accommodated big groups of thirty or more riders who wanted to enjoy the remote wilderness. They were nationally famous for the

Joe Murphy at about age six. PHOTOGRAPH COURTESY OF THE MURPHY FAMILY.

A group of guests on a Trail Riders of the Wilderness trip gather at the Murphy Cabin at Murphy Flat. PHOTOGRAPH COURTESY OF THE MURPHY FAMILY.

"Trail Riders of the Wilderness" program, which was sponsored by the American Forestry Association to host members and others on trail rides in the mountains and backcountry of the western United States. Through this program, the association hoped to show community leaders the value of wilderness protection. The first ride snaked through the newly designated South Fork Primitive Area in 1933, and it was guided by Joe Murphy from his ranch in Ovando. The group of twenty-two riders hailed from across the country and paid just $43.50 each to participate. The fee included everything, even Joe Murphy's pies baked at his "lodge" at Murphy Flat along the South Fork.

The association advertised the trip as "Six days of wonderment, of marvel, of undreamed-of beauty! Nature unchanged for centuries. Mountains that lose their peaks in the clouds, canyons that sink out of sight, virgin forests that unfold as the sea, cold snow water forming hundreds of unknown lakes in glacier basins, wild life in all its unspoiled beauty. These are some of the secrets of the South Fork Wilderness that await the Trail Riders."

Along on the first trip were many influential men and women, including officials of the Great Northern Railway with their official photographer, and Carmen Haider of New York City, a personal friend of Bob Marshall. Professors, teachers, business leaders, government workers, nurses, and parole officers rounded out the group. They met with Forest Service rangers along the way at Burnt Cabin and Big Prairie.

Joe pulled out the stops; he brought along six in the packing crew, including his oldest son, Harold, and fifty-five stock to haul the mountain of food and gear. Joe squired the excited riders for about 100 miles through his favorite spots: into the Danaher, then on to Big Prairie and Murphy Flat, where they had a layover day for fishing, swimming, and sightseeing. For dessert at Joe's Murphy Flat camp, they served fifteen cherry pies, plus a birthday cake for rider Nancy Page of Moorestown, New Jersey. In the next several days, the riders continued along Big Salmon Lake, up Big Salmon Creek, up over the pass, and down to finish at Holland Lake.

The party enthusiastically praised the wilderness. Particularly enamored with Big Salmon Lake (where they caught lots of cutthroat and bull trout), Fred Hornady wrote: "Big Salmon Lake was the outstanding body of water seen on our trip. It is estimated that less than 500 people see this beautiful sight each year, and it is such beauty spots which the party hopes will be preserved as wilderness areas." The members of the party were smitten with the South Fork, and the success of this first outing spawned fifty years of introducing the public to wilderness through Trail Riders trips. Joe Murphy had done it again.

Joe started most trips from the Murphy Ranch, in the foothills of the Bob's mountains. Proud of the ranch, Joe described it as "one of the most beautiful spots in the Rocky Mountains," with "hay meadows, rolling prairie land, magnificent trees [big ponderosa pines], sparkling mountain streams" all located 4,000 feet above sea level. Only ten miles from the Monture Ranger Station, as a jumping-off point it couldn't be beat.

Joe was popular with dudes. His demeanor was quiet, and he was calm and competent. Even with only a grade-school education,

Joe was the intellectual equal of anyone. At six foot, two inches, he was an impressive man, and looked the part of a Wild West cowboy. He could handle stock like nobody else. People on his trips quickly saw that they could count on Joe to make good decisions and lead them on a safe trip far into the backcountry.

Joe issued prospective guests a copy of "Murphy's Handbook," a well-written and thorough manual on what to expect and plan for on a fishing or especially a hunting pack trip. A few suggested items from Joe's handbook included: "At least three (3) suits of heavy, warm, woolen underwear with long sleeves and long legs; At least two (2) preferably three (3) heavy woolen shirts; At least four (4) pair of light and four (4) pair of heavy wool socks." From his years of experience guiding thousands of dudes, Joe learned that staying warm trumped everything. In the handbook, he also recommended two pairs of boots, one leather and one rubber, and on and on. He added, "For the packtripper's own benefit and protection, alcoholic beverages are not recommended on a pack trip. Alcohol just doesn't mix with wild horses and high-powered guns." This recommendation was the only one written in all uppercase letters. Joe provided toilet paper and noted that "[r]easonable quantities should be carried in hip pocket at all times." Probably from a bad experience, and maybe being face-tious, Joe also noted: "Highly scented talcs, shaving lotions, or smelly toilet waters are not permitted at the Ranch or in the Primitive areas of Flathead National Forest."

The handbook also presented an artsy map of the three primitive areas (designated in the early 1930s) that guests would move through: South Fork, Pentagon, and Sun River. The map caption reads, "Packtrippers' Paradise."

When the well-informed guests showed up for a pack trip, they spent the first day choosing which horses to ride, practicing horseman-ship, and checking out gear such as fishing rods and firearms. The next day, after a big early breakfast, guests traveled ten miles by truck to the ranger station, where their saddle and packhorses were standing by. While the ranch crew tended to the last-minute adjustments of packs, the "packtrippers" rode up the trail into Monture Canyon, framed by stately yellow pines. Riders passed through the timber for the first three miles, then rode six miles through more-open country to Burnt Cabin.

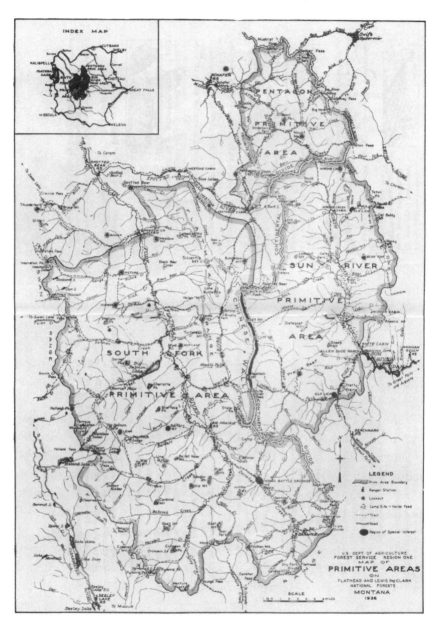

Joe Murphy provided Trail Riders with maps, sometimes highlighting their wilderness routes. This "Packtrippers Paradise" map offers a more general overview of three primitive areas that eventually became part of the Bob Marshall Wilderness Complex.

PHOTOGRAPH COURTESY OF THE MURPHY FAMILY.

Ruby Kirchbalm's cabin on Youngs Creek near the confluence with Hahn Creek. PHOTOGRAPH COURTESY OF THE MURPHY FAMILY.

A few more miles and everyone stopped to munch sandwiches, cookies, and fruit. Later, the riders moved through a steep burned area to reach Monture (aka Hahn) Pass, a high one at 7,800 feet.

The packtrippers descended into the South Fork drainage, and then into the main country of the Bob. On the way, Joe had the riders dismount and walk a few miles of the trip to loosen up and try to avoid saddle soreness. The packtrain continued down Hahn Creek, through a canyon, and down to its junction with Youngs Creek, where a well-established campsite was set up. The group had ridden twenty-four miles from Monture station, and they stayed in tents at this site.

Near this spot on Hahn Creek stood a homey cabin belonging to Ruby Kirchbalm, whom Joe knew well. Ruby had applied for and received a special-use permit from U.S. Forest Service ranger Ray Trueman in 1919 to build the cabin, which had a rock fireplace and even a closed-in porch. Along with Smokey Deneau, Ruby did some general packing and also packed for the Forest Service. She and Ranger Ray became close—really close. They eventually ran off together.

The next day, the riders descended Youngs Creek to its junction with Danaher Creek, which formed the South Fork of the Flathead

River. They rode on downstream and finished the eleven miles to reach Big Prairie Ranger Station. Joe had a very good relationship with Big Prairie district ranger Ray Trueman. In about 1920, Joe received a special-use permit from Ray to establish his main base camp near the mouth of the White River, downstream from Big Prairie. Joe called Ray and his crew "friendly rangers," and noted that hot coffee was always on at Big Prairie.

Beginning in the early 1920s, Joe's cabin and lodge, pole tents, and main home camp straddled a series of big, gorgeous meadows about seven miles downstream from Big Prairie Ranger Station. Located across the South Fork from the mouth of the White River, it came to be known as "Murphy Flat," and the name stuck.

Joe and his crew had built a main lodge or cabin about twenty-five by thirty feet in size, with a covered porch, as well as smaller cabins, corrals, a barn, and tent frames. The lodge boasted a large rock fireplace and offered all the frontcountry comforts in a spectacular backcountry setting, right on the shores of the best fishing stretch of

Joe Murphy at the well-crafted Murphy Flat Cabin.
PHOTOGRAPH COURTESY OF THE MURPHY FAMILY.

White River Sue was a hand-hewn mannequin the Murphy crew dolled up as a prank "date" for clients staying at Murphy Flat.
PHOTOGRAPH COURTESY OF THE MURPHY FAMILY.

the South Fork. This fine setup served as the base for Joe's hunting and fishing forays under his permit for many years.

According to Ranger Charlie Shaw, Joe's official U.S. Forest Service permit for Murphy Flat terminated "by mutual agreement" in 1937, a few years after designation of the South Fork Primitive Area. Three years later, this primitive area, along with Pentagon and Sun River, were combined into the Bob Marshall Wilderness. But Joe, and later his sons, continued to outfit from the Murphy Flat camp for decades. For example, when the Murphys broke camp near the end of the 1949 hunting season, their group comprised twenty-two hunters, and each had bagged an elk; this was an amazing accomplishment. The Murphys loaded their seven pack strings, with ten stock each, for the trip out. With more than 100 horses and mules, the Forest Service considered the Murphy outfit "the largest and best that has used the Bob Marshall Wilderness for any length of time." By 1948, the outfit had become "Murphy and Sons" when Harold, Tom, and Bob joined Joe full-time in the business.

Through the years, Joe's trips were known for politically incorrect pranks, as Joe and his boys worked hard to make their trips fun and unique. Joe was a born practical joker. One of the famed gags they pulled involved the beloved "White River Sue or Lou," a large doll made of wood and straw and dressed in lady's clothes. Sue lived at the Murphy camp along Murphy Flat, and she never came out of the wilderness. Joe and his boys told hunters that White River Sue was lonely, living year-round more than twenty-five miles from any trailhead. The lonely gal would end up in someone's sleeping bag every night, but you never knew who she would choose.

Another prank on the summer and early fall trips was the hopper invasion. The abundant grass at Murphy Flat was home to thousands of grasshoppers in the warmer months. The dudes often fished with "Joe's Hoppers," an artificial fly pattern that was a killer for cutthroat trout. It seems that the natural grasshoppers were attracted to the fishing dudes' flies, which somehow found their way into the dudes' sleeping bags. With the "lure" in place, the living hoppers would follow, filling the bags.

To toughen up the male dudes, Joe and his sons often used the time-honored hazing technique of "chapping." The dude would be lifted off the ground and toughened up by a number of slaps with leather chaps to his posterior. This proved to be very effective in reducing saddle soreness—or at least complaints about it—in inexperienced riders. Sometimes the wranglers lifted female dudes upside down and dropped spotted frogs into their pant legs.

While Dave Owen was Big Prairie ranger, he checked in occasionally with the Murphy outfit at Murphy Flat. On one visit, Dave's dog, a golden retriever named Mike, was miserable with a toothache. Luckily, one of the dudes at Murphy's camp happened to be a dentist, and he had a dental kit with him. He extracted Mike's bad tooth, and Dave thanked him profusely. Dave once bought a horse from Tom at the camp, and it turned out to be one of the best he'd ever owned. Eustace was a Thoroughbred–Quarter Horse cross, and Dave said he was typical of the fine stock that the Murphys raised and rode. Dave said that in his experience, over the years the Murphys were always willing to work with the Forest Service during their trips.

To say that clients trusted the Murphy outfit would be an understatement, even submitting to "chapping," which promised to reduce saddle soreness. PHOTOGRAPH COURTESY OF THE MURPHY FAMILY.

In the early days of the Murphy outfit, a classic trip that Joe squired illustrated his skill with clients, and his competence in all aspects of the mountains. Joe, twenty-nine years old at the time, had not yet formally established his permanent base camp at Murphy Flat. But the trip portended the quality and success for which the Murphy outfit would become famous.

On August 2, 1920, P. D. Wright, president of the Reed Manufacturing Company, and a companion, E. W. "Mac" McGill, arrived in Drummond by train from Erie, Pennsylvania. The two men contacted Joe Murphy, who was already building a sterling reputation, to arrange the wilderness fishing trip of their lives. They missed the "stage" to Ovando, so the next morning they hitched the forty-mile ride with a Drummond rancher. When they reached the little town, which they said included seven buildings, they stretched out after a rough drive that found them striking bottom on some of the bumps.

There they met up with Joe Murphy, a "dude wrangler" who they said, tongue in cheek, had "been driven to guiding" after suffering three dry years and three crop failures in a row. After exchanging greetings and packing the men's gear, the party mounted up and rode off by 11 A.M. They traveled over the foothills twelve miles to Monture Creek, where camp was already set up and being watched by Joe's sixteen-year-old brother, Bob. Fortunately, we know many of the details of this trip because Mac kept a journal, recording the events of each day in the wilderness. Mac's log provides a glimpse of the early years of guided packing into this vast wilderness.

Bob had caught some fish to supplement dinner, which greatly pleased the dudes from back east. When they dismounted, the two clients were already so sore that they walked "bow legged and draggy" like true cowpunchers, but a plunge in the cold waters of Falls Creek revived them. They slept soundly on balsam boughs.

The next morning at four thirty, Joe started rounding up the horses. Bob had breakfast ready by six o'clock. After breakfast, P. D. and Mac rode ahead on the trail while Joe rounded up the gear and started packing the horses. The trail narrowed and led the riders up the beautiful Monture Creek canyon. The two men had put some chocolate, field glasses, and cameras in their saddlebags; Joe was supposed to follow with big sandwiches on homemade bread. They found that separating themselves from their lunch was a bad idea.

At noon, P. D. and Mac stopped for a while, but there was still no sign of the small packtrain. They rode up the rugged trail and past a dead horse about 100 feet below the trail. "This did not allay our fears that something had happened," noted Mac. They rode through a burned landscape from the year before, with islands of larch, lodgepole, and spruce remaining. At times, the steep trail narrowed to just a few feet wide.

As they continued climbing and approached the pass into the Youngs Creek drainage, they decided to go no farther until Joe caught up with his pack string. As they climbed in elevation, the timber had been dominated by lodgepole pine, larch, and subalpine fir, along with whitebark pine in rocky, open areas near the top. The men, with only a small snack of chocolate since their early start, were as hungry as coyotes. At 2 P.M., they climbed off their horses, enjoyed the magnificent view of surrounding mountains, and waited for Joe and their lunch. P. D. weighed 216 pounds, and his horse seemed relieved when he dismounted.

Joe, Bob, and the lunch finally arrived, and Joe explained that they'd had trouble with the packhorses, though he didn't go into details on the holdup. He was in the early stages of training a new string. The outfit of ten horses and four men were now all together, and after the late lunch, the group left the pass and followed the trail down Hahn Creek for four miles. When they were within two miles of the "fire ranger's" cabin, Mac and P. D. rode ahead the last two miles to visit with the rangers. "One of the three men was married and had his wife there," Mac noted. "She wore bloomers and appeared competent and contented seventy miles from a railroad."

Plenty of time passed for Joe to have caught up with them, but he hadn't arrived. Two of the rangers volunteered to go back up the trail and check on the outfit. After another hour, Joe and Bob and the rangers arrived with the packstock minus one horse. The poor animal had stumbled on a steep sidehill portion of the trail, rolled to the bottom and into the creek, and broke a leg. Much to his chagrin, Joe had to shoot the horse. He then loaded its pack on his saddle horse and he walked the rest of the way.

The party continued on to a campsite along Youngs Creek near its junction with Jumbo Creek. Youngs Creek, along with Danaher, are the two major headwater streams that form the South Fork of the Flathead River. The men and horses had covered about twenty-three miles from the trailhead, and they were tired out. At 7:30 P.M. on a beautiful summer evening, they unloaded the horses, hobbled them, and turned them out to graze. Joe and Bob set up the camp stove and cooked a huge dinner: each man ate a pound of ham, six potatoes, and a quart of tea. The sleeping area was not level, so they laid out conifer boughs (Joe called them mountain feathers) and, turning in at 9:30 P.M., slept under the big sky and the stars.

At five thirty the next morning, Joe announced that breakfast was ready. After breakfast, the crew packed everything up and began to load the horses. According to Mac's description, all went well with the "peaceable animals." But P. D. and Mac witnessed firsthand the problems Joe and Bob had with two ornery packhorses—Baldy, a two-year-old mare, and especially Rattler, a 900-pound dark sorrel. It started to resemble a small-town rodeo. Three times, Rattler threw off his packsaddle; he reared, bucked, and plunged. Baldy "cut loose" and tried to throw her packs; she was tied to a sapling but bucked and fell over, rolling around with the packs. Mac called the event a "two-ring circus." Joe said that Baldy and Rattler just had to get it out of their systems and then they'd be fine.

Finally, according to the dudes, Joe reset the packs, worked the horses into line, and hustled them down the trail before anything else went wrong.

The packtrain moved down Youngs Creek and past Hole-in-the-Wall cave. The travelers looked across the creek and a few hundred feet up the cliffs where the yawning hole of the cave stares out like a blank eye looking over the landscape. A few more miles down the Youngs Creek trail led them to the Danaher Creek junction and crossing, at the official headwaters of the South Fork of the Flathead. Although this is one of the finest fishing spots in the Bob, the travelers didn't stop, but instead rode the final six miles to Big Prairie, where a ranger station sits in the middle of beautiful, large meadows and prairie. Joe and company made their way to the river just downstream from the 1916 ranger station and set up a beautiful camp among the ponderosa pines. A light rain fell but soon stopped and the skies cleared. There are no better conditions for fast fishing for cutthroat trout on the South Fork. Mac and P. D. unlimbered their fly rods for the first time. "The trout were rising fine," noted Mac, "and in a short time, we had a dozen weighing from one to two pounds."

The next morning, Joe and the travelers started out early, rode downstream through the large ponderosa pines at White River Park, past a tricky trail stretch at White River Butte, and then crossed the White River by noon. After that, the trail wound along above the river, crossing steep slopes at times. Joe had everyone dismount and lead their horses, saying that if a horse fell or stumbled down the hillside, the chances of survival were about as good as "the proverbial snow ball in Hades." He added that a broken arm or leg nearly forty miles from the trailhead over the rough trails would be "no Sunday school picnic, and not to be encouraged."

At one bend in the narrow, exposed trail, the party met a prospector on a horse, leading one pack animal. Joe called him a "lone wolf" with no home or friends, who had been drawn to spend months in the backcountry for the past twenty years. Mac said it was a "mighty poor place to even halt a packtrain, but there we stood." Somehow the "grizzled old prospector" turned his mount and pack animal around and found a place to allow them to pass.

Joe, Bob, and the dudes wound along the trail and finally dropped down to the South Fork. They forded the river, where a strong current lapped at the horses' bellies. At Salmon Forks they set up base camp in a beautiful flat near the mouth of Big Salmon Creek. They pitched both tents at about 3 P.M.; the camp already held a handy table of split logs built by the "fire rangers." After testing out the fly fishing, the men enjoyed a great dinner of a dozen one- to two-pound native cutthroat trout with all the fixings.

The next morning, Sunday, Ranger Smithers stopped by their camp and invited the men to eat a Sunday lunch with him and his co-worker a little over a mile away at their camp at the outlet of Big Salmon Lake. This lake, four miles long and sitting at 4,300 feet, is the largest in the wilderness. At exactly noon, Smithers emerged from the cook tent and shouted, "Come get 'er or I'll throw 'er out!" Joe, Bob, and Mac ate heartily, but P. D. outdid himself. According to Mac, he downed a pound of bacon, six potatoes, half a loaf of bread, pickle salad, macaroni and tomatoes, rice and raisins (which Smithers called "slum-gullion"), a quart of strong tea, half a huckleberry pie, and two kinds of cake.

After their "light lunch," the travelers began hiking the four miles up the Big Salmon Lake shoreline to the inlet of the lake, a renowned fishing spot; everything went well on the hike except for a "black hornet" incident, where Joe and Bob stepped into a nest. The day turned hot, and Mac noted that "the sun beat down on our foolish heads." The four miles seemed like forty, and when they got to the head of the lake, they had to bust brush and wade side channels to reach the point where Big Salmon Creek entered. They didn't catch a single fish in one of the best fishing spots in the Bob, maybe because of the heat or because they were too worn out. The four men hiked back down the trail along the lake, crossed Big Salmon

Creek on a log in the dusk, and arrived back at their Salmon Forks camp at 9 P.M.

The next day, the group fished and rested for their climb to Salmon Point where a fire lookout watched over the country. Mac and P. D. started the hike early. They retraced the trail partly up the shoreline of Big Salmon Lake and then headed up the switchback trail to Salmon Point, which at 6,995 feet in elevation stands above the lake like a sentinel. After twenty switchbacks and some off-trail scrambling, the two men neared the top of the mountain where the lookout was stationed. P. D. declared that he didn't think there was "such a blankety-blank fool on earth" who would climb to this lookout spot every day. But when they reached the top, "behold there was the fool, a smiling Scotchman, just starting down towards camp."

The two dudes enjoyed the breathtaking views of Big Salmon Lake's blue waters nearly 3,000 feet below. And they had a raven's-eye view of the high rocky cliffs of Charlotte Peak, standing above the far side of the lake. Mac said that the cliffs of Charlotte were sheer and looked like they were carved by a stonemason. To the northeast, they could see the mountains of the Continental Divide twenty miles away. Luckily, they had field glasses and also borrowed the lookout's field glasses for maximum views. What an amazing and inspiring place these game Pennsylvania dudes found themselves in.

Mac, P. D., and "the Scotchman" started the long climb down, picking four quarts of huckleberries along the way. P. D. huffed down the trail with "his pine stick as a staff, his knees bent, his face red and streaming, and his shirt tail flapping as he walked." At 6:30 P.M., the men arrived back at the Salmon Forks camp with weak knees and a strong appetite for the huckleberries.

After a day of rest, on August 14, the party started their trip to White River to explore its headwaters, cross over the Continental Divide at Larch Hill Pass, and camp on the east side. Mac aptly described the White River as clear as crystal, flowing over white rocks and gravel.

The riders rode up the South Fork, then the wide floodplain of the White River, and up the narrow canyon, entering into a huge burn from the previous year. According to Joe, no good trail had existed up the White before last year's fire, when fire rangers cut a trail to service the "hundred or so men" who fought the fire. The year 1919 was a bad fire year. In total, 150,000 acres burned in the Flathead National Forest. At 12,500 acres, the fire in the White River was one of the largest, and the Forest Service devoted a lot of effort to control it. The riders could see trenches and swaths made by the firefighters; Joe could relate stories of the fire, because he had helped pack supplies to the fire line. Most of the resources were packed in from Coram, a one-week trip.

"The so-called trail became a joke," noted Mac. "Thousands of small pines and tamarack trees were down everywhere you looked, and literally hundreds of them were across the trail." Thousands of small pines, ten to thirty feet high, had bent before the terrific heat of the fire, and their tops touched the ground.

Joe untethered the packhorses and let them find a way through the downed timber. He had brought the entire string, and they all worked hard except for Rattler; he had a sore back, so he didn't have to carry a pack. At times, Sandy, the sand-colored Airedale dog, nipped at the heels of the horses, adding to the "accompaniment of the accumulated cussing of Robert, P. D., and Mac." Joe, as always, remained calm and above the fray.

The travelers had an unobstructed view because the fire had swept the timber off the mountains. The canyon became narrower and rougher, but the riders persevered past the point where the White River below lost its flow; Joe explained that the river simply sank out of sight, then bubbled back up and reappeared downstream.

After more than twenty miles in the saddle, at 5:30 P.M. the men finally rode into Brushy Park's several hundred-acre expanse at the river's headwaters, "ready for supper and the mountain feathers." The men were too tired and sore to set up the tents, so they rolled out some tarps, pine boughs, and blankets. The weather frowned, and it rained most of the night. P. D. groused and complained, and for the rest of the trip he was known as "Hard-boiled."

The next morning broke with better weather. Joe fixed lots of fried trout, little ones rolled in meal, and added hotcakes and honey. The party rode on and crossed the Continental Divide at Larch Hill Pass, with the "China Wall" on their right. They could see for miles, even into the eastside prairies, and remarked that you could "almost set one of the small New England states down in one of the valleys and lose it." The men could see rocks "as big as houses" scattered under the wall.

The men rode along the 300- to 500-foot-wide bench at the foot of the Chinese Wall, certainly one of the most spectacular rides in the Bob. Two bull elk sprang out of a little valley about 150 yards away; one of the bulls was a six-pointer. Joe picked out a stunning alpine campsite at about 2 P.M. and set up the tent this time. At 4 P.M., they saw two mountain goats on the cliffs above them, although they were too tired and sore to check them out. Joe was treating these eastern dudes to an unforgettable adventure and the finest scenery in the West. And Hard-boiled and Mac responded by toughing out some pretty challenging travel conditions.

The next morning, Joe and P. D. climbed up a crack in the wall to look for goats. They saw none but rolled some rocks down on the campers to scare them. They did find several snowbanks and on one of the banks, several ptarmigans. They caught two of the birds and climbed back down to camp, holding the ptarmigans in their hands. "These are the snow birds," Mac noted, "a mottled gray in summer, the color of the rocks, turning to a snow-white in the winter." The men released the ptarmigans, and the birds flew back up into the cliffs.

The men also found many hoary marmots, or "whistlers," which Mac described as "about twice as large as a woodchuck, gray and beautifully colored with silver color on the neck and back." With his .22 pistol, Bob shot a marmot so the party could inspect it closely.

Mac also described the "rock rabbits" they encountered, "exact duplicates of our eastern rabbits, but only about the size of a small fist." Mac said that they were the color of the rocks, and the "cutest animal we saw as they hopped about eating grass . . ." Like now, pikas were abundant in the rock fields of the wall. These men, led to remote, little-visited country, were being treated to some of the best wildlife viewing anywhere in the West. And they loved it.

The travelers saw many ground squirrels, which they called "gophers." Bob shot many with his pistol. In the afternoon, Mac tried his hand at hunting with Bob's pistol. He didn't shoot anything but claimed to have scared a number to death.

At about 5 P.M., as often happens at the Chinese Wall, a mountain storm slammed Joe and his group and the horses. The wind howled up the canyons while lightning flashed and thunder echoed from peak to peak along the wall. The men gathered everything up, including their supper that they had spread out in camp, and retreated to the tent. It took all four of them to hold fast the flaps and ridgepole "to keep the tent from leaving us." Windblown dust filled the inside of the tent and sprinkled liberally over their grub. The men spread towels and shirts over their tin plates, but they loaded up with "black pepper." When the wind finally stopped, the crew started eating. They could brush some of the dirt off the food, but if they wanted to eat, they couldn't avoid eating a lot of sandy soil. Mac said that eating sand was good because it might discourage grizzly bears from eating them.

The next morning, Joe rounded up the packtrain and they rode north, back along the wall and west over the pass. They returned to their Brushy Park camp at noon and decided to stay over so they could try to get photos of elk.

At sunrise the next day, a half inch of ice covered their water kettle. Joe rounded up three horses, and he and the dudes worked their way up the mountainside to a mineral lick he knew about. The horses carried the adventurers past downed timber and steep gulches, well up the mountain. Finally, they tied the horses and continued on foot. After crossing a few ridges, Joe whispered to P. D. and Mac that the lick was just ahead.

"We had our cameras all open and ready," said Mac, "and practically crept up to where we could see into the depression. There was a little valley, and in the center a space probably one hundred feet wide and two hundred feet long, trampled like a barnyard, and a small pool of water at one end . . . but not an elk did we see."

The men crossed the lick area and worked over a few more ridges; they enjoyed watching a herd of nine elk, and viewed them with field glasses, but could not get close enough for a photo. Joe warned them that this was prime grizzly country. P. D. said that he'd heard that all you have to do is "stand perfectly still and try the power of the human eye on 'em." Joe replied, "Fine, you do that while we hunt trees, and I give you fair warning the nearest tree is mine." The men headed back to camp and just as they arrived, the rain started.

The next morning, August 19, the crew rose at 5:30 A.M.; snow dusted the peaks around them. Joe urged them to an early start, and they reached their Salmon Forks base camp by 4 P.M., after a twenty-mile ride.

Mac and P. D. wished to bring out a good supply of smoked fish, so the crew got serious. They fished up Big Salmon Creek and in the South Fork with good success. Joe fished downstream to the mouth of Little Salmon Creek and hit the jackpot with big cutthroat, and even saw some bull trout. In fact, he saw one bull trout so large that it scared him. Joe said that he would not go swimming near Little Salmon "where that whale was" in fear of losing a leg. That evening, some of the horses decided that they liked the White River grass better than the feed at Salmon Forks. Joe had to travel about five miles to find them and wrangle them back to camp.

Joe rounded up three saddle horses the next morning and some bags to hold the fish. Bob stayed in camp, keeping the fish-smoking operation going. Joe, Mac, and P. D. forded the river on horseback and fished their way down the rough banks, sometimes re-crossing the fast-flowing, clear river to reach better places to fish. At good river holes, the men dropped the reins on the ground and fished.

P. D.'s feet had been sore after all the wading they had done up Big Salmon Creek, so after one stop, Mac announced to P. D. that he had a plan. "The next time we ford the river, I am going to fish from my horse in the middle of the stream. Why freeze our feet when the horses are willing. I will catch them and you stay on bank and land them." P. D. said that it sounded like another theory that wouldn't work.

Mac rode out into the river at the next crossing, and at midstream he stopped his horse, Bones, with the water lapping the stirrups. He cast out about thirty feet of line, and a one-and-a-half-pound cutthroat hit his fly. As he played the trout, he struggled to make sure it didn't tangle up with the horse's legs; he held the fishing rod and the saddle horn in one hand, and by leaning way over was able to net the fish with the short-handled net. Bones stuck its nose around to smell the fish, and something set him off. Mac was startled and "reined him in with the strong arm bit, but he either went towards shore, walked on his hind legs, or backed up, all of which was appreciated by a man with a fly rod and a net with a fish in it in one hand, the reins in the other, and the extra fly on the leader flipping around. . . ." Mac's fishing trick, for him, had turned into a rodeo, and it was no less entertaining for P. D. and Joe.

Meanwhile, enjoying great catch rates, P. D. fished in the center of the river from the back of "Monty" and landed five large trout in about twenty minutes. Joe rode back and forth from shore and loaded each trout in a bag on his saddle horn. Mac struggled on Bones, and finally gave up on his own theory and fished from shore. The men continued to haul them in.

Joe left for camp about noon to join Bob and clean the fine catch of trout; they would salt them for smoking and keep the process going. Mac and P. D. did not take Joe Murphy for granted. He worked superhumanly hard to provide a great experience for them, and their respect for him grew and grew. He was calm and collected no matter what challenges they encountered.

P. D. and Mac ate lunch "in a beautiful little park" at the mouth of Little Salmon Creek, having covered about three river miles downstream from their camp at Salmon Forks. They ate a sandwich and a smoked trout apiece, and reveled in the sunshine deep in a remote area they had nearly to themselves. The men were in anglers' paradise, a long way from Erie, Pennsylvania.

Mac and P. D. had to be feeling pretty good about the day. They had caught dozens of big cutthroat trout, a treasure that would be smoked and preserved for packing out. They might never experience fishing this good again.

And, most importantly, the dudes had invented a new sport: trout wrangling.

After lunch, the two men decided to fish one more hour at the mouth of Little Salmon Creek. The cutthroat trout broke the water everywhere. Mac cast out into the large, twenty-foot-deep pool where Little Salmon Creek flows into the South Fork. He hooked a double—one cutthroat took his large dry fly, and one hit the sunken dropper fly. One fish broke off, which was okay, because "one fly was a plenty thereafter." After landing the trout, Mac made another cast and immediately hooked another pound-and-a-half trout. He started playing the trout and, suddenly, it went crazy.

The cutthroat raced from one side of the pool to the other. It raced toward shore, gaining speed as it approached the riffle of Little Salmon

Creek. Then Mac saw the object of the cutthroat's fear: a bull trout "at least three feet long" and swimming like a high-speed torpedo was within two feet of grabbing his cutthroat off his line. Mac called to P. D. to watch the "race for life." The cutthroat kept just ahead of the bull, finally reached the shallows of the creek mouth, and "actually seemed pleased" to slide up the bank to safety.

In about an hour of fishing, Mac landed twelve nice cutthroats in the pool, all of them at least a pound and a half. He caught one five-pound bull trout, so the two men got a close-up look at this big char that had migrated more than 100 miles upstream from Flathead Lake.

Meanwhile, P. D., fishing a little downstream, landed three doubles of cutthroat of two pounds each. While Mac cleaned the dozen cutts he'd caught from the pool, P. D. walked up and started casting, and he caught five more. Incredibly, the two dudes had caught seventeen nice cutthroat trout, each more brilliantly colored and prettier than the last, out of a single pool at the mouth of the Little Salmon. The fishing had been great in the morning, but this truly was the best fishing an angler could ever experience, and they both must have known that it could never be equaled.

P. D. and Mac loaded the cleaned fish in bags on their saddles. Tired and sleepy, they started the three-mile ride back to camp. Unfortunately, Bones was not done acting up. At one sandbar, he suddenly rolled and tried to shuck Mac, the saddle, and the packs. P. D. said that Mac let out "an awful outburst of vitriolic King's English" and got Bones back under control.

Back at camp, the large smoking operation was cooking along. Joe had built the smokehouse of four poles, with a top of small saplings, all covered with tarps stretched tight. The trout were salted dry overnight, then placed on the lower green cottonwood racks. Periodically, the fish were moved higher in the racks as new trout were added. After several days, the fish were well preserved.

Mac and P. D. testified that the process was well worth it, resulting in "the finest eating in the world if you like fish at all." They were excited to be able to pack out the fish and have it shipped back east to enjoy and savor the memories.

The next day, the party started to think about packing up for home. P. D. and Mac found eleven mountain goats at a lick along the

Murphy guests hold their string of fresh-caught trout, 1946.
PHOTOGRAPH COURTESY OF THE MURPHY FAMILY.

South Fork and were able to approach them closely. They also enjoyed seeing "fool hens" or Franklin's grouse, as well as blue grouse. In their two weeks in the Bob, thanks to Joe and Bob, the dudes had seen and experienced it all.

The men swung into their saddles early the next morning and said goodbye to Salmon Forks. They planned on riding up the headwaters of Danaher, over the Dry Fork divide, and down the North Fork of the Blackfoot. But after a twelve-mile ride, they approached Big Prairie Ranger Station and met up with a boy carrying a message relayed over the ranger's telephone. The message alerted them about a "sickness at home," so they changed plans and rode the same route they used to get in. They turned up Youngs Creek and rode until they reached their campsite of the second night along the creek; they had traveled "thirty-five Montana miles" that day.

After a cold rainy night, again without a tent at that spot, the horses smelled the barn and the men rode up Hahn Creek and over the pass. The weather had turned from rain to sleet to snow by that time. Joe rode ahead to bring the truck to the trailhead so P. D. and Mac could get a good start on their trip home. Things warmed up a little as Bob, P. D., and Mac dropped down Monture Creek and out into the foothills. They stopped at the first ranch house at eight thirty in the evening, turned the hardworking horses loose, and cooked and ate dinner. Joe showed up with the Ford and they loaded the gear.

In two hours, Joe drove the Ford forty-five miles over the mountains on primitive roads and paths to reach Drummond. Joe rousted the proprietor at the train station where Mac and P. D. could sleep a few hours waiting for the early train east.

Mac and P. D. were not anxious to go. They had grown close to Joe, who had performed so well for them and looked out for their safety all the way. They had seen amazing places and critters, and they loved the "water, the splendid fishing, and the big game."

"And thus, endeth a trip," gushed Mac. "A real trip. This was the most enjoyable and most worthwhile trip either of us ever experienced."

Joe and Bob had successfully squired two very important and influential people on the trip of their lives. P. D. and Mac would never forget it, and they would always talk highly of this place that would become the South Fork Primitive Area and then the Bob Marshall Wilderness.

On another classic trip, in 1921, Joe outfitted a party on a big game hunt in the upper White River country. One of the hunters, L. A. Holroyd, later reported on the trip in a series of articles in *The Montana American,* in the January and February editions of 1922. The four hunters arrived at Joe's ranch and prepared to ride into the wilderness on what would become the trip of their lives.

The party of eight men (Joe, three guides, and four hunters) on saddle horses and fourteen pack stock followed Joe's established, twenty-four-mile route up Monture Creek, over the pass at the head of Hahn Creek, and on to camp near Ruby's cabin on Youngs Creek. The next day, the riders covered another eleven miles to Big Prairie, then seven more miles to reach Joe's main camp at Murphy Flat, where wall tents were up and ready and his main cabin was taking shape.

Joe Murphy takes advantage of a warm seat to eat his lunch after a successful elk hunt. PHOTOGRAPH COURTESY OF THE MURPHY FAMILY.

The next day, while some of the sportsmen hunted in the area, Joe, his brother Bob, and several others worked on the main cabin, splitting out shingles and chinking and daubing the logs of the cabin so the men could enjoy the shelter if the weather turned bad. The "carpenters" needed one more day to finish the job. The other men visited Big Salmon Lake. They didn't get a shot at any elk but fished for cutthroat trout and caught "all they cared to pack home the four miles to camp."

When the men returned, a triumphant Joe Murphy was baking pies in the stove of his now-completed main cabin, or lodge. The workers had made tables, benches, and shelves, and had moved everything into the warm, snug lodge in the middle of the Bob. The famed and unique Murphy Flat Lodge had been established, and these men were the first to see it completed and to enjoy its fine hospitality.

The next morning, the hunting party headed up the White River, bound for the great elk hunting grounds that Joe already knew better than anyone.

The string crossed the South Fork just downstream from the mouth of the White River. As they climbed the steep bank across the river, the mulligan kettle, which had been hurriedly tied by its handle onto Bones' packsaddle, came loose and dangled into the horse's ribs. Bones began bucking. "One instant the kettle would be straight up in the air the length of its tether," noted L. A., "the next slamming him in the ribs or on the rump." After a good laugh, the men finally got ahold of poor Bones and secured the pot. The party reached their campsite in the upper White River, not far from where Joe had camped with P. D. and Mac the year before.

The hunters and guides enjoyed great luck hunting in the deep reaches of the wilderness. They took a number of very nice elk. For several days, the hunters would return to camp after bagging an animal, and then Joe and others would return to the kill site, quarter the elk, and pack the quarters back to camp where they would be hung to cool.

On one foray, L. A. and Joe came upon a bull elk. Surprisingly, they were able to closely approach the bull without spooking him. Both men had filled their elk tag, so they couldn't even consider shooting him. As they got right up to the unresponsive elk, they realized that there was something very wrong with the poor animal as he lifted his head. "What to hell," Joe said. "My God, the poor old devil is blind!" The elk had come out on the losing end of a harem battle with another bull; both of his eyes had been gouged out by the victorious bull's antler points.

The two men felt deeply sad about the bull's plight, but they could not dispatch him legally, an amazing, character-revealing nod to legal hunting regulations in this highly unusual circumstance. After Joe took a photo of L. A. actually touching one of his antlers, the two men left the feeding bull to his fate.

Joe Murphy, left, and a guest packing out a bull elk.
PHOTOGRAPH COURTESY OF THE MURPHY FAMILY.

Like so many of Joe's trips, this wilderness trip was epic: the party of eight men had the hunt of their lives and bagged seven elk and two mule deer. They had an exciting encounter with a big grizzly sow and two cubs. They had bonded as a group, got to see Joe at his best, and stayed a few nights in his one-of-a- kind, remote wilderness lodge.

L. A. eloquently summed up the trip soon after he reached home: "It was the most wonderful outing I ever had or expect to have. I bagged a five-point blacktail buck deer and a five-point bull elk. I saw a number of mountain goats and last, but by no means least, a big old she grizzly bear and her two cubs. We traveled some 150 miles on horseback, viewed some of the grandest, most magnificent mountain scenery upon this earth. It was a trip that is beyond my power of description, but one that will live with me until the end of my days."

Joe had inspired another group of people who would always support the Bob.

As Joe's reputation grew, he became the go-to guy for large or specialized parties wishing to traverse the Bob backcountry. In 1925, Professor J. E. Kirkwood of the State University of Montana in Missoula contacted Joe to pack on an extensive botanical survey across the Bob from Ovando to the Sun River country and back. The aim of the survey was to collect and identify plants and catalog the geology of the area. His colleague, university president J. H. Ramskill, and geologists C. H. Clapp and J. H. Bradley would round out the party of scientists. Joe would be assisted by two other packers: old-time Danaher trapper Virgil Woods and Gilbert Muchmore.

The party left Joe's ranch and proceeded to the Monture Creek trailhead on August 23. Joe had assembled a packtrain of twenty-two horses to pack the supplies and scientific equipment needed for the seventeen-day expedition. The party followed the usual route over the pass and down Hahn Creek to Youngs Creek camp, collecting flora specimens along the way. Many of the plants documented by Professor Kirkwood and his colleagues stirred great excitement. At the pass, he noted a "fine little stand of Lyall's [subalpine] larch, that rare and interesting species which is seldom found below 8,000 feet."

The packtrain proceeded down the Youngs Creek trail to Big Prairie and spent several days collecting and documenting geological processes. At this point, they had covered about thirty-five miles and were working out the kinks in their riding abilities. After a few days at Big Prairie, according to plan, the party split in two. Packer Virgil Woods and half of the expedition members stayed to study the geology of the Big Prairie area and the surrounding environs. They intended to "explore for fossils in the Devonian and Mississippian deposits of the neighborhood."

Joe led the second half of the party, including the botanists, to his home camp on the White River in preparation for the trek to its head-waters, then across the Chinese Wall and on to the Sun River country.

Professor Kirkwood became excited as he chronicled and collected the flora of this virgin country that had not seen a single plant collection. As the party rode up the White River, he gushed about the abundant "rattlesnake plantain, *Pedicularis racemosa*, dwarf birch, mats of *Dryas octopetala, Aster, Angelica*," and dozens of other plants. Each evening after the party camped, Kirkwood and the others carefully pressed each plant and added it to the growing first-collection of plants for the Bob. The men experienced the joy and pleasure of discovery and chronicling flora of a remote wilderness, and they must have felt some kinship to Lewis and Clark's exploration of the West.

The party passed Brushy Park, where Joe's "main hunting spike-camp" bordered the willow- and sedge-edged headwaters of the White River. After an early start one day, they headed over the Continental Divide at Larch Hill Pass. Kirkwood noted that the lodgepole timber disappeared and graded into orchards of whitebark pine. At the pass, Kirkwood experienced the joy of seeing another grove of Lyall's larch, and noted that they must be near 8,000 feet. As they topped the pass and looked out over the Sun River drainage, his aneroid read 7,900 feet. They had reached the Missouri drainage at the head of Moose Creek, perhaps the most scenic point in the Bob. The view inspired Kirkwood, a gifted writer, and, presented with this view for the first time, he penned one of the best descriptions ever written of the scene:

[O]n gaining the crest, a thrilling view was unfolded to our gaze. The eastern face of the divide dropped perpendicularly a thousand feet and reached away southward, mile upon mile. These huge cliffs, known as the "Chinese Wall," are the edges of strata dipping to the valley of the White River. They vary in alternate promontories and shallow bays, the former rising as peaks along the crest. It was a magnificent view which gained in impressiveness as we made our way around the end of the wall and down under its broadening shadow at the close of the day.

Joe must have felt a special pride to have squired such an important expedition in his home country. Throughout the trip, he listened and learned much that would help him become the most informed outfitter, guide, and packer in the early Bob. On this trip he shared the joy of discovery with these highly educated and thoughtful men, and they in turn developed great respect for the man who was leading them. The area was still six years away from being protected as a "primitive area," but a trip like this surely added to the decision to give these wildlands special status.

Kirkwood continued collecting as plant after plant fell to his scissor: blooming golden buckwheat, cinquefoil, beargrass, columbine, and "the beautiful gentian, opening fully only in the bright sunlight."

A Murphy pack string on the trail at the base of the Chinese Wall.
PHOTOGRAPH COURTESY OF THE MURPHY FAMILY.

Kirkwood was in heaven, and the entire party shared his enthusiasm and joy of discovery.

The party skirted the base of the Chinese Wall and dropped into the Sun River drainage. They saw large herds of elk, some mountain goats, and many signs of beaver as they spent days thoroughly exploring the forks of the Sun River. They met the second half of the party at Benchmark Mountain; this other group had been successful in locating and studying a number of fossil deposits. Crossing the Divide, they made their way into the South Fork drainage again, and down into the Danaher, which Kirkwood called Willow Creek. After a day of collecting plants among the beaver, the entire party rode up the Danaher and over the Dry Fork of the North Fork of the Blackfoot Divide. They rode down the North Fork and out into the plains at Kleinschmidt Flat, not far from Ovando. Kirkwood and his party had experienced a flawless, seventeen-day trip that more than met all their

Joe Murphy, left, with his sons and daughter Janie.
PHOTOGRAPH COURTESY OF THE MURPHY FAMILY.

objectives. The riders had made a safe, 200-mile loop through a good chunk of what would become the three primitive areas, and by 1940, designated as the Bob. Joe Murphy had done it again.

Pack trips with the Murphy outfit gained more and more notoriety. As the size of parties increased, their reputation grew. Murphy's trips featured some of the largest packtrains ever to use the Bob. The famed "Trail Riders of the Wilderness," associated with the American Forestry Association and dude ranches across the West, sometimes included several dozen riders and more than 100 stock. At its height, the twelve-day trips would start at Ovando out of Joe's ranch and

Monture Creek, tour through the Bob north and east, along the Chinese Wall, and back west to end at Holland Lake. Then after a few days to resupply, another group might be picked up at Holland Lake, the trip done in reverse, and emerge from the wilderness twelve days later at Monture Creek near Ovando and Joe's ranch.

For years, hardworking Joe and his sons did this over and over and over again, all around the Bob, with ever-increasing numbers of guests, making great friends and supporters of this jewel of a wilderness. Joe also made a big effort to ensure his guests had a chance to view wildlife such as mountain goats and elk.

Joe's daughter Janie cooked for these trips in the late 1950s and early 1960s. She believed that the trips built strong support for wilderness. "It brought people out of the cities, and from rural areas all across the country," she said. "The outgrowth of these trips was strong support for current wilderness and the desire to expand it." Janie said that some of the guests went on to champion legislation and support efforts leading up to the 1964 Wilderness Act.

Joe treated all his guests equally on these trips, whether they were corporate executives or couples who had saved for years to afford the $250 fee. Janie said that the guests made up a "melting pot" of American society at the time. Joe had the ability to make every guest feel special, and the guests admired him and his crew as genuine cowboys of the Wild West. For some of the guests, this was their first time riding a horse, and their hearts swelled with a sense of accomplishment to have covered well over 100 miles in the saddle.

Janie treasures her memories of these big pack trips. As a young woman, she asserted herself and took charge of the most important and anticipated item: the food. Once she had to scold the six-foot, four-inch wrangler who kept setting up the adjustable camp table so high that she could barely reach the top of it to prepare and serve the food.

Bison roast was a highlight of the Murphys' backcountry meals, typically on the menu for the second night. On one trip, the huge roast, wrapped in tarps and packed with ice, hadn't thawed enough to cut up and fit in the camp oven. Janie did what she had to do—grabbed an axe and chopped the roast into pieces, fit them in the oven, and cooked them to perfection. No one was the wiser. The Murphys raised bison on their ranch, which added to the Old West ambience of the trips.

Janie Murphy in the kitchen of a wilderness camp.
PHOTOGRAPH COURTESY OF THE MURPHY FAMILY.

Janie's reputation with the guests rose as they watched her bake and serve homemade pies in camp thirty or forty miles from the trailhead.

The wonderful backcountry meals, seasoned with the sauce of the wilderness, burnished the reputation of the Trail Riders trips and may have been one of the biggest draws. Each trip required nearly 100 hardworking packstock to haul all the food into the wilderness, and meals were a centerpiece of each day's camp routine, a bonding time for guests from a wide range of places and backgrounds.

Janie recalled only one conflict during all these wonderful trips, and it was a minor one. A group of guests from Texas were proud of their homeland, and they erected a Texas state flag at the Murphy Flat camp. Joe told them that their Texas pride was fine, but this was Montana, and the flag was coming down pronto. There were no hard feelings.

On every trip, riders experienced the stunning vistas of the Chinese Wall. Janie remembers riding across snowfields along the base of the wall. At one point, Joe would have everyone dismount and rope up to traverse snowbanks and get a better look at the scenery. With this experience, the guests had the feel of being pioneering mountain climbers in the midst of a vast wilderness. In fact, the wall is one of the most remote points in Montana.

To Joe's chagrin, Janie took to riding mules at one point. She thought mules were more stable and sure-footed, especially on snow. But Joe drew the line on that. "He told me, 'Janie, you can't ride a mule. It just doesn't look good. I'm the owner of the outfit, and my daughter is riding a mule. Can't have that.'"

Janie went on to become a highly regarded schoolteacher in Seattle. She missed the landmark pack trips, but out of respect for her dad, she never rode a mule again.

At some point before Janie's time, friction developed between the Murphys and the Forest Service over the improvements at the Murphy Flat site. Joe had been under the impression that he could maintain and operate his lodge and improvements at Murphy Flat under a ninety-nine-year lease. Maybe one of the rangers over the years had said something to that effect. But institutional memory often develops gaps when staff leave or retire, so it's easy to imagine that the "understanding" Joe had with the Forest Service would someday come into question. But officially, the Forest Service's intent was to end the developed use of the site.

"Grandad had a meeting with the Forest Service at Murphy Flat," recalled Tom Murphy's son, Ted. "A Forest Service ranger said that it was desirable to keep this here for historical purposes. My Grandfather asked the officials if he could use them [the lodge and other improvements]. The word that came out of his mouth was 'No.'" Practically speaking, this meant that the agency would take over the lodge and other structures Joe had built and used for years. "Grandfather said a few choice words and out came a match." Family history says that Joe burned down the main cabin lodge on the spot.

The Murphy outfit faced challenges. Harold and Robert entered the military during World War II, so Tommy had to stay and take care of the ranch with Joe. "The boys came back from the war," said Dennis Murphy, Bob's son. "Harold married Ann, a gal from back east, Tommy married Bonnie, and Bob married Doris. They had some hard times, but the business continued nonetheless, and at least some of the Murphy outfit continued to host trips into the 1980s."

A pile of rocks and a rusted fireplace insert are among the scant remains of the Murphy Cabin on Murphy Flat.

PHOTOGRAPH COURTESY OF THE MURPHY FAMILY.

Joe's end came at age eighty-one with a heart attack at his ranch near Ovando during the winter of 1972. "It was a cold day in late February and I was out feeding the cows," recalled Ted Murphy. "All of a sudden, I saw a big plume of exhaust coming from the direction of the truck." Joe had started the truck, had a heart attack, and his foot depressed the gas pedal, causing the engine to roar. Joe died a few days later.

Until his death in the fall of 2019, Ted had kept the flame of Joe's memory alive, operating his WTR Outfitters out of Ovando. Ted owned the old Charlie Young place, and his life was steeped in the memories of early South Fork history. Last year, one of his dudes bagged a monster of an elk in Danaher Meadows. Ted entertained his clients with stories of the early Bob passed down from Joe, including elk roping and wrangling, shortcuts to the top of the Chinese Wall, and riding big miles on horseback after dark, sound asleep, trusting his mount to know its way along the trail.

Joe always thought big, whether it was amassing 9,000 acres of land around Ovando, co-founding the Montana Guide and Outfitters Association, or doing crazy feats of packing into the Bob. Ted said that over the years, Joe had packed metal army cots, elaborate dish sets, and one-piece stoves into the Murphy Flat camp. The cots didn't come apart and were eight feet long. A stove still remains at the site as a relic of the history of Murphy Flat.

When the Forest Service told the Murphys they had to pack everything out, Ted said that it was impossible after all those years of using the site. "So, Harold and Tom told us to start digging a hole," said Ted. "Much of it is buried up there somewhere. Everything went in: china, silverware, just everything." Before the Wilderness Act of 1964, this is how the Forest Service itself disposed of non-perishables in the backcountry, so the agency could hardly complain.

With his half century of hard work and foresight, Joe Murphy stands as perhaps the greatest packer in the early days in what would become the Bob Marshall Wilderness. Joe was one of the first, a true visionary; he sensed the future of wilderness travel and the need to preserve this wonderful place. He could see it as clear as the water in a White River riffle on a hot August day.

Joe's clients always left with their souls touched and with respect and support for this beautiful place. For all that he did, the people he influenced, and the legacy he left, Joe Murphy stands as one of the biggest heroes of the Bob.

SOURCES

The Murphy family made it possible to write this chapter, and they graciously worked with me on content and photos.

Personal recorded interview by the author with Ted Murphy (now deceased), Lynn Murphy, and Dennis Murphy, February 21, 2019, in Missoula, MT.

Colleen Murphy Southwick and Janie Murphy Nicholson passed along important input and advice on the chapter, May 2019.

Interview by the author with Janie Murphy Nicholson, May 13, 2019. Several follow-up conversations, spring 2019.

Joe Murphy papers and collection, provided by Dennis and Ted Murphy. Includes history of Joe and his family, the Murphy Ranch, etc. The pamphlet "Murphy's Handbook" is a well-written and unique part of this collection.

Extensive letter from P. D. Wright, president of Reed Manufacturing Company, Erie, PA, to Joe Murphy, February 18, 1921. Taken from a diary description by Mac McGill of a 1920 trip with Joe.

Report on a 1921 hunting trip by L. A. Holroyd in a series of articles in *The Montana American,* in the January and February editions of 1922. Also reprinted in *Bugle Magazine,* 1987.

Shaw, Charlie. *The Flathead Story* (a history of the Flathead National Forest). U.S. Forest Service, October 24, 1967.

"Pioneer Trail Riders of the Wilderness." Forest History Society, Durham, NC. Description of the inaugural trip in 1933, then referred to as Trail Riders of the National Forests. Description written by Fred Hornady. See also: https://foresthistory.org/digital-collections/pioneer-trail-riders-of-the-wilderness

Kirkwood, J. E. "Botanical Explorations in the Rocky Mountains." *The Scientific Monthly* 24 (1927): 226–250.

Personal recorded interview by the author with former Forest Service ranger Dave Owen at his home, March 14, 2019.

Jumping into the Bob

*Parachuting into the Bob Marshall in the
early years with the intrepid George Ostrom*

IT TAKES SPECIAL ZEAL AND BRAVERY to step out of an airplane and launch into a burning landscape of trees, ridges, and rocks. In fact, when the first time comes, some smokejumpers are not sure they can do it. Maybe the chute won't open, or maybe it will tangle up in a tree or cliffside. An updraft might blow the jumper sideways over a ridge. There's a lot to worry about.

Smokejumpers have been extremely valuable in firefighting. They jump into remote blazes shortly after the fires ignite and put out the smoldering fire, or "smoke," before it gets rolling and hard to stop.

On August 18, 1953, George Ostrom and six other young men were flying in a Ford Tri-Motor airplane over a fire in Helen Creek, a tributary within the Bob Marshall Wilderness. The smokejumper crew had aborted a jump the day before because of the wind. Now, conditions looked better and the jump was a go.

When George first started jumping on fires, he was nervous and a little scared. But, as a volunteer army paratrooper, he found it exciting and grew to like it. Like other jumpers, he liked the adrenaline rush. Now, as a crew leader, he instructed other jumpers in how to reach the right position, keep their eyes on the horizon, and hang straight down to lessen the shock when the chute opened. He cautioned them about the many hazards that could be waiting in the landing area.

Smokejumpers prepare to board a Ford Tri-Motor, 1950.
PHOTOGRAPH COURTESY OF GEORGE OSTROM.

It was important to have a good landing, which meant swinging around and taking the impact on your behind, or maybe landing in a short tree to break the fall. Usually, jumpers leaped when at least 1,000 feet above the ground. They would step from the plane, feel the drop in their stomach, and count, one thousand one, one thousand two, one thousand three, and the chute popped open. If it didn't, it was time to consider other options. Total time between stepping out of the plane and putting feet on the ground was often only one minute, leaving mere seconds to sort out any problems.

In the plane over Helen Creek, George checked his gear along with the other young men and gathered his concentration. As smokejumper leader, he would jump first, see how things were, and then the others would follow. He jumped from the plane, pulled the chute, and floated down, watching the landscape for clues. The drifting young man experienced a peaceful float at first, looking out over the hillsides. But because of his drift angle, he started to worry about finding a landing zone. After a minute or two in the air, the ground rose up quickly and it didn't look good. George was about to sustain his first smokejumping injury.

To reach the status of a smokejumper crew leader on the Helen Creek fire, George had followed a spectacular road. Ahead of his age (at just seventeen), and with his father's signature and consent, he joined the army during his senior year at Flathead High School and shipped out to Europe. He loved the mountains of the Flathead and looked forward to returning and making a living there. George enlisted to be a paratrooper, so naturally when he completed his service in the army, he gravitated to the smokejumper corps. "I wanted to jump out of airplanes," he said.

During his years as a smokejumper, George jumped three times on fires in the Bob. The first fire jump in 1950 was on a small "start" (a new fire) east of Big Salmon Lake. This was less than a year after the Mann Gulch disaster near Helena, where thirteen smokejumpers lost their lives in an inferno. That had to be on the mind of every smokejumper.

George and another man jumped on the very remote fire, which, luckily, turned out to be a "two-man fire"—there wasn't much to

George Ostrom served as a paratrooper in Europe during World War II.
PHOTOGRAPH COURTESY OF GEORGE OSTROM.

putting it out and no one got hurt in the process. When he hiked down the mountain and got on the primitive phone lines at Holbrook Cabin, the dispatcher told him there were no fires, the jump list in Missoula was a mile long, and nobody was getting any action. The dispatcher asked him if he would mind working at Salmon Forks Guard Station, a few miles downriver, where the Forest Service wanted to build a mule corral. George was thrilled and said sure, he would take the assignment.

"I had another smokejumper with me," said George, "but he didn't like the wilderness, so he left." George couldn't believe that the other jumper didn't want to stay in the wilderness with him. "Can you think of a better place than Salmon Forks to spend a piece of the summer?"

George walked to the Salmon Forks Cabin, downriver at the mouth of Big Salmon Creek, a large fish-filled tributary of the South Fork of the Flathead River. He was excited to have the cabin mostly to himself, work to do, and prime fishing to enjoy.

The South Fork of the Flathead River was an angler's paradise, with easy-to-catch westslope cutthroat trout holding in its clear, choppy waters. And a one-mile walk from the station would take George to Big Salmon Lake, the largest lake in the Bob. Big Salmon basked in a big-fish reputation; it was chock-full of bull trout up to thirty-plus inches, and nice westslope cutthroat. George visited the lake often; it was a wild and beautiful place, sitting in a big bowl of a cirque. One day he was walking along the trail above the lake, came around a bend, and stood face to face with a huge bull elk. That part of the trail crossed a narrow sidehill. George, a bit nervous, stopped and waited and didn't know what to do. The big bull had a terrible time switching directions, but he finally turned himself around and got out of there. He didn't want to confront G. George Ostrom.

George found that building the rail fence and corral was hard work. Long, satisfying days of cutting and building fence in the heat were broken up by refreshing dips in the icy South Fork. One day, he was down by the river and watched a mother grizzly and two cubs walk along the shoreline. He was disappointed that he didn't have a camera. Later in life, he would be renowned for his wildlife photography.

George's appetite soared with his hard work in the warm weather. The station shelves held lots of canned food and non-perishables.

A packer leading a nice mule string brought in food and supplies for George after about a week. Supplies included canned hams, canned Boston brown bread, and other delicacies. George, a bit lonely, enjoyed visiting with the gregarious packer and received lots of good advice. To George's delight, the packer had brought in a chainsaw, a bonus from the Forest Service. This was before the Wilderness Act, so it was legal to use a chainsaw.

Fishing in the clear waters kept George fed with westslope cut-throat trout and an occasional bull trout. He hiked upstream and fished Big Salmon Creek near the Tango Cabin on one adventure. George had a telescoping steel fishing rod that was packed in for him. The rod was "as flexible as a galvanized pipe," but it came in handy when he latched onto a big fish. He hooked and landed a couple of ten-pound bull trout at the head of Big Salmon Lake, and he baked those. But what he enjoyed most were the smaller cutthroats, rolled in cornmeal and fried in bacon grease. The job had shaped up to be a fine gig for a twenty-two-year-old guy.

Later, the Forest Service flew in a couple of men to work trails. George welcomed the company at first, but only briefly. "Those guys had terrible body odor, both of them," said George. "I don't know what was the matter with them."

The two smelly trail crew workers moved into the cabin with George, but he refused to stay in there with them. So he found a tent and set it up a reasonable distance away and upwind from the station. George lived in the tent and didn't have anything to do with the odorous trail crew. They were there for several weeks.

George enjoyed his otherwise lonely stay at Salmon Forks. He saw very few people coming by on the west side of the South Fork. The fire season soon picked up again, so he had to finish up his work at Salmon Forks and rejoin the smokejumper ranks. To pick him up, the Forest Service flew a plane in to the "one-way" Holbrook airstrip, upstream along the South Fork. It had been a super idyllic stay for the young man who loved and connected with the wilderness. "I loved the whole dang thing," said George.

A few seasons later, in August 1953, two planes carrying smoke-jumpers approached the fire that had been spotted in the Helen Creek drainage, not far from the Black Bear Guard Station. Dave Owen and

George Ostrom, twenty-four years old, ready to board a 1952 Ford Tri-Motor airplane. PHOTOGRAPH COURTESY OF GEORGE OSTROM.

several jumpers were in a borrowed Ford plane. George, then twenty-five, was the crew chief and flew in a Travel Air with two other jumpers. He saw smoke boiling out of the fire.

"It was getting late and it was windy; we couldn't jump," said George. "So, I tried to reach the other plane on the radio, but their radio wasn't working properly. The other plane landed at Spotted

Bear, then later took off, planning to return to Missoula. I was in charge but couldn't communicate with them." Unable to reach the other plane, George's plane returned to Missoula.

Unfortunately, as it was lifting off, Dave's plane crashed near the airstrip at Spotted Bear. Several of the jumpers and the pilot sustained injuries. Forest Service officials at Spotted Bear provided first aid for the men.

Meanwhile, George's plane landed at Hale Field in Missoula. He headed to the smokejumper office. He had heard about the crash through radio communications.

"A man stepped out of the dark and asked me if I was George Ostrom, and I said yes I am." The man asked George if Dave Owen was on his crew. George told him that Dave was on the plane that crashed, and although several people were injured, Dave was okay as far as he knew.

The concerned man was Dave's father. He and George walked over to the office, found out more about the crash, and learned for sure that Dave was okay.

To help the injured, George said that officials got the "bright idea" of sending George and another man to jump on the Spotted Bear strip with medical supplies. But instead, as George recalled, a pilot named Kelly wanted to fly a plane in to land and pick up the injured. Kelly said he was sure he could land the Twin Beechcraft at the Spotted Bear airstrip, deep in the mountains, in the dark. Flying legend Bob Johnson was skeptical, but Kelly was determined and finally got the go-ahead.

After Kelly took off to retrieve the injured, George got in his car and went to look for replacements to jump the next day on the Helen Creek fire. He went to the smokejumpers' favorite bar where some of the guys were having a beer, and he assembled the list for a new crew of smokejumpers to jump on the fire the next morning.

Meanwhile, Kelly flew the 100 miles to Spotted Bear where the crew had positioned two pickup trucks, one on either end of the airstrip. Guided by their headlights, he managed to land safely. "He got in there with that heavy twin-engine plane and flew the most badly injured out," said George. "He was a helluva pilot."

The next morning, George and his new crew boarded a Ford Tri-Motor and flew back to the Helen Creek fire. As they circled above the fire, they couldn't see a good jump landing zone because of the steep terrain. But they dropped several chutes carrying all their tools and supplies, including three Homelite chainsaws in wooden crates. Then George jumped alone on the next pass to reconnoiter the terrain. This was the jump where he suffered his first injury as a smokejumper. He landed in a field full of alder and hurt his leg badly on large rocks hidden in the brush. He remembered a herd of elk, including a couple of nice bulls, spooking out of the alder as he landed. While the plane circled overhead, George began limping up the hillside.

The chute on one of the chainsaws hadn't opened, so that saw was damaged. When George hobbled up to a flat spot on the ridge, he saw a guy working on the damaged saw. George noticed something very familiar about him.

"It was my brother, Ritchey—he was named for the doctor who delivered our mother [when she was born] and me—who just got discharged from the Navy Air Corps," said George. "He had served an extra year for Truman in the Korean war." George said that Ritchey joked with George, needling him by saying, "I thought smokejumpers were always first on a fire."

George's brother and a Kalispell friend had reached the fire first by flying into the Black Bear airstrip, located on a bench just west of the guard station. Then the men walked a few miles on the east-side upriver trail and up the Helen Creek trail to reach the fire.

George found a better landing spot for his crew and put out ribbon in the form of an "L" to mark it. George's crewmates, going to school on George's jump and focusing on his marked area, jumped successfully, avoided injury, and joined the firefighter group.

George's leg had begun to throb, and it had swollen so badly that he couldn't put any weight on it. "My leg swelled up like a sausage," said George. "They had to cut my Levis to relieve the pressure." George was frustrated. Rather than continuing to lead the charge and finish the fire line, he now needed help to make it to the station. The crew radioed the Black Bear station, a couple miles away, and let the ranger know that they had an injured man.

Toad Paulin, the famous Forest Service packer, brought a horse from Black Bear Guard Station to the fire site to pick up George. It was very painful for George as they helped him up on the horse. "The first step that horse took, I let out a yell because it hurt so bad. There was no way I would be able to ride a horse down to Black Bear."

So Toad went into the timber and found a few lodgepole branches and made a pair of crutches for George to try. The crutches worked. He could walk with the aid of the crutches with much less pain and, slowly but surely, made it down the trail to Black Bear and hobbled across the pack bridge.

A man named Francis, a Native American that George knew from smokejumper operations, was at Black Bear Cabin. He rounded up a fly rod for George to fish with while he waited to be flown out from the Black Bear airstrip. They expected a delay of a day or two before the next plane landed, but the Forest Service would be flying in more firefighters to help with the blaze, and George could catch a ride out.

Fishing served as a nice diversion for the injured smokejumper leader in the cool waters of the South Fork. He caught several cutthroat trout from his perch, sitting on the rocky bank along the river. With his line in the water, George noticed a man approaching him.

The man was an off-duty state game warden who spent his time off in the Bob for commercial gain. He used a high-powered rifle to shoot big, shell-shaped fungi (called "conks" for their resemblance to conch shells), which were used for medicine, off tall larch trees and collect them. At that time, tamarack conks were worth a lot of money. The warden hassled George, telling him he should be issued a citation, saying that it was illegal to enter the Bob Marshall by aircraft to go fishing.

Francis saw the discussion going on and joined George. "Francis was one big, tough guy," said George. "He told the guy to gather his mules and get the hell out of there." The man shut up and rode off.

After a day, George hopped one of the planes going in and out and was transported to a Missoula hospital. He recovered quickly; there was nothing broken (although George might have been suffering from a hairline fracture) even though his leg had swollen to twice its normal size. After Ritchey came off the fire and out of the wilderness, he filled George in on how the rest of the firefighting operation went.

George's brother was a take-charge guy, so he became the leader of the crew still on the fire. More men were flown into the Black Bear airstrip, where they marched a few miles to the fire and joined the "mop up." The crew now included some inexperienced people who were not trained or serious about firefighting; the rumor was that they were recruited at a Great Falls jail. According to George, they were a "rag tag" group of men. One guy had a pair of fancy-looking cowboy boots that were lightly built and simply fell apart.

After a couple of days, the jumpers and firefighters had a line around the fire. Ritchey walked around the line, checking on the men, who were supposed to be mopping up within the line, making the line wider, trying to burn the fuel, and preventing any fire from escaping outside the line. Some of the men were sitting around "having a big time" at a beautiful ice-cold spring that poured out of the mountains not far from the fire site. George said that Ritchey came up to the group and told the men that they were being paid to work, not rest.

"Some guy made some smart-aleck remarks to my brother," said George, "so Ritchey picked up a Pulaski, swung hard to bury it into a log, snapped the handle off, and yelled, 'I told you to get to work!' He had no other problems."

The Helen Creek fire (in the report, referred to officially as the Black Bear Fire) amounted to a total of twenty-two acres that ranged up to 6,500 feet in elevation. The firefighters had it under control after a few days of firefighting; by August 24 it was considered "mopped up." By September 1, the fire was out. The Forest Service listed it as a class C fire, lightning-caused. Thanks to the overall work by the fire crew, which numbered a total of ninety-five, the Helen Creek fire of 1953 was laid to rest. Total cost listed by the Forest Service was $17,125. Interestingly, the report noted that the "Crack-up of Ford Tri-Motor on 8-16 prevented getting jumpers on Fire evening of 8-17-53. . . ."

That same year, the Tango Creek fire blossomed up in the Big Salmon Creek drainage. A call came in to send a DC-3 and eight jumpers to parachute on a fire near the Tango Cabin above Big Salmon Lake. The supervisor chose George as crew leader for the jump. So George and his crew loaded up in Missoula and took off for the fire.

"My God, what a fire," remembered George. "I looked it over, and I said, 'That's a trap, we are not jumping, take 'er back to Missoula.'" Tango Creek enters Big Salmon Creek after both of them wrap around opposite sides of a big, rugged ridge from the headwaters, causing twists, turns, and potential complexities of fire behavior. George served as spotter and crew boss, so he had the authority to call off the jump.

The crew landed back in Missoula and reported on the aborted jump. A new spotter, a big, headstrong man, asked George why he hadn't made the jump. George told him he judged it to be too dangerous—the fire was burning in a narrow canyon, with changing wind directions, and the presence of big timber that could crown—everything was wrong. The man kept pushing George, pointing out that it was a priority fire and in a key point in the Bob Marshall. George tried to answer his tough questions, then stood up and said, "I wouldn't jump that fire myself, and if I wouldn't jump, I wouldn't let anyone else jump either."

So the other spotter talked to the jumper chief supervisor and received permission to take a crew and try to land jumpers on the fire. He took off with his eight jumpers, flew over the fire in the DC-3, and, after looking it over, the men jumped. The way George remembers it, things went haywire.

"They lit running for their lives," said George. "They abandoned their tools, parachutes, everything they had, and it all burned. The men escaped and got out safely—maybe they got into a lake, I'm not sure."

George said that officials conducted an investigation of the fire and the events surrounding it. It appeared that it was man-caused, possibly started by a campfire in the drainage. Several groups had camped near the point of the fire.

Another fire George jumped on in the Bob was located near the headwaters of Youngs and Hahn Creeks at the headwaters of the South Fork of the Flathead. On this jump, one of his crew members suffered a bizarre injury. The early smokejumpers wore catcher's masks and high padded collars for protection. Parachuting into this fire, one jumper didn't have his collar secure. The young man tried to steer his chute to miss a tree that was coming up fast. But he glided into the tree, hitting it fairly hard. A stick went through his cheek and came out into his mouth, resulting in an extremely painful injury.

But this kid was tough. The smokejumpers had received intensive first-aid training, and they immediately went to work on him. George said they "bandaged him up" and he was able to do his part to help fight the fire in spite of the pain.

An adventurer all the way, George felt privileged to have jumped into the Bob only a decade after the country's first jump had taken place. He was following in the vein of Earl Cooley and Rufus Robinson, who made the inaugural jump on a fire in 1940. They operated out of Ninemile, west of Missoula, and had jumped from a Travel Air and floated onto a fire in Idaho's Nez Perce National Forest. The two men extinguished the small fire and hiked out of the wilderness. Missoula pilot Bob Johnson flew a pick-up plane on that first operation.

Montana's ties with smokejumping continued with the first training camp set up in the early forties at the Seeley Lake Ranger Station. The smokejumper base was then moved to Missoula, where George operated as a jumper and spotter. At one time, Big Prairie, deep in the Bob, served as a "spike camp" for jumper operations. Jumpers used a space in the historic barn there to pack their chutes and organize gear.

By 1954, George had become a senior and trusted jumper leader. He was asked to jump at the dedication of the U.S. Forest Service Smokejumper Center in Missoula. On September 22, George and one other smokejumper made ceremonial jumps. Originally, officials had planned on sixteen jumpers, but the wind was stiff so they pared the list down to George and one other jumper.

Under pressure to perform, George bailed out of a DC-3 and floated down to land at the field a few hundred feet from the speakers' stage. He steered into the wind and "planed" all the way down, using specially designed tails and "Derry slots" on the chute. These innovations were added to parachutes in 1945 to allow for better turning. He hit the ground hard and was "semi-knocked out." Other jumpers gathered around George and helped him get up and smooth out his jumper suit. "Then I got up on the speakers' stage with the bigshots," said George, "wearing all my jumper gear."

The other jumper wasn't so skilled and lucky. "Joe got blown around and landed towards Hamilton someplace," said George. "He never lit anywhere near there."

A huge crowd of people, estimated at 40,000, had gathered for the dedication. The speakers included President Dwight Eisenhower and Montana's Governor J. Hugo Aronson. As fate would have it,

George Ostrom gathering his chute after jumping in 1954 at the dedication of the U.S. Forest Service Smokejumper Center.

PHOTOGRAPH COURTESY OF GEORGE OSTROM.

at the speaker's platform George met and had a conversation with Montana's U.S. Representative and conservationist Lee Metcalf. George and Lee hit it off and talked for more than an hour about managing wilderness in Montana.

Lee had been greatly touched by his conversation with George, holding it in his mind for years. When he ran for a U.S. Senate seat in 1960, more than five years after their conversation, he called George in Kalispell.

Metcalf said that he thought he'd be elected to the senate, and Jack Kennedy would be elected president. He wanted George to come to D.C. and help him write the wilderness bill. He would serve as Metcalf's special legislative assistant and researcher on wilderness issues, specifically to prepare the justification of the bill (which became the 1964 Wilderness Act).

On his first day in Washington, George familiarized himself with the layout of the city and the offices he'd be working in. On the second day, George was sitting at his desk reading the "ORRC" report, a summary of information on wilderness in seven volumes. "I reviewed the long report for the gems that would help us support wilderness," said George. "Lee walked up to me and gave me another report to read about stream degradation and told me we had to stop that."

George spent two years, 1960 into 1962, in Washington, D.C., working with Metcalf on the justification for the bill; he was instrumental in the early stages of its preparation. George brought his wife, Iris, and their two young children to live with him while he worked for Metcalf. Eventually, after many attempts and years of work, the Wilderness Act was signed into law by President Lyndon Johnson on September 3, 1964. The Bob was included as one of the original areas to be officially designated under the act.

Besides helping to promote the early version of the Wilderness Act, George went on to be a champion of wildlife, wilderness, and wild places. Back in Montana, he became an award-winning newspaper editor and broadcaster. His rich voice and wit landed him in the Montana Broadcasters Association Hall of Fame, and he was named a distinguished alumnus of the University of Montana. George Ostrom is a household name in western Montana, especially with people who love wildlife and the wild.

George Ostrom (second from left) with Lee Metcalf in August 1962.
PHOTOGRAPH COURTESY OF GEORGE OSTROM.

It seemed like everything George took on blossomed big. He and Iris share a special bond that has lasted for more than sixty years after their first blind date. The couple raised four very successful children.

George has always looked out for the Bob. As a pioneering smoke-jumper, he fought remote fires within the wilderness. He also watched over the Bob from aerial fire patrols for a couple of years. At age sixteen, he manned a lookout for a season during World War II. And as a legislative assistant in Washington, he aided Lee Metcalf in his effort to help pass the Wilderness Act. In more ways than one, George Ostrom will always stand as a hero of the Bob.

SOURCES

Personal recorded interview by the author with George Ostrom at his home in Kalispell, October 10, 2016.

Personal recorded interview by the author with George Ostrom at his home in Kalispell, November 1, 2018.

Personal recorded interview by the author with George Ostrom, February 28, 2019.

Personal recorded interview by the author with George Ostrom, March 5, 2019.

U.S. Forest Service. History of Smokejumping. Online resource, USFS.

Montana History Compass. Online resource. Metcalf and the Wilderness Act of 1964, Part 1 and Part 2. Edited by Jeff Malcomson.

Wilderness Act of 1964, complete text. Public Law 88-577, approved September 3, 1964. Online resource.

Historical fire records, Spotted Bear District, U.S. Forest Service.

Official Black Bear Fire Report, September 9, 1953. Individual Fire Report, Ranger Report Number 11. Historical report supplied by Michael B. West, U.S. Forest Service.

Photographs from the George Ostrom collection, used by permission.

Best Packer of His Generation

*Bronc rider Bill Workman has packed in
the Bob for the U.S. Forest Service through
a long and storied forty-year career.*

ASK ANYONE ABOUT PACKERS in the Bob Marshall Wilderness and you will likely hear Bill Workman's name. He's been a government packer longer than anyone else in the Bob. Forty years ago, he joined the U.S. Forest Service packing team and learned from all the old-timers, including Gene Brash and even those who packed when Gene was a boy.

Bill comes from a long line of packers, including his grandpa and his dad, who both packed for the government for years.

He brought special skills to his packing and stock handling duties: he was a very successful rodeo cowboy, specializing in bronc riding. He's won a bunch of belt buckles, but it's hard to get him to talk about it. "Even as a little kid, I always knew I'd be a cowboy," he said.

In high school, he went to rodeos with his uncles who were good bronc riders. "It took me a few years to learn," said Bill. "Even though I'd been riding horses all my life, not everyone picks up riding broncs right away. Some people do, but not me."

His fifteen years of bronc riding, including winning Lincoln County rodeo championships and other events, contributed to his ability to handle stock and stay in the saddle. He even spent a year rodeoing for the Western Montana College team in Dillon.

A young Bill Workman rides a bucking bronc.
PHOTOGRAPH COURTESY OF BILL WORKMAN.

As Bill was fond of saying, "I can ride anything with hair on it." He even entered a bison bull riding contest and was not thrown. His ability to stay in the saddle has probably saved him from injury in a number of tight spots with pack strings in the wilderness over the years.

During his career in the Bob, Bill has packed 24,000 mule loads and ridden 40,000 trail miles. He's stayed 220 nights at Schafer, 370 nights at Big Prairie, and 755 nights at Black Bear, for a total of 1,345 nights at wilderness cabins. That has to be a record, but who's counting? Bill's loads have kept the Bob's west-side crews humming along, moving their gear, their food, and everything else needed to maintain the Bob's trails and environs for four decades. He's definitely the Bob's current packing hero.

Born in Kalispell, March 17, 1956—St. Patrick's Day—his mom considered naming him Patrick after a baby his grandmother gave birth to years before on the same date; that baby lived only a few days. But Bill was named after his grandfather, who was also a forty-year government packer. He's lived up to the name.

Bill and his family lived in the Pinkham Creek drainage near Eureka, down toward the old townsite of Rexford (which was inundated by Lake Koocanusa when Libby Dam was built). The family bought a piece of land where the Tobacco River joins the Kootenai. Both sides of his family always had lots of stock. "We rode horses since we were really little," said Bill. "We were chasing cows as soon as we could, keeping the ranchers' cows up on the range. Dad would take us up in the hills. When I was eight or ten, I went on a few of those trips in the Wolverine–Bluebird country." (Wolverine and Bluebird Lakes are northeast of Eureka in the Whitefish Range, near the Canadian border.)

Bill's grandfather packed for the U.S. Forest Service for four decades, mostly on contract and mostly in the Rexford District; he kept copious notes and shared lots of packing stories with Bill. He once told Bill how he rigged up a portable phone that he could attach to the number 9 phone wire strung through the backcountry. As he grew up, Bill lived and breathed horses, mules, and backcountry packing.

Bill's dad, who is now in his eighties, was his main teacher of specific packing techniques. He packed for the U.S. Forest Service and the National Park Service for eight or ten years at Ant Flats near Trego and St. Mary on Glacier Park's east side. He got his outfitting license about 1970, and he still has it.

As a teenager, Bill worked for his dad's outfit at what eventually became the Spotted Bear Ranch. His dad outfitted for them, then

Leading a pack string with oversized loads.
PHOTOGRAPH COURTESY OF BILL WORKMAN.

started his own business. Bill packed for him during high school in summer and fall at Dean Creek, Spotted Bear, and Damnation Creek.

"I spent too much time up there in the fall, so I would have to make up school," said Bill. "I was learning to pack horses when I was fifteen or sixteen, and I started packing for Spotted Bear Ranch at age eighteen."

A student of backcountry history, Bill noticed things from the past on the landscape. "There were a lot of old things still around in the '70s," he said. "Once when coming down from White River, I stopped at Murphy Flat, looked around, and picked up a colorful porcelain coffee pot, still in good shape, left over from old Joe Murphy's camp. I didn't want to stop and put it on a pack right then, so I put it in a hollow log and planned to come back and get it. Never tried to find it again and I suppose the log has burned up by now."

In 1980, Bill began his career as a government packer with Glacier National Park at St. Mary. He finished up the summer season, then heard about a fall packing job with the U.S. Forest Service at Spotted Bear.

"The second Forest Service packer at Spotted Bear was leaving to go back to school," said Bill. "So, they asked if any Park Service packers wanted to come work for the Forest Service. I was going to get laid off anyway, and I was the youngest packer there. Dave Owen and Fred Flint picked me up and I've been at Spotted Bear ever since."

One reason Bill got hired was his letter of evaluation from the Park Service. They noted that they knew they were getting a good hand with Bill, but they didn't know they were getting a packer as good as Artie Biegler, who was highly regarded and Bill's uncle. With that recommendation he was "in like Flint."

At the time, esteemed old-timer Gene Brash was packing in the South Fork, so Bill was assigned to pack in the Middle Fork. In the off-season, he attended college at Western Montana College in Dillon, competing on the rodeo and wrestling teams. "I couldn't ride broncs very good, but they didn't have anybody any better," he said. "I rodeoed and wrestled for them, but next year I quit school."

Bill went on to rodeo around Montana for fifteen years, about half of that time while working for the U.S. Forest Service. Some years he competed at thirty or forty rodeos, and during a few of those years he was never thrown. "I wouldn't say I was great, but fair; partly cloudy anyway. Won some belt buckles, Tobacco Valley rodeo three times. I rodeoed a lot, slowed down when I got my government job. Always wanted to be a packer, and I wanted to do a good job at that. And to be a government packer, to me, was a little step up. Especially since my grandfather and my dad had both done it."

At one competition in about 1988, Bill was catapulted off a bronc and landed hard on his shoulder. He had to get an operation, which kept him out of his packing job for a month or so. He never did get on any broncs again after that. "I slowed down when I realized how important my job with the Forest Service was to me. I didn't want to be injured, or be in Billings at a rodeo on a Sunday night and have to be at Spotted Bear ready to go on a Monday morning."

Bronc riding, Bill said, might help you as a packer by making you more comfortable in tight spots. "But I doubt if it helped much," he said. "I know a lot of good packers who never rode broncs. If nothing else, you might get pretty good at falling off or getting out of the way of something."

Packing in the wilderness. PHOTOGRAPH COURTESY OF BILL WORKMAN.

Bill met his wife, Gail, on the rodeo circuit. Her brother rodeoed, so Gail accompanied him and met Bill at the high school rodeos, although she was several years younger. Gail was a natural and she joined the Flathead High School Rodeo Team.

When they were first married, Bill was still working seasonally for the U.S. Forest Service, and they stayed at Diamond R Guest Ranch or other places around Spotted Bear, or simply camped out. Gail volunteered for the first six years, helping Bill with the mules. Gail finally hired on with the U.S. Forest Service at Spotted Bear in about 1987. She also rode the backcountry with Bill, once only a month before their daughter Chelsea was born.

Bill took over the head packer position for Spotted Bear District after Gene Brash retired in 1997 and has been the lead ever since.

Over his decades of packing, Bill spent hundreds of nights at Black Bear Cabin, which served as a nice stopover point for his trips in and out of Big Prairie. It offered a place to relax and gather energy for the next day's loading and packing. Mostly, stays over the years at Black Bear were uneventful. But there was one major exception, and it would require all the skills Bill had learned on the rodeo circuit.

"I'd come down from Big Prairie, and I was lying on a bunk reading my book," said Bill, "and a couple crews showed up, including the river crew. When they came in the cabin, they said, 'We saw a moose down by the river!' They were all excited. Well I thought that's cool, but I've seen plenty of moose, so I wasn't going to go down there." Bill did wonder a bit though, because he never had seen a moose in the Black Bear area.

The next morning, Bill and another packer, Nick, who had come in from Meadow Creek with a load of hay the day before, hoisted packs on the stock and rode down from the cabin corrals to the pack bridge across the rushing South Fork of the Flathead. They were planning on riding out to the trailhead at Meadow Creek.

As Bill rode across the bridge leading the stock, he saw a medium-sized bull moose still down along the river, back on the cabin side of the river. Bill thought it was unusual for a moose that was seen the night before to be still hanging around the river. He got across the bridge, tied up, and waited for Nick. The two men walked over to the riverbank and looked across the river at the bull, standing along the river's edge and looking forlorn.

"His ears were droopy, like a sick calf, and I thought maybe he was a little sick," said Bill. "We figured he'd come out of it, so we mounted up and rode the trail up the hill on our way out to Meadow Creek and Spotted Bear."

After riding less than a mile, the two packers gained the ridge and topped out on the bench above the station. When they got up on the bench, their radio came alive. One of the crew had checked on the moose and called out to Spotted Bear to report that the moose was hung up in the number 9 wire of the old phone line. Spotted Bear District ranger Deb Mucklow came on the radio and asked them to take a look and see if anything could be done to help him, and that she would call Montana Fish, Wildlife & Parks to see if they could help. Bill came on the radio and said that he and Nick would go back and see if they could do anything for the moose.

If anyone could wrangle this moose it would be Bill. The three-time Tobacco Valley Rodeo bronc riding champion rode back down the trail to the rescue.

The packers tied up their mules up on the bench and rode their horses back to the bridge. As they sized up the situation, Bill got on the radio and asked Deb again if the state might come to dart the bull and tranquilize it.

The moose was about 100 yards upstream of the pack bridge. Bill, Nick, and two other crew members, Ben and Elisheba, came down to help. Bill thought that maybe they could snug the bull against a tree and remove the wire. They got down to the river and saw that the moose was standing in big rocks toward one edge of the river; there were no trees nearby. The wire was wrapped around his neck and antlers and even wrapped under his chin. Things didn't look good.

"Deb radioed in and said the Fish and Game isn't going to helicopter in and try to tranquilize and remove the moose," said Bill. "She said if you can't get him loose, you have permission to put him down so he doesn't remain caught up there for days or starve to death. Well, you could see the look on the faces of those young people when they heard about putting him down, and I knew we couldn't do that. I knew we'd have to figure something out."

The bull had tangled up in the phone line up by the cabin, but the line was loose, so he had run down the bank into the river and about halfway across until he hit the end of the line. When he couldn't go any farther, he came back to the rocks on the edge of the river. The line got wrapped around a boulder in the river, which shortened up the length that he could run. It looked like an impossible mess, and posed significant danger to the rescue crew, especially given the typical fiery nature of cornered moose.

The moose was standing partway out in the river, about eighty feet from the bank. Even though there were no trees growing in the boulders at the site, there was one uprooted tree, about ten inches in diameter, that had floated down the river, complete with its root wad. The tree was lying along the rocks perpendicular to the current and near the bank. When the moose ran out into the river, the wire had crossed the tree, and he was standing fairly close to the root wad, which sat in the river.

"Worst case, a guy could cut that line and the moose could run off," said Bill, "but he'd be dragging that line, maybe a couple hundred feet of number 9 wire, and he'd probably just get hung up again. You could do that, but it wouldn't be much good."

When Bill went down to take a closer look, the moose ran farther out into the river. Bill could see that if they could get him back to the root wad, they might be able to lasso the bull's antlers, snug him against the roots, and then cut the wire. A long shot, but it looked like the only decent alternative. It sounded matter-of-fact, but think about roping a moose in an open area and imagine how hard it would be. Everything would have to go just right, and not just anyone could do it. It would take a pretty good roper.

For this plan to work, they had to figure out a way to scare the moose from out in the river back toward the downed tree. Bill and Elisheba, who was a river ranger, dragged her downriver boat to the river and launched it upstream of the moose. The plan was to float down past the bull and scare him out of the river to the tree and root wad along the bank.

"I wasn't worried about Elisheba, she's the river ranger," said Bill. "I started to float with her, but that kayak wasn't very big, and I can't swim, and I didn't want to hold her back and get her in trouble, because that bull could reach us if he wanted to. So, I got out and told her to just float on past him and see if she could scare him out of the water toward that tree. And I said, 'I would go with you but I'm afraid my spurs would poke a hole in your raft.'"

The moose didn't react to the first float-by. So Bill hollered to Elisheba to try it again, only this time get a little bit closer. She walked back up the river and floated past again, and this time the moose slogged back toward the bank and got out of the water fairly close to the root wad. "I asked her to just stay below the bull a little bit, park her raft there and keep his attention. At this point I thought I might be able to lasso his antlers if things went just right."

The moose focused on Elisheba, giving Bill his opportunity. He began to sneak up to the root wad, keeping it between him and the bull. Each time the bull turned toward Bill, he froze. Their plan was working. Bill worked his way upriver, reached the log, and slowly worked his way toward the root wad.

"I was a little afraid he'd come around that root wad and eat me or something," said Bill. "All I could see in my mind is that picture on the wall at Schafer [Ranger Station] of a guy being attacked by a moose. Eventually I got up to where the wire ran over that log, just behind the root wad, and I could have cut it then, but he'd be running off with a length of wire, so I didn't want to do that."

Luckily, the bull mostly focused on Elisheba standing with her raft out in the river. The rodeo star carefully climbed up on the log and crept along it to the root wad.

Bill didn't have a proper lasso rope, which affected his throw. "Up at the station I found a big soft rope, not really the best rope to lasso something with, but that's all we had," he said. "I've done some calf roping before, which helped, but I rope only when nobody's watching because I'm a piss-poor roper. But if something's just standing there, I can usually rope it."

In this case, Bill was lucky to have roping experience and skill; it's doubtful if the average person would even try to rope a potentially dangerous bull moose at close range. "It may have seemed foolhardy, and it did cross your mind that something could happen," said Bill. "But I figured if something went wrong, I could handle it."

Bill was now up on the log and planned to throw the rope over the top of the root wad. It was now or never; he launched the rope.

"My intention was to lasso both antlers and snub him to that log. So I threw the rope, but only got one antler. I took all the slack out of it I could get, pulled and wrestled him toward the root wad, and tied off that one antler. There was plenty length of rope, so I cut it and made another loop and I lassoed the other horn, wrapped that rope off on the wad, and took up the slack. Of course, the moose was not taking this lying down. He started getting a little wild."

Meanwhile, Nick and Ben had ahold of the wire up on the bank, and they were supposed to haul on that wire and wrap it around a tree if the moose tried anything, which probably wouldn't have worked. Bill called Nick down to the river's edge to help him try to snug the moose against the log, and Nick scampered down to help wrestle the rope tighter.

"I had one rope fastened to top of the root wad, one at bottom, and between the two of us we got some slack out, worked him right up to those roots and tied him off," said Bill. "We were both a little scared. That bull was struggling, just grunting and groaning; his eyes were wild and bloodshot, just red. We were *all* a little scared."

Now that the moose was more or less snugged against the wad, Bill reached around to snip the wire, using a set of nail nippers from the barn. The downed tree was moving some because of the struggles of the bull.

"So, I got up close and cut the wire right where it attached to his antlers, and I cut the piece where it was stuck under his throat, but had to leave the wire on the antlers. Then I told Nick that all we needed to do is cut those ropes and run."

Bill asked Nick to take the length of rope that was closest to the bank and dally it around a tree, which he did. "I was thinking," said Bill, "that once I cut the rope that bull would be loose, and if he came to get me, it would at least slow him down to give me a chance to get out of the way."

Bill cut the ropes that bound the antlers, jumped off the log, and ran for the bank.

The moose never moved—he just stood there. He had gotten used to the idea that he was caught up in the wire and didn't know he was loose.

"We actually had to go back down there," said Bill, "and toss a few rocks at him. He finally trotted across the river and up the other bank on the opposite side from the ranger station. He had two pieces of rope dangling from his horns, probably three feet long. That's what

I had to leave on him, but he seemed fine. That should have been the end of the story, but it wasn't."

Bill's wife came back to work at Spotted Bear soon after the moose rodeo. Deb, the district ranger, had told her about Bill's heroic lassoing of the bull moose. She said, "I can't wait to see pictures." And Bill said, "Well you won't see any pictures; there were four of us there and do you think anybody thought of taking any pictures?"

A week later, Bill was preparing for his regular packing trip into Big Prairie. He and Gail drove up to the Meadow Creek trailhead, where they unloaded the mules from the trailer and started placing packs, as always keeping the packs even on each side of the mule. The last mule got out of the trailer and Bill began loading him. The mule kept looking around behind him.

"I thought maybe he was looking at a bear," said Bill. "I turned around and I saw a moose walking up the road, and I said, 'Oh, it's a moose.' Gail was on the back of the truck and she looked up the road, and said, 'Yeah, and it's your moose, too."

The bull was walking up the access road with white ropes dangling from his antlers. Gail snapped a photo as he reached the sign for the "Meadow Creek Turnoff." In the photo, the moose is at a distance, but Bill said you could tell "what it is and where it is." The moose had traveled about ten or twelve miles by trail downriver from where Bill roped him the week before. Who knows which route he followed to emerge from the wilderness and end up at the trailhead at the exact time Bill and Gail were loading up for the next trip. "Gail said he was coming back to thank me," said Bill, "and maybe he was."

Bill said that it had been a really good feeling to turn him loose, especially with the young crew members watching. "There was no way I'd want to shoot him, and I never really figured we'd have to shoot him," he said. "We were going to turn him loose one way or the other. We could have cut the wire anytime, but it would be tough for him with all the wire he'd be dragging."

When Bill and Gail saw him at the trailhead, the bull still had the rope and some wire wrapped and wadded around his antlers. It looked like the antlers would stay together when the bull shed them, so they would likely fall off together. Bill was hoping that someone might find the sheds and that he'd hear about it, but nobody ever did.

Crossing big water on a bridge in the Bob Marshall Wilderness.
PHOTOGRAPH COURTESY OF BILL WORKMAN.

No matter how good a packer is, dangerous situations will inevitably arise that can't be avoided. In one of Bill's closest calls on his packing runs, he and his string went "over the side" on White River Butte a few years ago. When the wreck started, he thought he might be a goner.

It was in the fall, on one of those bone-chilling backcountry days. He'd left Black Bear Guard Station in the drizzling rain and rode up the east-side trail bound for Big Prairie. Bill led his string of eight mules through the stately ponderosa pines at White River Park. Right on schedule, they reached White River Butte where the trail cuts across a steep sidehill, about five miles from Big Prairie. There's one nasty point on this sidehill, where about sixty years earlier, even legendary Joe Murphy had narrowly avoided a bad wreck.

"You reach that one place where the trail cuts across the face," said Bill. "Seems there's always part of that trail that sloughs off, and there's a little point right after you've passed the worst of it. So, I got up to that point, and the trail is muddy and slick, but my horse, lead mule, and I figured we had it made, we'd gotten through the worst of it. There's another seventy feet of sidehill and I have to get my mules through it, but you've passed the worst, and I always take a big sigh of relief when I reach that point."

But on this day, things stopped going right just when everything looked good. In fact, things were about to go very wrong. Bill and his string were about to meet the black-clad backpacker.

"I was feeling pretty good and looked around the corner and about thirty feet away there's a little seep that runs across the trail," said Bill. "There's a backpacker dressed all in black with his butt up in the air, drinking from that seep. Well my horse saw him and instantly stepped off the trail. And just that quickly he made my lead mule do the same thing. It's just one of those things, and it's so steep there, and muddy, that I knew we were in for big trouble."

Once Bill's horse stepped his two front feet off the trail, it started a chain reaction. If it had been dry, Bill might have held things together. But with the slick mud on the nearly vertical slope, everything just went.

"It was just spooky," said Bill. "You don't see somebody bent over on the trail very often, dressed all in black, black raincoat, black rain pants, backpack sitting there too. I can't really blame my horse. I can't believe all the stuff I thought in that instant, it happened so quickly. I was thinking he's sick or hurt, I hollered at him, didn't want him to come anywhere close to me. I'm thinking, me and my horse and my lead mule will go off the mountain, but I didn't want my whole string to go so I hoped the pigtail would break."

Bill, his horse, and the lead mule started to slide off the mountain. All three of them were wide-eyed. Luckily, a pigtail broke after six mules so the entire string wasn't yanked over the side.

"I was scared, but with a lot of effort I was able to stay in the saddle," said Bill. "I didn't think I'd get killed, but I didn't know how we'd make it all the way to the bottom and stay on our feet, thinking something is gonna happen and we're gonna get hurt. I could see about forty feet below us the phone line was sagging, about chest high to a horse, so we are gonna go through the phone line too, and I'm thinking this isn't going to be good. But for whatever reason, my horse cuts sideways, across this thing, so now instead of flipping head over heels down the mountain, I figured we'd just tip over and slide down that mountain."

To Bill's surprise, he was able to hang on, and his horse was able to stay on its feet and "hog" across the steep sidehill slope right through the worst of it. With the lead mule still in tow, they slid around a little tree and reached a "teeny bit of grass," which provided just a bit of traction, allowing them to stay on the slope. They had paralleled the trail in the opposite direction they'd originally been heading.

"But I heard all kinds of noise and clatter behind me and knew that I'm going to have an awful wreck to pick up and just hope none of the stock are killed. But when we hit that little patch of grass it was just enough traction to hump back up to the trail. I slow the horse, the lead mule comes up, and I am looking back, and here comes another mule and another mule, and when it's all said and done, I've got six mules of my nine mules, we are going the wrong way, but we are okay. So they had followed and went down off the trail, cut across like we did, and were balled up below that little tree. The other mules thought they'd better follow our route; what a bunch of sure-footed stock. But when we made that cut, I heard mules getting drug off the trail, dragged some of those timber rails that were pegged into the trail, and they rolled down at us, so I had feared the worst."

At that point, Bill knew he had six mules at least, and they had all survived. Next, he had to check on the other three mules. He had to ride a ways to turn the string back around and tie them up. Just then, Big Prairie called him on the radio and asked when he'd be in. He told them that he was on White River Butte, had some issues going on, and might need help, but he'd let them know.

"I tied up everything and grabbed my gun and radio and started running back up the trail," said Bill. "The mules had seen the others go, so they followed and went across down off that trail and were balled up by that little tree. I slid down on my butt to that tree. I was able to untie one lead rope from one mule and grabbed the end of the lead rope and started scrambling up the hill where we came up. The other mules made it up and I took 'em down and tied them up with the string."

With his string secured, Bill ran back up the trail to check on the black-clad backpacker. He was just coming around the corner.

"Of course, I'm pissed at the whole thing, but not necessarily mad at him," said Bill. "He said, 'Man, I didn't know what happened to you, I figured you were down there dead. It got so quiet and I didn't hear anything else. Something to be said for having four legs.' And I said, 'Something to be said for just breathing.' And he laughed."

Bill walked him down the trail past the stock and told him there were no hard feelings. Then Bill led his string up the trail to Big Prairie and explained why he was late. The ranger, Guy Zoellner, said that he always worried about going off the trail at that sidehill. Bill told him not to worry and joked that there was now a trail there if he ever needed to use it.

"Once my horse stepped his front feet over that steep slippery edge, I thought we were in for something bad," said Bill. "But all it cost me was a half hour. I didn't lose a single pack, just had to wiggle a few packs back straight. I've had mules down, but as far as big wrecks I've never had one. That one could have been terrible."

It was the Bob's worst mule wreck that never happened. The rodeo star had done it again.

As Bill has learned, in the backcountry, packers have to be ready for anything, especially when they least expect it. Horses and mules are quirky, and their behavior is often unpredictable.

On a hot day one August, Bill led his mule string along the trail on the timbered bench above Black Bear Guard Station. He'd been on the trail all day, coming downriver on the east-side trail twenty-one miles from Big Prairie. The run takes about six and a half or seven hours, and he was almost ready to ride down the approach to the cabin and cross the pack bridge over the South Fork. Bill was looking forward to sitting in the Black Bear station with his feet up, drinking Kool-Aid, and taking a breather. He led the string off the main trail and onto the side trail to Black Bear.

"I was about halfway across that flat before you drop down to the pack bridge, and there was a little black bear off the trail about forty yards; he was just digging in the dirt, not causing any trouble. My horse saw him, my mules saw him; they don't care, and we were just going along fine."

But one of Bill's mules, Zack, evidently was sleeping as he moved along. He woke up with a start and saw the bear, then stopped for a second, and when he stopped, the string was still moving so he got yanked.

"He went to trotting a little bit," said Bill, "and the trotting motion tightened the pack rope and it got across the handle of a fire extinguisher I had in his pack. So all of a sudden that pack started going 'shoosh, shoosh, whoosh'; it was loud, and the fire extinguishing gas was spraying out all over the place."

Predictably, Zack blew up, got wild-eyed, and started to buck. "So here was this mule just blowing up and going crazy," said Bill, "and he likes to buck anyway; [it] scared the rest of my mules. And I couldn't get off the trail to circle them to slow things up, because the phone line was down on one side of the trail, and there was downed timber on the other side. He broke his pigtail with a few mules attached, and when he'd buck up, the pack would go up and then down, and a big cloud of white smoke would whoosh and spray out of that pack. He finally threw the damn thing off."

Bill waited until things settled down, then put Zack's pack back on him, rearranged the fire extinguisher, and gathered the mules together. He got the string going again, looked ahead, and saw another little black bear on the side of the trail.

"I didn't need any more issues," said Bill. "It was hot and I wanted to be done, didn't want another blowup. So I rode up and ran that

Bill Workman unloading a mule at Big Prairie Ranger Station.
PHOTOGRAPH BY JOHN FRALEY.

second bear away from the trail, rode back, grabbed the string, and we were back on our way, heading for the Kool-Aid. Zack was a good mule, but he did like to buck."

In this instance, Zack woke up on the wrong side of the saddle blanket and the sudden view of the little bear just didn't sit well with him. Bill didn't hold it against him or take it personally, an attitude that seems common to great handlers of stock.

"That mule, Zack, was a way good mule, but he was the only mule I ever saw who could buck and still stand in one place," Bill said. "Let him get over it and he'd be fine. He's retired now, had him twenty-two years. Did a lot of good work for me."

Every packer in the backcountry hauls a lot of food. The whole issue of food supplies and packing attracts a lot of discussion among the crews and packers. Food is important to everyone, and it's especially critical for hardworking backcountry crews who burn huge numbers of calories each day. Crews in the Bob can order almost anything they want, within reason, because a fed crew is a happy crew. It's reached the point where the "warehouse" at Big Prairie, which is part of the ranger station, looks like a well-stocked grocery store. Between the warehouse and root cellar, there's enough food at Big Prairie alone to feed a Boy Scout troop for years, as long as they don't mind a few expired dates on some items.

"Crews can have anything they want now," said Bill. "Fresh veggies, watermelon, avocados, all kinds of fresh fruit. But I also have to pack all the gear, propane, tools, and so forth. Sometimes you can't get all the food in there in one trip, and you have to bring some the next run. It's not like anyone is going to starve."

Gail is in charge of the food warehouse at Spotted Bear. The stations send out their orders, and then Gail buys it all and stocks and organizes the shelves. The warehouse has a walk-in cooler and freezers and, like Big Prairie, looks like a grocery store only even bigger. With everything organized, it's efficient to fill the orders for the various crews.

"It's gotten a little crazy the last few years, in my personal opinion," said Bill. "We used to have two kinds of crackers; now with so many choices they can have any crackers they want, so we have cases and cases of them back there. We spend way more time food packing than we used to—whether that's good or bad, it's not up to me." During the packing year as a whole, Bill estimates that food now makes up more than half the packing weight.

With all the fresh food, the weight and bulk of supplies has increased. By the time the food gets into the backcountry, it can lose some of its freshness. But some of the major stations have propane coolers and freezers, which helps keep food fresh.

Bill has had some unusual requests from crew members who require vegan diets, but he and Gail go all out to meet their requests. The lack of fat in these diets, he believes, challenges these crew members who are working so hard day after day. "They work as hard," said Bill, "but they seem to be in bed and napping by 4 P.M., while everybody else is fishing or hiking. Then maybe they'll get up for supper, but I'm not sure they are getting enough fat in their diet without eating meat. But I suppose they know best, and we are willing to pack anything."

Bill Workman and his team keep the pantry at Big Prairie well stocked.
PHOTOGRAPH BY JOHN FRALEY.

Over the years, Bill has come to prefer mules over horses for packing. Growing up, his dad didn't have mules, he just packed horses. And, Bill acknowledged, individual animals can vary: there's good horses and good mules.

"I started packing mules and got so I'd rather use them," he said. "Some will say they are way superior. I don't necessarily believe that, but there's some things mules are better at, in my opinion. One thing, if you get in a bind, they might not panic like a horse does, and you have time to say something or do something. With a horse, you just have to let things quiet down, whether the horse passed out or died or whatever, before you can even go help him."

Mules are great for packing, but Bill would still rather ride a horse, hands down, and he even questions the validity of riding mules.

"You've got mule people bragging up mules," Bill said. "There's probably good riding mules, and nowadays there's lots of people who ride mules. I like what my uncle, who trained horses and rode broncs forever, told me years ago about guys bragging on their mules. 'Yeah,' he said, 'they tell me their mule can go there, do this, do that, ride here or there. I don't care how good they are, at the end of the day you're still riding a mule.'"

Mules still have a bad reputation with some shoers, and others, but Bill thinks their disposition has improved over the years because of better selective breeding. In the old days, they might breed a mare that wasn't much good but at least they could get a mule out of her, and they might end up with an ornery mule. Not that you can't still find some like that.

"If a horse is calm, you can walk up and pet them," said Bill, "and they don't care who it is who walks up and pets them. Mules, even if they seem as gentle as can be, not a mean bone in the body, but they might say, 'Well I don't know you and I'm not going to let you catch me or pet me or whatever.' And there's some horses that way, but generally that's true. Mules can be more standoffish."

Across the stock world, mules have the reputation of not forgetting mishandling and save it up to get back at you later. They don't forget.

"If you need to kick a mule, because he needs kicked at that moment, he might put up with that. But if you kick him for the hell of it when he knows he doesn't have it coming, at some point he might kick you for it later. With a horse, more like a dog, you can do things to it you shouldn't. If you do something that doesn't need to be done, a horse might say, 'Okay, that's just the way humans are,' just like a dog might. But a mule, he'll keep that in the back of his mind and he'll get you sooner or later."

Bill has had a couple of really good horses that stood out over the years. His first good government horse, a nice-looking Morgan named Buster, didn't want anything to do with him at first; he was hard to even catch. Buster had only half a tongue. Bill didn't know the story behind his missing tongue but figured it must have had something to do with a misplaced bit. Bill didn't like him at first because Buster had bad habits. As he put on trail miles though, Buster smoothed out and proved to be maybe the most intelligent saddle horse Bill had ever seen.

"When the trail's straight, you just go," said Bill. "But if there's a little creek you have to cross, you slow down enough so that all your stock have a little extra time to cross. It takes a certain amount of time for all nine head to cross. When I'd get to a place like that, Buster learned to slow down on his own until all the stock crossed; sometimes he'd count wrong, only gave time for eight to cross, but really he got way good." Over the years, Buster gave Bill a lot of good service, and he was Bill's horse of choice for his daughter to ride when she was young.

Throughout his career, Bill had only one really bad mule, and his name was Miller. The Forest Service bought Miller and his brother, Curly, from a ranch in eastern Montana late in the year and overwintered them. The first trip of the following year, Bill was assembling his string and included Miller and Curly for their first check-out run. Bill had to have help getting them saddled and packed. The mules were both young and had never been touched outside of wearing a halter to get them to the Flathead from eastern Montana. Bill would have a couple guys saddle the mules with him in the Spotted Bear barn. Then they loaded up and drove the twelve miles to the Meadow Creek trailhead to load the packs for the trip into the Bob.

"They were just terrible," said Bill. "You had to be careful not to get kicked or stomped on. It took a while to get them packed, and then you had to tie them together so they didn't get away. I left the trailhead with these two in my string, and we're knocking little trees over before we get very far; they are scared of this and that, but I actually managed to get to Black Bear in pretty good shape."

The next morning at the Black Bear corrals, it took Bill three times as long as usual to saddle and reload the packs on his string because of the shenanigans of Miller and Curly. It was only the second day they'd packed. He was able to walk up to Miller and catch him. But that mule hated wearing his packs, and Bill felt that he would kick if he had a chance.

Bill finally got Miller and the rest of the stock loaded. He didn't ask the trail crew to help him because he was afraid the two green, contrary mules might hurt somebody. Bill gathered up the stock and headed over toward the pack bridge to start his run to Big Prairie. Miller had a load of oats on him, but the load jingled around, riding a bit high. Not wanting to see the mule blow up on the pack bridge, Bill stopped to better secure the load. He tied the string up but, being in a hurry, didn't cross-tie Miller with a rope around his neck and his hind foot between two trees like he usually did.

"I thought it would be easier to just take off his pack and then reload it," said Bill. "He let me take it off; I didn't even set it down, adjusted it, started loading it back on. Well he squiggled around, took aim, swung his hoof around and cow-kicked me in the chest, right in the heart—hit me pretty damn hard. It knocked me on my butt and I hit hard."

A "cow-kick" is like a roundhouse punch—swung from the side rather than straight back. But it still delivers a heavy blow. Bill couldn't breathe at first, and the young trail crew members thought he might be dead. "I told them, 'No, I ain't killed,' but I couldn't catch my breath and it hurt so damn bad I couldn't do anything. I was worried that even if I got him packed back up and headed back up the trail, I could die on the trail and those kids would be stuck."

Bill told the stunned crew that they'd better lay over for a while. He called Big Prairie on the radio and told them that he had an "issue" and would be late. Spotted Bear overheard the radio call and asked him what was going on. Bill was worried, because he believed the kick initially stopped his heart. He didn't know what else he had, maybe internal injuries, and it still hurt so bad he couldn't do anything.

"I didn't really know what to do," said Bill. "I didn't want to ride up the trail and keel over, leave those kids with all those mules, especially the ornery mule brothers. So the next thing I know they've called in a helicopter."

Bill couldn't do much, especially with his left arm and side, so he got the crew to help him unpack the mules, including the brooding pair, Curly and Miller. Not long after, they heard the helicopter landing up on the flat of the old airfield above the cabin. The crew helped Bill walk up to the bench just as the EMTs were dragging the litter off the chopper.

"They said, 'Where's the patient?' and I said, 'That would be me,'" said Bill. "I asked, 'I don't need to get on that, do I?' and they said, 'Nope, just get in.' On the flight, they checked me, and my blood pressure differed between my left and right side, but nothing else major that they could pick up. I had a pen in my pocket, half metal, half plastic, right where the shoe hit. It broke the metal part and ran it

Bill Workman and a pack string heading out from Big Prairie.
PHOTOGRAPH BY JOHN FRALEY.

into my chest enough to give me a scar to remember it by. And on my left chest, I had a perfect bruise print of Miller's hoof. Another packer came in next day to take care of the stock."

Bill reflected on the close call. "When he kicked me, it knocked me up in the air holding a short pack. I was lifting that short oat pack; it was a cow-kick around to the side, not straight back, or it would have been worse. Kicking ahead and to the side, it was still a hellacious kick but not as bad as if he'd caught me with a hind leg kick behind him. That could have killed me. Still, I was hurting, couldn't even sleep that night, couldn't lay down, had to sleep crunched up in a damn easy chair. Way bruised. It took a few days to recover and get back in the saddle."

After Bill got floored by Miller, it became a good-natured joke. Whenever Bill asked for help to put the packsaddle on Miller at the Spotted Bear barn, he got to saying, "It's Miller Time." Most of the time people like hearing that phrase, but not when it applied to the killer mule. Some crew members ran the other way when it was Miller Time. Some crew members showed up just to watch the rodeo.

Showing his patience, or maybe out of stubbornness or pride, Bill used Miller a couple more years, just to say he could. Miller never quite got over the desire to kill Bill once in a while, and he'd throw fits on the trail every so often. Finally, Miller threw one of those fits as Bill and the string were heading up a treacherous, narrow, steep section of the trail near Henry Anderson Creek, just upstream from Mid Creek on the South Fork trail. Bill jumped off and landed into the mules milling around, and luckily none of them had flipped over and rolled down the mountain.

"I got the mules safe, tied Miller to a log on the sidehill, put a foot rope on him, got the packs adjusted, and finally got back on the trail," Bill recalled. "That was it. He could have cost a lot of good mules their lives. After that I decided not to keep him. Guess it hurt my pride as much as anything, having to give up on a mule, but I was just worried about him killing my good mules. I think we paid $700 apiece for Miller and Curly. Miller cost us a lot. Curly, on the other hand, got good, and after twenty years I still use him."

Not all wrecks were dangerous, and some were downright light-hearted, like the flying hay bale incident. Bill and Gail were leading the string around Whitcomb Peak, heading toward Schafer Meadows. Bill had a mule that, when she had to go, just stopped dead in the trail and did it. On this steep sidehill trail, the call of nature hit her. When she stopped, the other mules tugged and she flipped over on her back. She was loaded with hay and was rolling around on her packs. Bill was faced with the dilemma of getting her up without losing her load or having her or the other mules go over the side.

"So I did get one pack off her and got the rope untied on the other side," said Bill. "It was kind of a grassy, beargrass slope, and even though it's steep I know she's probably not going to roll too far or get hurt. I was able to roll her over the pack, but then she jumped up and bucked around, and a pack with a hay bale came off and went bouncing down the mountain." The bale bounced end over end down the mountain, and every time it hit the ground, it went higher and higher in the air until it seemed to grow wings and was literally flying down the slope until it was nearly out of sight. "I was watching it and I didn't know whether to laugh or cry," said Bill. "Gail's laughing, but I'm thinking it's a long way to go down there to get that bale of hay."

The bale finally came to a stop at the bottom of the slope, at least 1,000 feet below. They thought about it for a minute, then secured the pack string and started heading down. "Now I had a mule with nothing to pack on one side," said Bill, "so we decided we'd go down and pack the bale up the dang hill. We went all the way down there, and we tried packing it up that steep beargrass slope, and finally said, the heck with this, unwrapped it, and left it there. But I did have a bunch of tarps on one mule for picking up a camp on the way in. I put all the tarps together on one side to balance the now odd bale of hay. When we stopped to pick up the camp, we were able to even things out." Bill and Gail continued riding on to Schafer minus one bale of hay but with yet another story to tell.

Bill had a few dogs over the years that kept him company on the trail and herded critters when they had to. His last dog was a female border collie, Shania. Bill's daughter, Chelsea, wanted to call it Shania after country singer Shania Twain. Bill and the dog became great friends.

"She was a way good dog," said Bill. "A good herder and great trail dog. I had her fifteen years and she went with me up until the last couple years. She was stove up, been kicked and run over a lot. Around the home place she did a lot of cow work too; she was really good at that. Winter and spring, she helped me with my work for ranchers in town."

Shania was valuable help for Bill in the backcountry beyond just being a companion. Loose mules sometimes run into a string and can cause havoc. Shania didn't let that happen to Bill's string.

"If I got into Murphy Flat and Cheff's mules were there, she wouldn't let them get close to our mule string," said Bill. "And one time, at Salmon Forks, Shania saved me from a likely wreck in the river. I was packing supplies into a crew there, and we were crossing the South Fork. I had the lead rope in one hand, a pair of wading shoes that I was getting out for a crew member in the other, then somebody called me on the radio and I had that under my arm. There was a bunch of outfitter's mules at Salmon Forks and they all started coming into my string as I was trying to come out of the water. I thought I might be looking at another rodeo, because loose mules can cause you a big mess when they come running into your string."

The area was open with no trees, and Bill was fearing the worst as it started going down. But Shania had swum the river, dove into the loose mules, and ran them back to their camp. Luckily, Shania was always a good swimmer. She could swim the South Fork even early in the summer when the water was high, although she might get swept downstream a ways. Shania worked hard for Bill and covered thousands of miles with him for fifteen years. He had a hard time putting her down a few years ago when she couldn't walk any longer.

Looking back on forty years, Bill feels lucky and grateful for his long and wonderful career. "I do think I came around at about the right time," he said. "When I started, all those old-timers were still around; I met them and knew them and learned. People starting today, the oldest they're going to know is me, or maybe Smoke [Elser]. I was lucky to meet Toad Paulin, people like that, Johnny Christenson, my dad, my grandpa, all those ties to the older generation. I met most of the old outfitters and packers when I worked with my dad: Montgomery "Monte" Kennedy, the old Big Prairie packer, and Bill Chilton, the old Schafer ranger and packer, one of the best. And I was Gene Brash's understudy for years."

Bill has ridden through the years and made a smooth transition to the modern Bob, and he has earned the respect of the upcoming generation. Nearly everyone who packs in the Bob mentions that they learned something about packing from Bill Workman.

"When you grow up in the Bob country," said Bill, "you can take it for granted. But when all the new people come on and say how grand it is, I say you are right. I owe all I have to it, because it's been my livelihood. It's bred into me, I'm following my dad and grandad."

According to Bill, packing in the Bob has changed, but it's still rewarding. "When I first started there was lots more horse use in the Bob. Back then, everybody knew how to pack in their camp; that's what they did, and a lot more people had stock. Over the years that's kind of gone away. Maybe the kids aren't as interested, maybe the people who knew how to do it are gone. I just think it's a different generation.

"I like all of it at times: the country, the stock, packing, the people. I like it best when my packs are on my mules, things are going good, it's a good day, the country's good, the people you meet. It's been a good ride.

Bill Workman leading a pack string across a river in the Bob Marshall Wilderness. PHOTOGRAPH COURTESY OF BILL WORKMAN.

"Whether it's the riding or the packing, you always want to be the best. I'll leave that to somebody else to judge. I wasn't the best bronc rider, but I always wanted to be, of course. As far as packing, I kept that goal in mind on every trail mile I rode."

SOURCES

Personal recorded interview by the author with Bill Workman, April 2, 2019.

Follow-up conversations and notes from Bill Workman, spring 2019.

5

HEROES OF THE BOB

Bud Moore's Wilderness Experiment

Pushing seventy, Bud Moore trapped fur the old-fashioned way deep in the Bob Marshall Wilderness.

SOFT SNOWFLAKES FILTERED LAZILY DOWN around Bud Moore on a lonely slope deep in the Bob Marshall Wilderness. Bud had just tracked down and shot a mule deer buck on a high ridge above the Little Salmon Creek drainage. It was late November 1983. Bud was alone, but he wasn't lonely. After more than a half century in the wilderness, he felt confident and spiritually fulfilled. On this trip, it would be a long time before he'd see a trailhead.

Bud field-dressed the beautiful buck and prepared to drag it down the ridge back to camp along the creek near the mouth of Palisade Creek. Good thing he didn't have to pack it all the way out: it was a twenty-mile trek up Palisade Creek, through the Bob, and over the top of the Swan Range to the trailhead.

"Daylight was fading with darkness near at hand," Bud wrote later. "Working there in the snow, I was the only human in that natural universe."

An expert on wilderness, Bud had retired about nine years earlier after a forty-year career with the U.S. Forest Service. He knew wildlife and he knew trapping. On this special trip, he would officially demonstrate the lost art of long-line trapping in wilderness. A life well-lived had led Bud to this point: perched on a remote slope above a remote camp in the heart of the Bob, doing what he loved to do, sighted in on a higher purpose.

*Bud Moore at the U.S. Forest Service Brushy Fork Cabin in the Lochsa
country, circa 1937.* PHOTOGRAPH COURTESY OF THE MOORE FAMILY
AND THE UNIVERSITY OF MONTANA ARCHIVES.

William "Bud" Moore began life out in front. He was the first
of nine children in his family, growing up on a homestead in the
Bitterroot Valley near the edge of the Selway-Bitterroot Wilderness
and the Montana–Idaho border. He surprised his teachers by obtain-
ing his eighth-grade diploma in just five years. A brilliant and profound young man, that's all the school education he needed.

Bud was born in 1917 and spent his childhood in a "hunter-gath-
erer" family, growing crops and harvesting deer, elk, and fish. Often,
old-time trappers coming and going from what is now the Selway-
Bitterroot Wilderness would stop by to stay with his family, and they
inspired him with their stories. He grew to love the mountains and
wild country.

Traps hang from Bud Moore's shed. PHOTOGRAPH BY JOHN FRALEY.

"As soon as I was big enough, at twelve, I crossed over a pass into the Lochsa country," said Bud. "I remembered getting up high in the South Fork of Lolo Creek and looking down into the Lochsa drainage all by myself and loving it."

Bud learned to be self-sufficient, and his father demanded to know his whereabouts only under certain circumstances. "He told me that if I was alone that's fine," said Bud. "He knew I could take care of myself. But if I went with another kid, he wanted to know where I was going. If there were two or more other kids, he wouldn't let me go at all."

At age seventeen, Bud convinced the U.S. Forest Service to hire him as a firefighter and forest guard in the Lochsa drainage in Idaho, a spectacular waterway that hosts migratory salmon and resident trout.

Bud Moore loved being in the wilderness, a lifestyle that kept him strong throughout the decades; shown here (above) in shorts at Big Salmon Lake in 1980 and (top of next page) at Hoadley Reef near the Chinese Wall in 1970. PHOTOGRAPHS COURTESY OF THE MOORE FAMILY AND THE UNIVERSITY OF MONTANA ARCHIVES.

(This was the rugged drainage that nearly broke the Lewis and Clark Expedition on its voyage to the Pacific in September 1805.) During the winter, Bud ran his own trapline in the Lochsa country. "Back then, trapping was a big commercial business in the backcountry," said Bud. "The Forest Service controlled trapping through their cabin permits." Bud bought two traplines and joined them into one eighty-mile-long trapline with seven or eight cabins spaced out in a loop that he repeated about once a week.

Like some other old-time trappers, Bud was in business to trap every winter, work for the U.S. Forest Service in the summer, and make a life out of it. But World War II, the South Pacific campaign, and two purple hearts interrupted Bud's plans.

When Bud returned home from overseas, he worked again for the U.S. Forest Service, this time as assistant ranger in the Powell and Missoula Districts; he became ranger in charge of the Powell District in 1948. Bud said that he was one of the last in the nation without a degree to be grandfathered in as a professional forester. Bud and the U.S. Forest Service clicked—he skyrocketed through the ranks, filling many high-level positions, leading him to a stint at Harvard Business School. Upon his retirement in 1974, Bud received an honorary Doctor of Science degree from the University of Montana. Considered

Bud and Janet Moore near their cabin home in the Swan Valley.
PHOTOGRAPH BY JOHN FRALEY.

an expert on fire management, Bud served on a Forest Service task force in Washington, D.C., charged with reducing fire casualties like the thirteen firefighters killed in the Mann Gulch fire in 1949. Bud helped the group develop standard firefighting orders, based on the Marines' standard orders, that are still in use today.

Bud rose to increasingly higher positions in the agency, such as deputy supervisor of the Lolo National Forest; training and safety officer at Ogden, Utah; director of U.S. Forest Service training in Washington, D.C.; and assistant regional forester for fire and air operations in Missoula. Bud said that he worked hard to bring the Forest Service from "fire control" to "fire management." Bud retired from that job in 1974, at the age of fifty-seven.

"I wanted to get away from the government while I still had some energy," said Bud. "I felt that I had moved the agency from fire control to fire management, recognizing the benefits of fire to the ecosystem. Rather than taking on a whole new set of objectives, I decided to do something on my own. Working for the government sort of neutralizes you as a person." Bud also had in mind his desire to write a book about his beloved Lochsa country in Idaho, where he had long-line trapped as a youth and served as the Powell District ranger after the war.

Bud returned to the land, an approach that had always served him well. He and his wife Janet entered the venture together. Bud and Janet bought eighty acres in the Swan Valley, perched between the Mission Mountains and Bob Marshall Wilderness Areas; they set out to manage it, along with some other lands, and live on it. The first thing they did was select a site for their log home. The writer Norman Maclean, a good friend of the Moore's and a summer resident of nearby Seeley Lake, joined them for a picnic near a small lake on the property in about 1974.

"We turned around and Norman was gone," recalled Janet. "Then we saw him heading like a homing pigeon to a knoll across the lake. He was poking around the ground with a walking stick. When we caught up with him, he said, 'This is where you'll build your cabin.'"

Bud voted no on the site, but Maclean and Janet voted yes. It turned out to be a good site. With the help of family and friends, Bud dug the entire foundation of the 2,000-square-foot log home and outbuilding, and fashioned the structures using a gin pole and leverage to handle the logs.

Bud's friendship with Maclean began when Maclean was working on his first book, *A River Runs Through It and Other Stories*. Aware of Bud's reputation as an expert on fire and the Bitterroot Mountains, Maclean asked him to read "USFS 1919: The Ranger, the Cook, and a Hole in the Sky," a story he planned to include in the book. Bud edited the story as he had edited many manuscripts during his years with the Forest Service.

"I gave him the red ink," Bud said. "I pointed out that with a number of changes, he could make the story more accurate and still preserve its entertainment value."

Bud returned the manuscript to Maclean, then didn't hear from him for weeks. "He finally called me," said Bud, "angry that I had given him such a hard time on the story. He said to me, 'Remember Bud, *I'm* the professor.'"

"I always believed," said Janet, "that Norman viewed Bud as living the life he would have led himself, had he not ended up as an English professor at the University of Chicago."

Bud Moore reminisces in his home office. PHOTOGRAPH BY JOHN FRALEY.

Later, Maclean asked Bud to review an early draft of *Young Men and Fire*, the story of the Mann Gulch tragedy. Again, Bud was hard on Maclean's manuscript. "I advised him to reduce the details on fire modeling and other technical stuff in the book, to make it flow better," Bud said.

In the book, Maclean acknowledged Bud's help, calling him "the old-timer in the Forest Service I feel closest to." Maclean described driving the thirty-five miles to Bud's place. Before they talked about the book, Maclean dug out a bottle of "Ancient Age" from the trunk of his car, noting that when mixed with spring water, the water is "just as good as the whiskey."

"Afterwards," wrote Maclean, "I went back to my cabin to write on the effects the tragedy of the Mann Gulch fire had on the know-how of firefighters. What I wrote comes next, and Bud Moore was the first to check it."

Bud's love of the land led him to apply principles of sustainability on his eighty acres in the Swan that he referred to as the "Coyote Forest." He built a small mill, logged light on the land, and demonstrated it to whoever would listen. In a way, Bud was an unheralded father of an emerging concept at the time among land managers.

"Ecosystem management is billed as new stuff," Bud said, "but the Forest Service old-timers I learned under were pretty close to it." Bud explained the concept as "keeping all the parts."

Another facet of Bud's return to the land was returning to trapping. Bud believed that furbearers and predators did not have a strong public following. "The main thing that drew me back to trapping was not trapping itself," said Bud. "Trappers are most knowledgeable about furbearer habitat needs. To be credible with trappers, one has to trap. So, to help trappers organize in support of their resources is the main reason I returned to trapping."

Bud "picked up some rusty traps" and started trapping fur in the drainages of the Swan Valley. Bud wanted to get an idea of the ability of the land in the Swan and in the Bob to produce furbearers. He ran a number of shorter traplines in the Mission and Swan Mountains to practice his trapping skills and learn about the furbearers of the area. He commented to the state on seasons and limits. He looked ahead to major trapping forays into the Bob, to relive his long-line trapping adventures as a young man in the Selway-Bitterroot.

Bud said that he was motivated to trap again in part to improve trapping practices and ethics. He and Janet worked with others to form the Montana Trappers Association (MTA). "I felt that cleaning up the trappers' act was job number one if we wanted our heritage to continue," Bud said. Janet signed on as a lobbyist for the new association, and they both urged legislation to begin a trapper education course. When a course was started by MTA, Bud worked on lesson plans and helped train the first instructors.

Bud said that Janet did most of the organizing and paperwork for the organization, while he served more or less as senior advisor. "I figured when I left the Forest Service, I left all that administrative mishmash behind me," said Bud. "I didn't want that to drain time away from what I wanted to do on the land." Janet was anyone's intellectual equal. Beginning in 1979, she lobbied for years for the

Bud Moore and Koyak near Bud's Palisade camp in October 1983.

PHOTOGRAPH COURTESY OF THE MOORE FAMILY
AND THE UNIVERSITY OF MONTANA ARCHIVES.

Montana Trapper Association, developing effective, one-page briefing sheets for legislators. Other lobbyists called her the "talk of Helena." With her successes, Janet went on to serve three terms in the Montana Legislature from 1987 to 1991, fighting hard for wildlife conservation.

Once Janet had settled in with MTA, Bud was free to focus on showing that wilderness trapping was a valid and important use of the backcountry. "I wanted to keep the old style of trapping alive," said Bud. "I wanted my fellow trappers to know there's another way to trap without snowmobiling right up to the set."

Bud believed that trappers were instrumental in developing the wilderness ethic and should continue that heritage as an example to others. "There were lots of trappers who loved the wilderness for wilderness," said Bud, "not just to exploit it for fur. It was the lifestyle."

Always a doer, Bud organized an expedition in the Bob to promote his ideas. "I made up my mind," said Bud, "that I wouldn't speak out on anything unless I really learned the country and lived it. You have to think like a coyote to trap a coyote."

True to his word, Bud planned to spend several months trapping American marten in the Bob during the winter of 1983–1984. To do this he obtained an exemption from the Forest Service to maintain two tents as a base camp from which to establish trapping "spur lines" in the Palisade and Little Salmon drainages.

During the summer, Bud scouted the area. He located a spot to set up his camp along Little Salmon Creek near the mouth of Palisade Creek. Prime marten habitat surrounded his camp. Side drainages held old-growth and downed timber, favorite features for marten. The Little Salmon drainage is rugged and wild, with side drainages spilling into the big main drainage.

In October, Bud and his malamute, Koyak, crossed over the Swan Range, down to the Little Salmon near the junction with Palisade Creek. He lightly cleared an area on a bench above the creek and established the tent pole and tarp camp. Bud put up two small wall tents: one for sleeping and living space and one for the pelting of furbearers and storage. (Bud didn't want to share the fleas from the marten pelts in his sleeping area. He also needed to keep the marten bait and smelly lure out of his living tent.) He stretched a large plastic

Pine marten pelts. PHOTOGRAPH BY JOHN FRALEY.

tarp over both tents. Bud also dug a toilet and made other preparations to keep a clean camp.

A local friend and packer helped pack in most of Bud's supplies. He brought in a small stove, food, trapping supplies, fur stretchers, and everything needed for his long foray into wilderness trapping. The packer dropped off the supplies, and then left Bud alone again in the wilderness drainage.

After several days of work, Bud readied and secured the camp, hoisted and cached supplies, and then hiked back out over the Swan Range.

On Thanksgiving Day, Bud and a friend, Mike Stevenson, arrived back at the wilderness trapping camp after a several-day snowshoe trek over the mountains from the Swan Valley. Lots of work needed to be done to prepare for the December–January marten trapping season. Mike came in to help break trail, then trekked back out the next morning.

All alone, Bud went hunting for mule deer on a high ridge, but, as Bud said cryptically, he was "foiled by a mountain lion." It was crucial that Bud have success, because he needed the meat for his sustenance and the scrap for his marten bait. "It's a long way to the butcher shop when you're back there," he said.

The next day, on a high ridge above camp, Bud killed a beautiful muley buck while the snow filtered down around him. He dragged the buck toward camp for processing, eventually quartering the animal to carry it over the downed timber and brush.

To prepare for the opening of trapping season on December 1, Bud split slender pegs into various lengths to use in his trademark "peg sets." For each set, Bud selected a dead tree, pounded in longer pegs, and added some fir boughs to form a roof over the set and cover the bait. Two short pegs held the No. 1 foothold trap, while pegs on the sides guided the marten into the trap as the furtive mustelid sought the bait. Bud developed this set design as an improvement to the old notch set in the trunk of the tree. He made his sets in dead trees, and discarded the pegs (split from natural materials) when finished. Bud called this "no-trace trapping."

Bud began setting his traps and spur lines in the lonely, frosty woods on the opening day of trapping season. Bud enjoyed amazing views of the high mountains in every direction, and he had solitude in great measure. It took him several days to snowshoe along and visit all the sets arranged in spur lines, then he would do it all over again. On his line up Gill Creek, he eventually made more than thirty sets, and it proved to be his most productive drainage. Bud was demonstrating the old-time values of long-term trapping in an isolated, inaccessible landscape.

Bud stayed safe while crossing streams; a misstep and dunking in a creek while trying to cross a snow bridge would be dangerous in temperatures that sometimes dipped well below zero. During these frigid temperatures, handling traps and making sets sometimes became nearly impossible. Bud had earlier learned the technique of lighting a stump or snag on fire to thaw out his hands and stave off major frostbite. He made it through the winter with only one case of moderate frostbite on his thumb.

From his first check, Bud had good success catching the large mustelids, which measured about two to three feet long and weighed two

Bud Moore checking a marten trap during the winter of 1983–1984.

or three pounds. His sets were targeted for marten, and that's what he caught.

For Bud, it was a special thing to see a beautiful, dark marten hanging in a set that he'd carefully designed and built. To arrive at this success, everything had to click: the location, the set design, the bait, the lure. Bud felt a sense of pride when it all came together to catch what he called "a fine piece of fur."

Each night, Bud would skin his catch in the fur tent, stretch the hides flesh side out, and allow them to dry in the heated tent. When the hides were tacky, Bud turned the hides fur side out and produced clean pelts, beautiful and almost as light as a feather. American marten provide an elegant and valuable fur, also known as sable. Bud took pride in taking great care with the pelts so they would yield the best possible value—something he considered important to honoring his catch.

Bud trapped and prepared the pelts of thirty velvety-furred marten before taking a break and mushing out for Christmas. He packed his bale of fur over the top of the Swan Mountains and back down to the valley. Furbearer report records showed that Bud checked in thirty marten pelts for tagging with Montana FWP warden Guy Shanks on December 28, 1983. This was a great catch.

In early January, after a rejuvenating stay at home, Bud and Koyak mushed through sloppy snow for several days back over the Swan Range and in to his Palisade camp. The weather had warmed and Bud expected that "the fur would be running." And it was, especially in Gill Creek, where Bud nabbed a good catch of marten not long after he returned to the Palisade camp.

In the meantime, word about Bud's trip into the heart of the wilderness in winter had attracted a lot of attention from Swan Valley residents and others who found it unusual that Bud, described by Janet as "pushing seventy," could handle such an adventure. Some were concerned about his safety.

"If I'd known everyone would get so stirred up, I might not even have gone in," Bud said. "There were all kinds of speculation about what might have happened to me, but I was warm and active, piling up fur and enjoying it to no end."

The media also learned of Bud's trip. Several reporters from the *Missoulian* newspaper decided to snowshoe into Bud's Bob Marshall Wilderness camp in late January and cover his story.

"One day I was heading through the snow up the spur line to Lion Pass along the Swan Range," said Bud, "and I saw something red up there; I couldn't believe my eyes." Bud found a small stuff sack attached to a tree near one of his marten sets. The sack held a few items meant for him, including a "nice little bundle of first aid supplies" and two or three big, chewy fruit bars. "That was great," said Bud. "I sat down and ate a fruit bar right on the spot."

Bud learned from a note the crew had left that it had taken them three days struggling though deep snow just to cross the Swan Range and reach the closest marten set, and that they were probably overloaded with gear. "They reasoned," Bud said, "that if they wallowed all the way down to my camp and then had to make it all the way back out, they'd be long overdue."

Later, Bud sent the *Missoulian* editor a note thanking them for making the effort to cover his expedition, and for bringing the fruit bars. In his note, he said that the reporters' efforts under tough winter conditions made the *Missoulian* look good. "They did run a nice picture of Lion Creek Pass," said Bud.

The media attention and buzz around the Swan Valley prompted a number of people to contact the U.S. Forest Service and others about rules and safety. This type of long-term camp was generally not allowed in the wilderness, which is why Bud had called the Forest Service in July 1983. He talked to the Spotted Bear district ranger, Dave Owen, and explained his goals and purpose for the expedition. Finally, on January 13, 1984, well into Bud's trip, a letter from Owen arrived in Condon:

> Dear Bud: This letter will belatedly serve as a follow-up on your telephone request back on July 19th, 1983, outlining your trapping plans for the winter 83-84 particularly use of a site in the Palisade Drainage. Normally we expect little concern relating to that activity, however the media coverage of your operations have generated a number of inquiries related to duration of use of a site, caching of equipment and the like.

After this first paragraph, Owen went on to cite administrative rules and guidelines. He then more or less issued Bud a retroactive approval and noted that it was consistent with the Wilderness Act. Owen wrote, "This letter will serve as the appropriate authorization to occupy an undesignated campsite in the Palisade Creek drainage for the purpose of trapping furbearers during the time period November 1983–March 1984. . . . The authorization recognizes a use of wilderness land that covers a span of 100 years or more, the primitive means of conduction the activity are consistant [sic] to the provisions of the Wilderness Act of 1964." Owen went on to list conditions to restore the site after the trapping foray was complete. Better late than never, Bud had his official approval and the Forest Service had covered itself.

Bud closed up the Palisade camp by the end of January. He tidied everything and loaded his pack with his precious marten pelts and a few supplies. After a few days and a big push over the Swan Range, Bud and Koyak would be back home. He would return in summer with pack stock to no-trace the site and remove the remnants of his camp.

Bud ended up with about sixty marten that winter. When he came out at the end of January, Bud checked in thirty-one more marten pelts with Warden Shanks on a form dated February 3, 1984. Bud's trip demonstrated exactly what he'd hoped: traditional long-line trapping in a wilderness setting is doable and a heritage to be celebrated.

After resting the area, Bud again trapped the upper Little Salmon drainage within the wilderness. During the winter of 1985–1986, he made a half dozen loops along his trapline, starting and ending the sixty-mile loop in the Swan Valley.

"I crossed the Swan Range twice a week that winter, making about six trips," said Bud. "It's a pretty hard lift over those ridges." A number of people wanted to accompany Bud that winter because he was coming out so often. A series of physically fit, mostly young men accompanied Bud to help him carry the load and to learn his no-trace trapping techniques. At sixty-eight years old, Bud was driven by the spectacular high-country views in winter, and by his love of backcountry, solitude, and trapping.

On these in-and-out trips, Bud avoided bad avalanche areas near Smith Creek Pass by crossing the pass near Owl Peak, between Lion and Smith Creek Passes. "You could go over Smith and down the other side, but then there's huge avalanche slopes coming in from either side, and you have to cross that son-of-a gun, and I don't know how you do it. I wasn't willing to risk it."

So Bud went up Lion Creek, where he had a camp, then cross-country up over a little pass skirting 8,250-foot Owl Peak into the head of the Little Salmon, and down to his old Palisade camp. The route covers a fair amount of open country with potential avalanche danger, but as Bud said, "it's tough but you can do it." If you're Bud Moore, that is.

Bud then set spur lines out of the Palisade camp—one spur line up a smaller drainage, one down the Little Salmon. Then, on the way out, Bud would reverse direction on his snowshoe trail back up over the pass to his Lion Creek camp and down to the Swan Valley. This made for a tight loop, limiting the coverage of his trapline. The experience showed that staying at a camp in the heart of the wilderness, like he did in 1983–1984, was a superior way to run the trapline.

"Bud made national news on those trips," said Janet. "NBC, ABC crews, all of them wanted to come out and go in there to cover him, but they couldn't find any reporters who were tough enough to carry their equipment and still make it."

Bud Moore on his Swan Valley cabin's front porch.
PHOTOGRAPH BY JOHN FRALEY.

Janet was a big supporter and proud of Bud, but he steadfastly refused to talk about his superior condition and talent for wilderness travel. "Humility is so important in wilderness," he said. "If you make a few mistakes by overestimating your ability you can end up a corpse. You need to remember that you can always cross that pass the next day. I always wanted to make it out to sell my furs."

Later, Bud made several attempts to convince the Forest Service to make the extended-stay idea official in the regulations for the Bob, but he was not completely successful. The Forest Service did confirm that recreational trapping in the Bob with the fourteen-day stay limit for one camp was consistent with wilderness values. Bud noted that Dave Owen's letter explained the rules as he would like to see them. A follow-up letter from district ranger Greg Warren stuck with the fourteen-day camping limit. Bud said that the new rules make it "impossible for a trapper to operate in all but the fringes of the Bob Marshall Complex."

But Bud noted that the right of recreational trapping and managing furbearers in wilderness still holds through state management and responsibility, and this was included in the cooperative fish and wildlife management plan for the Bob in 1994. "It's the only hope that the trappers have," said Bud.

Bud had taken his best shot and made progress for wilderness trappers. He was "hooked on the spell that wilderness creates on natural land." He gave his heart to the Little Salmon traplines before his advancing age shut the backcountry down for him. He demonstrated traditional long-line trapping techniques and wilderness travel in winter. Bud took on the bureaucracy, and although he didn't come up with the decisive victory he had hoped for, he made progress. Even Bud couldn't win them all.

Bud, a conservation icon, passed away on November 26, 2010, at the age of ninety-three. Janet had preceded him in death on April 7, 2001. Bud left a monumental legacy in his long conservation career, with hundreds of people seeking him out for advice and counsel; his son, Bill, called it the "Bud Thing." To start learning Bud's lessons, read his magnum opus, The Lochsa Story, *his autobiographical, landmark book on land ethics in the Bitterroot Mountains.*

SOURCES

Personal interview by the author with Bud Moore; notes by the author December 6, 1995.

Extensive recorded personal interview by the author with Bud Moore at the Coyote Forest, April 16, 1996. I relied on this interview to a large extent. There were many shorter interviews and meetings with Bud over the next decade and more for various projects.

Personal interview with Bud Moore; notes by the author, June 13, 1996.

Moore, Bud. Three-page single-spaced letter from Bud to author John Fraley (at that time FWP's representative to produce a Bob Marshall Wilderness fish and wildlife management plan; Greg

Warren was the Forest Service representative), October 19, 1994. In these comments, Bud mentions Dave Owen's approach and Greg Warren's more restrictive approach to wilderness long-line trapping.

Warren, Greg, Forest Service district ranger. Letter to Bud Moore and Mike Stevenson outlining the continuation of more restrictive caching and length-of-stay regulations for the Bob Marshall Wilderness, applying to trapping and other uses, March 11, 1991. The letter does confirm that trapping is a permissible use in the Bob as long as the fourteen-day restriction is followed on a specific campsite.

Montana Department of Fish, Wildlife, and Parks. Marten harvest registration form for William R. Moore, thirty marten; December 28, 1983; another harvest registration form for Bud, thirty-one marten, February 3, 1984.

Moore, Bud. "No-Trace Trapping in Wilderness." Manuscript, 1980. Copy given to Fraley by Bud. Eventually appeared in the magazine *The Trapper.* Bud said he wrote it for trappers.

Fraley, John. "Bud." *Montana Outdoors* 27, no. 6 (November/December 1996). I included some modified portions of this article for this chapter.

USFS and Montana Fish, Wildlife & Parks. *Fish and Wildlife Management Plan for the Bob Marshall Wilderness Complex,* John Fraley and Greg Warren, eds., 1994. Signed by district rangers and FWP supervisors around the complex.

Letter from Montana HD 65 representative Janet Moore, March 25, 1987, regarding furbearer management, specifically lynx.

Owen, Dave, U.S. Forest Service letter giving approval for Bud's Bob Marshall Wilderness extended stay for the purpose of marten trapping in the Little Salmon drainage, January 13, 1984.

6

HEROES OF THE BOB

First Couple

Over the past thirty years, Greg and Deb Schatz have ridden 25,000 miles in the Bob Marshall Wilderness.

DEB AND GREG SCHATZ CAME TO MONTANA more than thirty years ago determined to become the best wilderness packers they could be. Through steep learning curves and horse wrecks, they found the secret to achieve their goal: never give up.

Deb and Greg met at Minnesota State University–Moorhead. Their experiences with livestock were a common bond. Greg had learned to pack in a New Mexico wilderness with burros, and Deb, who grew up on a farm with stock, was impressed that he knew how to tie complex knots. They married, then headed to Montana in 1988.

Now, more than thirty years and tens of thousands of miles on horseback later, Deb and Greg could be considered the "First Couple" of the Bob. After a rough and humorous start, and with their "never give up" attitude, the couple have become some of the best packers around. Few couples have spent more time in the Bob, ridden more miles, or given more back to the wilderness they love.

Greg and Deb have dedicated their lives to traveling and packing in the Bob, often packing in youth groups, trail crews, and others. They've found that safety and success in the backcountry requires total focus, which comes naturally. "Horses and packing are what we do," said Greg.

It hasn't always been easy. The rocky start to their Bob Marshall packing career would have been enough to discourage most people, but not Greg and Deb. Looking back at it, they now find it funny.

"I'd learned to pack a little bit in New Mexico," said Greg. "We moved up here and joined Back Country Horsemen of the Flathead and got all this advice. Of course, we were broke and in our twenties and just starting out, so we bought green horses because they were cheaper. We bought a $350 horse, Scruffy, to use as a packhorse. So, we practiced with him, and he was a little bit flighty."

"A lot flighty," added Deb.

When they tried to load Scruffy, he would circle around. Any noise would scare him, even just a rope scraping across the pannier.

Scruffy's "real" name was Smokey. When the Schatzes first got him, an experienced packer, Russ Barnett of Outfitter Supply in Columbia Falls, came over to help with Smokey. When he got there and saw the horse, he asked what we were doing with "Scruffy." He didn't think that he looked like the type to be a good packhorse and he was right; Scruffy was too thin, a Quarter Horse. So the Scruffy name stuck.

They started out making mistakes. "We had these army panniers," said Greg. "We didn't know any better, but they were way big, twice as big as they should have been."

For a first trip, they were advised to try the Summit trailhead near Marias Pass. "We thought: good trail, flat, lots of grass, good first trip," said Greg. "So, we got up there, and there was an unlocked, barbed wire gate between the road and the trailhead, because of a grazing lease. Fortunately, we closed the gate behind us when we got in there." In a bit of foreshadowing, Greg noted, "We didn't have the money to buy collapsible buckets, so we just tied a metal bucket on top of the load."

We loaded up, got on our horses, took two or three steps," said Greg. "And here came a train. And the trains, when they reached Marias Pass, blew their whistles. This was a new sound, and Scruffy lost it. He pulled back, ripped the lead rope out of my hand, and started bucking and running around the parking lot, bucket banging around, so it was going really bad."

Deb was riding Cisco, and Greg was riding Dusty. "Cisco and Dusty didn't do anything," said Greg. "They were kind of like,

'Whatever, we don't like Scruffy anyway.'" At least they had closed the gate behind them, which helped corral the spontaneous rodeo.

Finally, Scruffy stopped, and Greg and Deb unloaded him, then reloaded him. At this point, Scruffy was really jumpy. Greg and Deb swung into the saddle and rode down across the creek, and then they started hitting the mud.

"There were cattle and four-wheelers using the trail," said Deb. "Every low spot was full of water and mud. The first two miles were horrible."

"Dusty decided she didn't want to get in the mud; she refused," said Greg. "And she couldn't get around the mud, because the trees were right there. Then Cisco went ahead and Dusty followed Cisco, then Scruffy balked at the mud."

Deb had to go back around Scruffy and encourage him so he would go through the mud. She had to lead the horses individually. Greg was still leading Scruffy, but with a lot of rope out. "Scruffy was smashing into trees," said Greg. "It wasn't pretty."

"Every time we got to one of those muddy areas, it was a production," said Deb. "And it went on for two miles with maybe 100 of those muddy dips."

It took the crew hours to go the first mile.

"You're supposed to go three miles an hour," said Greg. "But it took us three hours to go one mile. So after about six hours, we had made it two miles, and finally reached the Two Medicine River."

The discouraged travelers set up a small camp along the river, while rain drenched them. They had planned on being in there five or six days, but by the time they set up camp and it was still raining, they agreed to leave the next day. The soggy riders decided to forgo all the day rides they had planned.

"After that, we started riding Scruffy and we packed Dusty, and all of a sudden everything was good," said Deb. "Scruffy was still a nut, but he was a lot happier being ridden." And ride they did—having survived that first trip, the Schatzes began packing into the Bob on a regular basis, amassing many trail miles and learning the territory.

Scruffy liked being in front. He had the entire Bob memorized. Not only did he have it memorized, he knew what areas they had camped in and wanted to return to those.

"He could connect the dots, somehow, in his head," said Greg. "And he had an incredible memory of the trail, where he had stepped over downfall, whatever. It could be a month later, he'd figure it out."

Scruffy, with racing in his blood, showed great promise in skijoring. He loved to pull and race. The only problem was that Scruffy wanted to compete when he was in the pack string. If the packhorse behind him sped up, he would think, "We're skijoring, let's go." He would run past Greg leading the string, while the other packhorse ran past Greg on the other side, nearly knocking him out of the saddle. After a time or two of that, Greg put Scruffy in the back of the pack string.

On one trip in the early 1990s, they headed into the Bob at Benchmark for a planned one-month trek. But they came out after two weeks and went to Augusta to get Dusty checked out by a vet because of an infection on her neck.

After Dusty was patched up, Greg and Deb headed back into the Bob to Gates Park, and after fourteen miles of knee-deep mud, they reached Gooseberry Park where they met Forest Service ranger Al Koss. Because of the mud, their mounts needed shoes badly, but there were none at Gooseberry. Al offered to let them use the horseshoes at Schafer. Deb and Greg rode another fourteen miles and camped just short of Schafer Cabin. They decided to have dinner before going up to the station to shoe the horses. They dug into the boxes and found a dish with mostly dried mashed potatoes, but the cooking directions had worn off the bag.

"We messed up the whole thing," said Greg. "We ended up having partially dried mashed potatoes, way too many of them, but we forced ourselves to eat them because they're hard to get rid of," Deb recalled. "It was terrible."

The bloated riders went up to Schafer Cabin to get the shoes and ran into a jovial Al Koss, who said, "You should come in and have dinner with us! We made lasagna!"

Greg and Deb went into the station. On the large table sat two huge cake pans of lasagna; only four people were there for dinner. But the couple were so stuffed they couldn't eat a morsel.

"They had green salad, too, and we hadn't eaten anything fresh for a while. But we couldn't eat anything," said Deb. "In fact, we were so full, that when we went to bed that night, we wondered what might happen to our stomachs. When these potatoes hydrate, would we wake up bloated?" After a few days at Schafer, Greg and Deb soldiered on, planning to ride to Gates Park via Chair Mountain.

Greg and Deb were learning to pack using manty loads; the packers in the Back Country Horsemen had urged them to use manties, not panniers. (Panniers are boxes made of wood, leather, or plastic, and manties are canvas tarps that the packer wraps around a load and secures with ropes.) On the ride from Schafer to Chair Mountain, a gorgeous trail, they were packing using this technique when they ran out of film for their camera.

"I looked at the packs and wondered where the film was," said Deb. "Which manty is the film in? Which side is it on? Do we at least know that?" Deb finally dug out the film. The sidehill was steep with beargrass, and some of the load was sliding down, but they were able to re-manty everything and kept going.

The couple came down Red Shale Creek and rode on to Gates Park where they did some more shoeing. By the end of the trip, Deb had the knack of horseshoeing. Greg complained about being too tall to bend down, so Deb nailed on the shoes while Greg held the horse.

"We reset about four shoes," said Deb. "Twenty minutes, I had the shoe on. We learned to know where the shoeing tools are in the pack and to take extra shoes. We learned how to manty and where to put certain things so they didn't fall out of the corners. You just learned a lot of tricks."

Deb and Greg learned that the manties were superior to pack boxes or panniers, especially on sidehill portions of the trail. They avoided rubbing on brush, and the load could swing if they hit a log or something, while boxes had no give when they hit objects. Manties keep the weight higher on the horse and off the ribs. Plastic boxes are really hot, while manties breathe. Packhorses that are loaded with panniers or boxes can even have their ribs flattened; the panniers hang down lower and the horse's ribs can become deformed.

All in all, the month-long trip stood as kind of a "coming of age" pack trip. Greg and Deb had some setbacks, but they came away from the trip with a lot more knowledge, skill, and confidence.

Seeking to improve their technique, Greg and Deb attended a Back Country Horsemen convention not long after that trip. It was crowded and they were last in the lunch line. They were looking for a place to sit, and Deb suggested taking a seat alongside three important-looking people. Greg said, "We can't sit over there, that's Smoke Elser." But Deb dragged Greg over and they joined them anyway. Smoke, a legendary packer, instructor, and author (see Chapter 13), warmly welcomed the young couple.

"We learned a ton of things from Smoke about packing," said Greg. "How to manty, how to load." Later, Greg took Smoke's packing class at the Ninemile Wildlands Training Center in Huson. Smoke lined up the twenty students, one on each side of a mule, and guided them through the loading process. "Every time there was a Smoke Elser packing demonstration in western Montana, we were there," said Greg. "He knew the mistakes we were making and he didn't even have to see us packing. He's been doing it so long, he could read people. He realized that we wanted to learn, so we picked up lots of stuff. He was our greatest teacher."

The next time the Schatzes set out on a long sojourn through the Bob, they had the packing thing down. The couple came to learn a standard routine when they packed: get up, graze the horses, pack them up, head out, ride, choose the next campsite, handle the horses the same every day, and set up a highline in a good spot at each camp.

"It gets to be a routine for you and for the horses, and everybody kind of settles down," said Deb. "It's like you live there. We pick the camp based on the horses, highline, water, grass, not so much on where the cooking area is, or where the tarp will be. I don't go back there to eat, I don't go back there to cook. We go back there to ride."

Deb and Greg use sideline hobbles to limit the horses' mobility when they are grazing near camp. They check on the horses every twenty minutes. The average grazing time is about two hours in the morning and two hours at night, but they watch how long it takes them to get full. Each horse eats about twenty pounds per day, and if the horses start moving around it shows they are getting full, and they go back on the highline. Deb and Greg never leave the stock out overnight. "That's just asking for trouble," said Deb.

Because of good management, the couple has never had stock run off. "Why did we never go more than twenty minutes without seeing our stock? It's simple. In twenty minutes, a horse can go a mile. With sideline hobbles, their front leg is tied to the back leg so they have to walk. Scruffy learned to dangle one leg and run with the other three. But he wears out after a while. We graze them so they have to pass us if they try to head out. They have incredible memories and they want to go home, and they know the entire complex where all the trailheads are."

On the next month-long trip, they brought three packhorses: Dusty, Willy, and Cisco. Greg was riding Scruffy. Deb decided she wanted to try plastic panniers to test them out for an all-ladies trip she was planning. Decidedly anti-pannier, Greg was doubtful about it.

Cisco was a solid horse and had never caused any real problems. But when trying something new like plastic panniers, it's advisable to test it at home: put on the panniers and lead the horse around. Instead, they had picked up the panniers at Outfitters Supply, right on the way to the Benchmark trailhead. "What could go wrong?" said Greg.

At Benchmark, on the east side of the Divide, they loaded up the horses and prepared to head out on the trail. They didn't realize how noisy plastic panniers could be, with things like a water pot banging against the side of the pannier. The couple rode out from the trailhead and after a few hundred yards reached the suspension bridge across the West Fork of the Sun River. Greg was leading Willy and rode onto a little ramp that leads to the bridge. Willy stopped for a second, and to catch up she trotted a few steps. Behind her, Cisco trotted to catch up, with Dusty following. At this point, the whole crew was still on the suspension bridge.

"Cisco never carried panniers, wasn't used to the noise, and he started to buck," said Greg. "And Dusty was thinking, what's behind me bucking, I better get out of here, and pulled up behind Scruffy. Then Scruffy thought he needed to get out of there, thinking, 'I'm a racehorse, I'm fast,' and he took off. I was hauling back on Scruffy's reins as hard as I could, and we were three across heading over the bridge, and hit the wing of the bridge on the other side. At that point all the horses were bucking, and gear was strewn everywhere."

The horses settled down and the couple gathered up the gear and got repacked. As planned, they headed up toward Stadler Pass and then cut north and hit Grizzly Basin. But the area was muddy, there was no place to camp, and three feet of snow lingered in places.

It was near the Fourth of July, but it had been a big snow year. So they turned back and retraced their steps, with the horses lunging back through the snow down to the South Fork of the Sun. At one point, Willy lunged and landed on Scruffy's tail, pulling some of it off, quite a piece, adding to their woes.

"There was lots of downfall; we had to cut our way in, and more on the way out," said Greg. "We made it back down to the river, and after all that, we had to camp about a mile from the suspension bridge. That was all the first day of the trip." But always determined, Greg and Deb, as planned, persevered for a month in the Bob. And lucky for other wilderness travelers, they became an unofficial, two-person trail crew for the duration of the trip.

"We figured that we cut seventy-five miles of trail all by ourselves," said Deb. "And that was just what we couldn't go over or around." They used a two-foot-long handsaw, which, although tiring, proved to be pretty efficient and could be kept sharp with a chainsaw file. For safety, Deb would hold the string while Greg used the saw. He would take 100 cuts, take a break, then repeat. Some bigger logs required 400 strokes to cut, and if a log fell right, the horses could step over it after one cut, although depending on the horse, that could be tricky.

The travelers camped at the West Fork of the Sun for a few days, then headed toward White River Pass, which at least one string before them had crossed that season. Deb and Greg realized that their trip would be a grand adventure: challenging, but with so many high points. They were rewarded by views of immense fields of blooming beargrass on the way up to the pass.

As the riders approached the pass and crossed it, they had to negotiate six-foot drifts. It was early in the morning, so the snow was firmer, but the footing was touchy. Enjoying the spectacular scenery of the south end of the Chinese Wall, they rode over the Divide and down the White River, bound eventually for Salmon Forks on the South Fork of the Flathead where they had agreed earlier to meet Beth Hodder and a Forest Service crew. Beth had invited Greg and Deb to help on ideas to revamp an outfitter camp. When they got to the river crossing, a sign warned that the river was too high to cross. Greg was skeptical, but when he looked at the river, he was convinced: the water rushed six feet deep at the crossing, which even under good conditions can be tough.

Crossing a pack bridge in the Bob, Greg atop Scruffy, followed by Twister.
PHOTOGRAPH COURTESY OF DEB AND GREG SCHATZ.

So the couple turned around on the east-side trail along the South Fork and crossed the White River, heading for Big Prairie where a suspension bridge crosses the river. The river at Big Prairie was bank full. They rode down the west-side trail, cutting downfall as they went, to reach Salmon Forks where they met the Forest Service crew.

After working on the outfitter camp revamp, the next planned stop on their trip was Big River Meadows, a gorgeous flat in the headwaters of the Middle Fork, where they had planned on meeting another friend, Marie. The riders left Salmon Forks and started for Black Bear, where a suspension bridge crosses the South Fork. They had planned to go over Pagoda Mountain but were informed that the trail was impassable. They rode across the bridge to the east-side trail and back up to the White River, upstream to Brushy Park, then cut their way over Larch Hill Pass, down Rock Creek, Gates Park, up over Sun River Pass, and on to Big River Meadows, cutting downfall all the way. The couple would get up at daylight and cut their way down the trail until dark, then set up camp. The riders had to keep moving because of the blowdown, or they wouldn't make their rendezvous with their friend, Marie, at Big River Meadows. They finally met up with Marie, and were also planning on dropping in at Badger cabin to put up some trail signs for the Forest Service.

"We hit this incredible downfall," said Greg. "We cut for hours, and it's starting to get dark. We had to bail on that project. We camped at Strawberry Creek, then went out the North Fork of Birch Creek, and out of the wilderness. We were in for a month, hundreds of miles, but we could have quit the first day."

At one point on the trip, near Grizzly Park, they ran into a trail crew at about 9 A.M. Greg had been cutting since dawn. "Where have you guys been?" Greg asked them. "We couldn't get across the river," they replied. Greg made it known that he wasn't happy, and he said it accomplished something. He said the trip illustrated to the Forest Service how accessing the wilderness from different points could make trail work more efficient.

Deb and Greg also discovered that after a month in the backcountry, everything seemed to move at hyperspeed when they came out of the wilderness. Driving out the trailhead road, then the highway, each step was more foreign. In the wilderness, life moved at a slow, easy pace, but outside, everything seemed to be in a hurry. And, Deb noted, she really missed the twenty-four-hours-a-day comradery with the horses. "The horses feel like partners," said Deb. "When we go into the Bob, your life is literally in their hands. You might be going along a steep drop-off and things could go right, things can go wrong. You just have to trust they will do what you want them to do."

"We were asked once, what else do we do besides horses," said Greg. "And we explained that our entire lives are tied up with horses. That's what we do.

"We've ridden 25,000 to 30,000 miles in the Bob," said Greg. "For one stretch of twenty years we averaged about 1,000 miles a year. We've been lucky. Never had to put a horse down, never had a serious injury, either us or our horses. We spent a lot of time with knowledgeable people in the Back Country Horsemen. We would learn from their stories what to do and what not to do. That shortened our learning curve, and when we faced a challenge we could figure out what to do. And we have great horses. Deb has a sense of picking out horses."

Deb and Greg got into volunteer packing in a big way to give back to the wilderness and to show people, especially challenged youngsters, the value of wilderness. They also packed in other trail crews for the Bob Marshall Wilderness Foundation and Montana Wilderness Association.

"We did the first horse packing for the foundation about twenty years ago," said Greg. "We thought, 'We have some volunteers who are going to keep the trails open, and we can pack? Let's not be stupid about this.'"

"Trail budgets were continually being cut," said Deb. "So we wanted to help. Packing in a crew is a lot more efficient than cutting it yourself. And we could introduce people to the Bob.

"For the youngsters, there was an amazing difference in their attitudes when you packed them in compared to when you packed them out," said Deb. "They had been doing things they'd never done before, and they were so proud of themselves, what they could accomplish. At the trailhead on the way in, they didn't see the value of it. Their phones weren't going to work, they have to carry their packs. But when they get in there, they say, 'Wow, I walked six miles or seventeen or whatever miles today.'"

Deb and Greg would pack in and drop the groups, then go on their own pack trip and pack the crew out at the end of the weeklong stint. They would join the group for the last night before departure. Often the kids would want to show them the work they had done clearing trail—the log they cut or the brush they cleared. The trail crew members knew that the horses had packed in their tools and some of their personal gear, so they took pride in showing Deb and Greg that they cut the trail with the horses in mind.

"It was so neat to hear what they had to say," said Deb. "One girl told me that she had never 'peed in a hole before.' Just basic things that the rest of us take for granted."

Greg and Deb estimated that over the years they've packed about seventy-five groups of youngsters into the Bob. In total, they packed in maybe 100 trail crew groups.

"I've done ladies-only trips with the Foundation, Hope Ranch, Girl

Scouts, Montana Academy, and others, just girls, more than a dozen of these trips," said Deb. "It makes an impact on the kids when they see ladies doing everything with the horses. I make sure there's a project involved that they will work on."

Once Deb and Greg packed in a group from the Hope Ranch. "It was their first time in, and they were scared," said Greg. "We lost them at one point because of a mix-up around Gibson Reservoir. And we had all their gear, tents, and so on. Luckily, we found them near a campsite near Circle Creek, where there's a little Forest Service cabin. They had ridden across the reservoir in Click's pontoon boat and headed to the cabin, while we rode the fourteen or so miles on the trail around the reservoir. I found a master key among my others and it worked, so I got in and called their crew leader on the radio. We found out we had just missed them in a nearby meadow, so we met them there with their tents and food. They had been scared, with rain clouds building and claps of thunder. So everything turned out okay."

After several days and a short side trip, Greg and Deb rode back to pick up the crew. Greg was chatting with several of the young ladies, and they were excited. They had worked so hard and did all kinds of great work; they probably talked for forty-five minutes. But when the adults showed up, they zipped their lips. They weren't going to let on how much fun they'd had. They didn't want to open up in front of their adult leaders.

On one landmark trip, Greg, Deb, and a friend, John, agreed to pack for a Montana Wilderness Association (MWA) trip as part of the Continental Divide Trail rehabilitation program. A fire had swept through Bowl Creek in the upper Middle Fork and burned the trail corduroy logs, so MWA had a contract to replace them. Someone else packed the crew's gear in, and Deb and Greg packed in loads of gravel for the trail project. On the return trip, they would pack out the crew's gear. The trip didn't start out well, but it ended in national fame.

"We got all set up at the trailhead, loaded the horses," said Greg. "We had ours—Twister, Dusty, and Scruffy—and had borrowed three more, Shotgun, Whisky, and Houdini. We were going up Teton Pass, pretty steep, when all of a sudden, all the packhorses were trying to pass me on Red Rocket. We get everybody settled back down. It was hot and the horses were tired."

Hauling gravel for a trail project, Deb Schatz uses the pack string to tamp down the new tread. PHOTOGRAPH COURTESY OF DEB AND GREG SCHATZ.

When the group reached Teton Pass, they thought it would be good to fly-spray the borrowed horses because they were hot and bothered by bugs. They tied the first horse off and tied the others to him, then started fly-spraying.

The first horse handled the spraying well. The second horse was good, but when Greg started spraying the third horse, the horse lost it, pulled loose from the pack string, and bucked down the trail out of sight through the trees. Teton Pass is relatively flat on top, so the crew just waited until the bucking stopped and then got him back in line.

The riders dropped over the pass and reached the trail crew camp at Grizzly Park, a beautiful meadow perched along Bowl Creek, a clear and fish-filled headwater stream of the Middle Fork of the Flathead. John was inexperienced using hobbles, and he was riding his wife's horse, which usually is a bad idea.

"In general, only under extreme circumstances do you ride your wife's horse," said Greg. "You are asking for trouble because you relate to the animal much differently."

The horse wasn't used to hobbles. Greg told John, "Whatever you do, don't put the rear hobble on first because if he starts kicking, he'll swing the hobble and run around with it. Always put the front hobble on first."

It was a picket hobble with a long chain, and John's horse pulled the picket out and started running through camp with the chain flying around. The trail workers had returned to camp and their eyes were really big, watching John running after the horse and the chain whipping around.

"We just stood back and protected our horses," said Greg. "Whatever happens in a wreck, you don't want to be in it. Let it run its course and go from there. The horse finally ran himself out and we got things put back together. And we thought, we have to pack gravel tomorrow, this is going badly." The horse wouldn't eat that night, but it seemed to recover all right by morning.

The next morning the crew hiked a few miles up the trail to the project, back toward the pass. The packers rode up to where the crew was, and then stopped and looked.

"We were riding up to the work site, and we saw a lady sitting there along the trail," said Greg. "And it looked like she had a little bear with her, covered by her coat, a black furry thing. We hadn't seen any animals in camp, and the Forest Service has strict rules about not having dogs along. We were wondering what was going on."

The trail crew had found two dogs that were apparently lost. They weren't backcountry dogs, and they couldn't find their way out. Maybe they had followed a pack string in, or chased an animal.

"The lady was taking care of one of the dogs," said Deb. "Their pads were all torn and they were cold, shivering, it was wet and rainy; everyone got their fleeces out and gave them to the dogs."

The trail crew leader, Sonny, radioed the Forest Service to relay a phone number on one of the dog tags. They were able to reach the dispatcher in Choteau and notify the dogs' owners in Conrad. The owners had rented a cabin near the trailhead, and when the dogs ran off they had spent days looking for them. But their black spaniels were nowhere to be found, and the owners had pretty much accepted the dogs weren't coming back. One of the dogs was an older female, and the other was her offspring.

The dogs, too, were on the verge of giving up, so the first challenge was to get them the two miles back to camp. Deb and Greg put the dogs in empty gravel bags with their heads sticking out and slung the bags on either side of Dusty's packsaddle.

"But, horses being prey, they don't want to get eaten by a predator," said Deb. "We put these predators on Dusty's back, and her look was like, 'You have stooped to a new low asking me to pack dogs.'"

The packers got the dogs back to camp and fed them some rice. One of the ladies in the crew had a dog rescue operation down the Bitterroot Valley, so she knew how to handle dogs in distress. The dogs hadn't eaten in a long time. Someone had to stay in camp to watch them, because the crew was going to be there three or four more days.

"After a while, the dogs sat in everybody's laps, wanting to be petted," said Deb. "It was a dog-loving crew. The dogs were set up sleeping in Sonny's tent on horse pads."

The gravel, dug out of a deposit near Bowl Creek, proved to be just what was needed to repair the trail, and everyone felt good about getting a lot of work done over the next few days. The crew packed up and was getting ready to head back over Teton Pass and out to the trailhead. An extra horse was not available to pack the dogs out, so the trail crew decided to carry the dogs out on a pole between them, suspended in empty gravel bags. But one of the dogs soon got out of the bag and walked out on her own. The older dog rode in her bag quite a ways before she too got out and walked.

"The dogs' owner met us at the trailhead," said Deb. "We made the transfer, but the dogs didn't seem that happy. We got back home Sunday night and I took the next day off. I got back to work on

Tuesday, and my co-workers asked how the trip went. I started talking about the dogs and they said they'd already heard about the dogs. I thought that they couldn't have heard that story because I just got home."

It turned out that one of Deb's younger co-workers, Lauren, was in the family who owned the dogs, and she had grown up with them. The person who had picked up the dogs at the trailhead was not a favorite of the dogs, so that's why they didn't seem that happy when they got to the trailhead. But Lauren was thrilled to have the dogs home safe and sound.

"So after a few weeks, the story was going around and started hitting the newspapers," said Greg. "Sonny got a call from his mom who was riding the subway in the D.C. suburbs and saw a story in the *Washington Post* about the rescue. Across the top of the front page along the masthead was a picture of Ted Cruz, a picture of Hillary Clinton, and a picture of me with Cisco, Scruffy, and the two dogs in sacks strung on the packsaddle. We started checking around and it made all the major newspapers in Seattle, California, and other places. It had over one million likes on Facebook."

After nearly thirty years of hard work and dedication in the Bob, Scruffy, Cisco, and Dusty had finally earned celebrity status and made the national limelight.

All told, it's been a wild and wonderful ride for Deb and Greg. "We've always felt that if you have horses, you need to use them," said Deb. "We keep our horses active, and just like with people, it keeps them healthy all around."

What motivates the couple? "It's the horses, the packing, the country; it's all that," said Greg. "There's nothing better to me than a thirty-five-mile trip in a day with the pack string—all the horses are getting along, you look back over your string, it's all going right; it's the art of it. It's people like Smoke and all the old-timers. When we pull our trailers into Choteau or Augusta or Lincoln, we enjoy visiting with all of them. It's the rich heritage; it's riding up the trail from the east to that big cirque below White River Pass with a sea of beargrass blowing in the wind.

"We rode forty-two miles one day and pulled into the Trail Creek trailhead in the Spotted Bear River drainage about ten thirty at night.

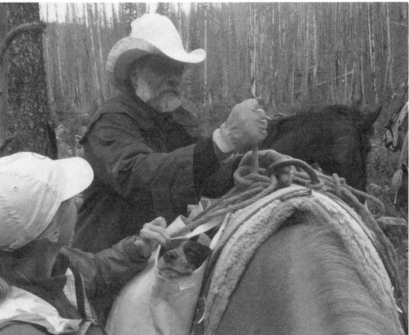

In 2015, the Schatzes helped rescue two dogs, lost in the wilderness, that were too tired to walk out on their own. PHOTOGRAPHS COURTESY OF DEB AND GREG SCHATZ.

Deb and Greg Schatz at Prairie Reef in the Bob Marshall Wilderness,
2014. PHOTOGRAPH BY MANDY MOHLER, COURTESY DEB AND GREG SCHATZ.

An old-timer came out of his camper and gave us ice and helped put our horses up. Over the years, we had seen him many times. He had packed for decades, but he could no longer do it, and it was special for him to visit with us and help us when we rode into the trailhead. We could share the trip together and he could relive all those years in the Bob."

"I like to get way up on the ridges, go right to the edge, eat my lunch," said Deb. "I love to sit on Haystack Mountain on the Chinese Wall; it's my absolute favorite, and I love Prairie Reef, any of those. I hang my feet over and stay up there a couple hours, then I'm good for a while. Seeing the boulders as big as a house at the foot of Chinese Wall, it's all special."

After three decades and about 25,000 miles, Scruffy, Cisco, and Dusty—the celebrities—are retired from packing now. They are living a well-deserved life of leisure at the Schatzes' ranch. But younger horses have taken their place on the trail.

In the Bob, Deb and Greg are just getting started.

SOURCES

Personal recorded interview by the author with Greg and Deb Schatz, January 25, 2019, FVCC.

Follow-up session, February 16, 2019, at the Schatz's ranch.

7

HEROES OF THE BOB

Pat McVay's Bob Marshall Secret

Pat McVay's secret to a long life was one shot of whiskey per day and two long summer trips in the Bob per year.

A HUNTER EDUCATION INSTRUCTOR SINCE 1957 (he was Montana's first), Pat McVay of Kalispell always loved fishing, hunting, and traveling through the backcountry on horseback. He figured that the spirit of the Bob gave him extra years, and he turned out to be right. Pat passed away in 2020 at 100, and in his heart he loved to relive his long horse trips through the country's flagship wilderness.

After he retired from his work at Hungry Horse Dam in 1975, Pat made about twenty summer pack trips through the Bob Marshall. Between those summer trips and fall hunting treks, he covered thousands of miles and spent close to a year of his life in the Bob.

Pat and his good friends Gene and Ruth Sullivan and Mylet and Mumford "Mumps" Kenyon often shared mounted forays through the Bob. Their lives were lengthened too: Ruth enjoyed 87 years, Mumford lived to be 95, and Mylet is still vibrant at 102. There must be something to Pat's longevity theory.

The riders usually entered the east side of the mountains and exited the west side. They loved the open expanses of the forks of the Sun River, which offered great grass for the horses much of the way. They entered the Bob at Benchmark, Gibson Reservoir, and other trailheads. They climbed Prairie Reef and explored along the Chinese Wall. They rode through Pretty Prairie, Gates Park, and all the great campsites and sprawling meadows along the east front.

Right to left, Gene Sullivan, Mumps Kenyon, Pat McVay, and another rider in the Sun River Country. PHOTOGRAPH COURTESY OF PAT MCVAY.

On one particular trip in July about forty years ago, things were going great for the wilderness riders. They had entered the Bob at Benchmark and planned to exit at Monture Creek. Friends had dropped them and their stock at Benchmark and shuttled their rigs to the Monture trailhead. The Bob would be their playground for about twelve days, and every day they'd see fresh country. Pat and his crew felt freedom, independence, and the joy of the wilderness.

They rode scores of miles and set up a half dozen camps in the drainages of the Sun. They watched the sun rise, rode along the maintained trails, drank fresh spring water, ate steaks cooked over the campfire the first few nights, and enjoyed good fishing in the rivers and streams.

At one of their camps, an official-looking person identified herself and walked into the campfire area. She checked on the condition of their camp, food storage, and horse highlines. The McVay outfit passed her test with aplomb. "A woman on Prairie Creek came around checking our camp, giving us instructions on what we could and couldn't do," said Pat. "She just showed her authority a little bit. We just listened to her." It was the first time anyone had ever checked his camp, so Pat was a little skeptical. He felt that it intruded a little bit on their backcountry solitude, but accepted the fact that as use was increasing, care was needed to maintain the wilderness he loved.

On this trip, like all the others in the Bob, Pat and the crew reveled in the ride. "I loved riding horseback through that country," said Pat. "The horse could watch where he was going, and I could look at everything else. Didn't have to pay attention to what the horse was doing. I'll always remember riding up the North Fork of the Sun with great timothy grass flowing by up to your knees."

Pat rode Rowdy, his big bay horse. The party had four other saddle horses and a few packhorses and mules. The trip had been relaxed and

Pat on his buckskin, Peco, in the Sun River country.
PHOTOGRAPH COURTESY OF PAT MCVAY.

The Chinese Wall, looking north. PHOTOGRAPHY BY HEATHER FRALEY.

uneventful, with beautiful weather. Then, riding up the trail toward the pass over the Chinese Wall, the action and pace began to pick up. Gene saw a man, who all of them knew from the NBC nightly news, walking toward them down the trail.

"We were coming up the east side on the trail, relaxed and enjoying ourselves," said Pat. "Had this one sorrel mule, ornery bugger, she would kick. Got up there and this guy was walking down the trail, giving little room to the stock. Sullivan said, 'Well hello, you look like Tom Brokaw.' Brokaw looked at Gene and nodded, and he started walking past them on the trail. Gene said, 'Watch that sorrel mule, she's a kickin' SOB.' And Brokaw slid off that hillside to get the heck away from her and avoid getting kicked. He might have been mad about it; he never offered to be sociable or anything. Then we passed his wife walking down the trail a half mile farther along. We told her that Tom was a ways ahead of her on the trail, but she told us that she was in no hurry to catch up; maybe she was mad at him. They were both walking with packs. Not sure if they were with a string or outfitter somewhere."

The weather smiled on the riders as they rode west toward Larch Hill Pass, which bisects the north end of the Chinese Wall. The wall, a twelve-mile-long escarpment that forms part of the Continental Divide, runs south to north from White River Pass to Larch Hill Pass. This dramatic, serpentine, Paleozoic limestone reef stands more than 1,000 feet high and fin-like, as maybe the most profound and calming view in the Bob. There's really nothing quite like it anywhere in the Rockies. The wall seems to spring out of the landscape, its vertical side facing east, and it can act as a giant lightning rod. In fact, this incredible landmark has a bad reputation for fireworks.

As the party approached Larch Hill Pass at an elevation of 7,713 feet, they noticed that the sky was darkening. "When we came near the pass a helluva lightning storm surrounded us, just came out of nowhere," said Pat. "It got dark and foreboding all of a sudden, so quickly. We were intent on keeping our string together and calming down the horses. I looked over at Rowdy and saw sparks dancing back and forth between his ears. It was a scary experience and we tried to hurry without spooking the horses.

Pat McVay in his favorite straw hat; Gene Sullivan stands near the packhorse, at the foot of the Chinese Wall deep in the Bob Marshall Wilderness. PHOTOGRAPH COURTESY OF PAT MCVAY.

Ruth and Gene Sullivan in camp on a long trip through the Bob Marshall Wilderness. PHOTOGRAPH COURTESY OF PAT MCVAY.

"Things were rattling around us; one bolt of lightning hit a big snag about fifty to seventy-five yards from us with a huge pulse of energy and a boom," said Pat. "Seemed like a God-awful blast of thunder. We could feel a force from it. This scared hell out of the horses and we struggled to avoid a runaway . . . they were so spooked and scared. We hurried down as fast as possible, but we didn't want to add to the feeling of rush and alarm. We were damned scared, the most I've ever been scared on horseback. I wanted off that mountain."

The adventurers held on to the string and dropped down the trail as fast as they could to outrun the storm, over and down into the head of Juliet Creek, and finally on down to the junction of Pego Creek and the White River at Brushy Park, having dropped 2,000 feet of elevation. After about fifteen minutes, like a miracle, the sky opened up and cleared. The upper White River had welcomed Pat and his party.

"We worked to set everything up near a small spring about twenty-five yards from the banks of the river," said Pat. "Had a certain routine we went through: take care of the horses, set up the tents, then string the tarps over the cooking and eating areas."

Pat enjoyed camping with the Kenyons and Sullivans. Gene and Ruth had been friends for years, and they shared the love of packing and the Bob Marshall. The friends had great conversations around the campfire, and they liked to share a "toddy" or two in the evening.

The weather broke clear and beautiful after the storm. It was time to fish, because the group always preferred to eat fish for an early breakfast. The lightning scare on top of the wall was fading from the adventurers' minds. "I was looking forward to fishing," said Pat. "I thought how nice and relaxing it would be after our scare on top of the wall and the pass."

Pat dug out his flies and tied on his favorite size 12 to the leader: a grizzly king, which he described as "fuzzy." Any fly works well in the upper White River, but since Pat had confidence in the grizzly, he probably fished better with it. Pat was a flexible fly fisherman, noting that "if the grizzly's floating, it's a dry fly, and if it sinks, it's a wet fly."

Pat had his favorite "little bamboo" rod along that had belonged to his dad. It had multiple sections and had been in the family since before World War I. For backup, he also had a small telescoping steel rod.

For Pat, fishing was a spiritual matter. He was the fisherman of the group, just like Silas Goodrich was the fisherman of the Lewis and Clark Expedition. In his journal, Lewis noted that Goodrich was "remarkably fond of fishing," and famously caught the expedition's first westslope cutthroats near the falls of the Missouri. Lewis called them "very fine trout." Now, over the Divide and not too far away, Pat was ready to catch some very fine trout of his own.

Pat looked over at the horses. The travelers always took great interest in their welfare. Rowdy and the crew were happily cropping grass. Feeling great about everything, Pat headed for the stream.

The upper White River running through Brushy Park is crystal clear and offers a number of runs and small pools as it meanders through the willow flats. Brushy Park can only be described as stunning to the angler's eye: it holds a beautiful, spring-fed, meandering stream dotted with beaver dams. Geologically speaking, tributaries like Juliet, Pego, Rooney, and Seep Creeks add their flows, gushing from the drainage's limestone, full of dissolved ions to feed the food chain.

To call the fish-bite good in the headwater streams of the South Fork is like calling the Chinese Wall a good feature of geology. Usually, like the wall, fishing is superb and sublime. And that evening, it was spectacular. Whether it was the clearing after a storm when lots of terrestrial insects have blown into the stream, or something known only to the cutts, they seemed to go wild after the rainstorm quit, the weather calmed, and the sun again lit up the valley.

The fish were actively feeding on the surface, sometimes launching themselves into the air and coming down on top of the insects lazily floating in the choppy current. Cutts have adapted to live in unproductive waters in part by mouthing everything that floats by to find out if it's something to eat. If they don't spit out an artificial fly fast enough, the fly embeds in their jaw. This characteristic makes cutthroat seem "dumb" and easy to catch, but really this behavior is the product of millennia of evolution, allowing the species to survive and thrive in the chill waters and short growing season in the Flathead basin.

Pat made his first short cast, laying out the fly in a choppy section at the head of a pool. The "fuzzy" fly attracted a splash and take by a nice, unsuspecting fish; Pat could see the silvery form rise to the fly, seize it, and flip its tail to force its body back underwater. The fish came quickly to the shore. In the middle of the Bob, at least twenty miles from any trailhead, Pat was in paradise.

Examining the chubby trout, Pat noted the bright red slashes under its throat, marking it as a cutthroat. In this isolated drainage, no non-native fish had ever set fin. He could be sure the vibrant fish was indigenous; its ancestors have thrived in the upper White River for millennia.

As Pat moved from run to pool, fish after fish splashed at his fly, and the breakfast menu began to take shape. It took Pat little time to catch about a dozen eight- to twelve-inch cutthroat for the crew's anticipated breakfast. Often, a couple of fish tried to take the fly at the same time. All the fish sported the characteristic red slashes under their chin.

"So, I had enough for breakfast," said Pat. "I cleaned them, cut off the heads, and lined them up in the dishpan. I put some water and salt in the pan with them and sat them on the panniers over by a tree and didn't think much more about them."

It was a beautiful evening and the travelers gathered under a stretched tarp to relax.

"We were sitting there having a tiddly and we looked out and saw this ol' doe mule deer wander into camp," said Pat. The campers enjoyed watching the beautiful animal calmly walk around camp. But they weren't too happy about what the doe did next.

"She wandered around a little bit, walked over and looked at the packs and then she came back to the dishpan. I couldn't believe it. I said, 'Hey Gene, she's eating our fish!' So five of us watched her eat every damn one of those cutthroat out of that pan."

Pat said the piscivorous mule deer would eat a trout, look over at them, then eat another one. "We were kind of stunned," said Pat. "We just sat there and thought about it for a while. But I'd never seen anything like that before, none of us had."

The crew turned in for the night, tired from their eventful day. They were a little miffed at losing their fish, but, on the other hand, they realized that they had witnessed something unusual and special. They forgave the bold muley doe.

Next morning, as sunlight filled the White River drainage, Pat collected his fishing rod and flies and caught a second batch of cut-throats. This time he protected the fish in a pack box until Ruth got busy cooking them.

"We were finally going to eat some White River cutts," said Pat. "Ol' Ruth really knew how to cook fish, and nobody loved eating fish more than Gene."

Pat and the crew enjoyed their breakfast of fish while the horses ate their oats from nose bags. They lingered around the fire, reluctant to leave this beautiful campsite at one of the keystone points in the Bob.

After breakfast, the party left Brushy Park and rode down the White River about seven miles to Needle Falls. These falls are an anomaly—not only are the falls narrowly restricted as the water plummets over the edge of the cliffy stream channel, but nearly an equal stream of water comes gushing out of a hole in the limestone wall on the east side of the river canyon. The riders recognized it as truly one of the wonders of geology in the South Fork. "No matter how many times you see it, it still seems crazy how that water shoots out from the side of that cliff," said Pat.

After a few miles, the riders reached the junction with the South Fork of the White River and swung around into the big, wide floodplain of

Ruth Sullivan, right, excelled in the cooking of westslope cutthroat trout.

the main White River. The White River channel and flow are unique in the South Fork. Heavily influenced by the limestone in its drainage, its cobbles give a white cast to the stream bottom. And when the water is high, the entire flow can take on a white appearance. The stream meanders across a wide floodplain, and it is mostly shallow. Woody debris in the channel, a few cliffy pools, and undercut banks provide some of the best fishing for nice-sized cutthroat in the South Fork.

Pat and the crew rode about another five miles down the White River Trail to the junction with the South Fork of the Flathead River. The party set up camp among the big ponderosa pines in the meadows of the South Fork–White River junction area across from Murphy Flat.

One of the first orders of business for the travelers was fishing the incredible pool near the mouth of the White River. The river is a major, high-quality spawning stream for large migrant bull trout that swim upstream from Hungry Horse Reservoir. Bull trout are a char sporting lighter spots on a darker, olive background. They are excellent to eat, strong fighters, and voracious predators. (Forty years ago, anglers eagerly fished for bull trout on the South Fork. But in 1998, bull trout were listed as threatened under the Endangered Species Act. Current Montana fishing regulations allow harvesting of bull trout only from Lake Koocanusa and Hungry Horse Reservoir. The South Fork of the Flathead is catch-and-release only for bulls, and then only during a limited season.)

Pat already had competed with a mule deer for cutthroat on the upper White River. Now at the river junction pool, he had to fight a bull trout for his cutthroat.

"I was playing a foot-long cutt and an ol' bull trout grabbed it," said Pat. "I just fed him line, fed him line, then reeled him right up to the shore. Just as I was ready to grab him, he spit out the cutthroat." Pat lost both the bull and the cutthroat, but the crew caught plenty of fish for supper that night.

The next day, the party rode up the South Fork of the Flathead, through White River Park's stately ponderosa pines. A few of the pines still showed visible scars from the harvest of cambium for winter food by native Americans many years before. After reaching Big Prairie, the party visited the ranger station and then allowed the stock to graze upstream along the river flats where there was plenty of good grass. Eventually, they rode on to the junction of Youngs and Danaher Creeks, a vibrant point of geography in the Bob. At this confluence, two magnificent, trout-filled streams come together and race downstream to form the South Fork of the Flathead River. Few places in the entire Bob can offer this level of fishing for native westslope cutthroats. These river-dwelling fish are the largest and most long-lived westslope cutthroat trout found anywhere.

The crew camped along Youngs Creek; they had it all to themselves. Gene fastened a bell on a couple of horses and turned the stock loose to graze. He kept two horses in camp. Pat went fishing.

"I got back to camp," said Pat, "and I told Gene, 'Where are the horses, I don't hear any bells.' Gene said, 'They're up in the little meadow above the trail, lots of good grass, they like it up there.'

"We listened and still couldn't hear the bells, so we checked on the horses and realized they were gone. We quickly jumped on the bare

The White River near its junction with the South Fork. This is near the pool where the big bull trout grabbed Pat's cutthroat.

PHOTOGRAPH BY JOHN FRALEY.

backs of the two horses we had and started up the trail, thinking that we would catch them quickly. We rode through the fading light and got well up toward Youngs Pass before we caught up with the horses. We got back to camp at one or two o'clock in the morning. I tied the horses up and crawled in the sack. I felt a little sore, but not too bad.

"Next morning when I got up it was really painful," said Pat. "I had a blister on my butt from riding bareback. I didn't want Sullivan to know about it because he would kid the hell out of me if he found out about it, so I kept pretty quiet.

"Ruth asked me why I was moving so stiffly, so I said that I sure wore a blister on my butt last night, and she said, 'I had to doctor Gene for one this morning. He had the same thing.' He didn't mention his and I didn't mention mine."

The crew packed up camp and prepared to head up Youngs Creek. They readied the string and, as usual, had to use a few tricks to get the mule to behave. "We put a blinder on her and tied up a leg, then put on her pack boxes, then we picketed her to a small sampling that would bend over and give," Pat said. "When we got ready to go, we untied her and dropped the blind once she was moving in the string."

The group rode up Youngs Creek about six miles, past Hole-in-the-Wall to Hahn Creek. They found a good campsite to rest up for the ride out to the Monture trailhead.

"Right about dawn the next morning, we heard a huff," said Pat. "And here comes a black bear running right through camp. Ran right into camp, never looked sideways, and out the other side. Never paid any attention to us. We figured he'd been hit by lightning, or he was being chased by a griz. But we never figured it out."

Pat was proud of their record with bears on their trips over the years. They always kept a really clean camp, and always carried a .44 Magnum, just in case. But in all the trips through the Bob, they'd never had a bear problem in camp and never had to use the .44.

After breakfast, Pat, Gene, and the others swung into the saddle for the twenty-plus-mile ride over Hahn Pass to the Monture trailhead and their waiting vehicles, ending another gem of a trip.

The friends would share many more trips and miles as the years marched on. It's hard to argue about Pat's theory that these trips, and the shots of whiskey the travelers enjoyed each evening, lengthened their lives. Pat and Mylet became centenarians.

Looking back over a half century of trips into the backcountry, Pat said, "Gosh, I wish I could do it all again. It's all so real in there. Everything that happens is unplanned. Nothing in this world is better for the spirit. I never wrote anything down, I just kept it in my heart."

Left to right, Pat McVay, Gene Sullivan, and Gene's son Terry near the base of the Chinese Wall. PHOTOGRAPH COURTESY OF PAT MCVAY.

SOURCES

Personal recorded interviews by the author with Pat McVay, November 7, 2018; December 1, 2018; and January 20, 2019; and various conversations, spring 2019.

Blood, Lex. "Geology of the Flathead." Flathead Watershed Sourcebook, http://www.flatheadwatershed.org/natural_history/geology.shtml.

Volunteer Man

*Fred Flint has worked and volunteered
for over forty years in the Bob.*

FRED FLINT IS THE BOB'S VOLUNTEER CHAMPION. After a thirty-year career working for the U.S. Forest Service, he jumped right back into the Bob as a volunteer. Working and volunteering for more than forty years, Fred has seen it all: bears, vermin, unusual people, horse wrecks, and more wilderness sunsets than a person could hope for. And, arguably, through it all, he's still maintained his sanity.

"I love volunteering in the wilderness," said Fred. "It's a place you can go and be by yourself if you want to; there's real solitude off the beaten path. As a volunteer you can work at a relaxed pace." Fred travels thirty-two miles into the Bob and watches over Big Prairie in the spring when the crew is out for several weeks of training. Each fall, he helps out for about a month at Schafer Meadows in the Middle Fork drainage. Few people know these haunts as well as he does. He greets and manages visitors, cuts wood, and does trail work and miscellaneous tasks around the stations. Fred's work has saved the Forest Service many thousands of dollars.

Fred was born in Missoula in 1944; his parents were from Philipsburg. His dad served in World War II, then left the service, and the family lived in Butte and other places in Montana for a while. His dad reentered the service during the Korean War, and the family traveled all over the West.

Fred Flint on Chair Mountain in the Middle Fork country, 1978.
PHOTOGRAPH COURTESY OF FRED FLINT.

He began working for the Forest Service in the Nez Perce National Forest in 1961 and continued there for four summers. After a few other jobs, a degree in forest management at the University of Montana, and a stint in military service, Fred signed on as a dispatcher in 1969 for the Lolo National Forest, where he ran into ranger Dave Owen. Fred worked seven years in timber management on the old Kanisku National Forest, then he moved to Spotted Bear in 1976 to work for Dave. When wilderness coordinator Jack Dollan left the district, that job was available, and there was another opening in frontcountry management. "Dave gave me the choice between the two," said Fred. "I pondered it for fifteen seconds and told him I'd take the wilderness position."

Fred worked for years in the Spotted Bear and Hungry Horse Districts, where he was responsible for river recreation, the Jewel Basin hiking area, and the snowmobile program. He retired in 2002 after a thirty-year career. Then his real career began. Ranger Deb Mucklow asked Fred to volunteer in the Spotted Bear District. He had three conditions: no paperwork, no supervision of people, and no management of nasty people. Deb said okay, and it's been a great relationship that's gone on now for more than seventeen years.

Fred especially likes volunteering at Schafer Meadows Guard Station, and he's done it as a retiree for each of the last seventeen years. He spends a month there each fall, so that makes one and a half years of his life at Schafer. His duties include packing supplies around where needed, maintaining the station, and visitor contacts. "When you retire you gotta have something to do," he said. "And that was a part of my job I really liked." He finds it a satisfying way to give something back, and the district makes him feel appreciated and valued.

Schafer Meadows is unique among the backcountry workstations in that plane landings are still allowed on its 1,000-meter airstrip, and many pilots, both private and agency, take advantage of this privilege, grandfathered in when the Great Bear Wilderness was established.

The Schafer Ranger Station in the Great Bear Wilderness.
PHOTOGRAPH BY JOHN FRALEY.

"You've got to take Schafer for what it is," said Fred. "Would I like it better without the planes? Probably. But the rules say airplanes can land. People come in there and enjoy the place in their own fashion. Some fly in and then hike, travel away from the station; some come all the way to visit over a cup of coffee. It's a little loud, but you live with it."

Private pilots are good partners; they sometimes bring in newspapers or dinner for the work crews, and they are willing to help out in a pinch. There's a limit on the number of private landings per year, and administrative landings are kept as few as possible. Sometimes the airstrip is used for emergencies or during fire season, but supplies for the crew are packed in, just like at the other workstations.

Schafer is totally different than Big Prairie, which serves as a major hub for crews during the busy summer wilderness season. One summer night, Fred remembers that there were thirty-five people for dinner. Most of his volunteer time at Big Prairie has been during the spring, to open up the station and watch over it before visitation picks up.

The Bob's expanse lends itself to this unique network of workstations or cabins. On the west side, in the South Fork, there's Basin, Danaher, Big Prairie, Hahn, Shaw, Pendant, Salmon Forks, and Black Bear (Holbrook burned in 2003); stations in the Middle Fork drainage include Spruce Park, Granite, Schafer, Gooseberry, and Sabido; the North Fork and Webb Lakes Cabins serve the North Fork Blackfoot drainage. On the east side, administrative sites include Pretty Prairie, Gates Park, Indian Point, Carmichael, Welcome Creek, and Green Fork. Most other wildernesses are smaller than the Bob and can't match this network of workstations.

Fred calls the Bob the "upside down wilderness" because for much of it, travelers enter by going up over the passes from east or west, and then down into the major expanse of wilderness. This contrasts with, for example, the Mission Mountains Wilderness, where travelers go up, past the boundary, and into it. Those up-and-into wildernesses lend themselves to a ten-day hitch and back out. But in the Bob, the cabins are a great resource and allow extensive trips for work crews and better service to the public. There is a cost to these administrative sites—sometimes there's opposition to keeping the structures in a wilderness area and a desire to see the cabins just go back into the

Fred Flint on Tillson Peak, 1994. PHOTOGRAPH COURTESY OF FRED FLINT.

ground. But the stations have been deemed necessary to manage the expanse of the wilderness complex.

To operate in the ranger districts without the workstations would be almost impossible given the large crews and big distances involved. Trail maintenance and public safety are key, and they are ensured by the cabin network.

Fred noted that safety standards have changed over the years. With the old radios and repeaters, you didn't expect to hear from people unless there was a problem. Now crews carry all kinds of communication devices, and workers check in to work centers every day. In the area of the workstations, modicums of civilization, with corrals and barns, are allowed to exist. But they're still in the wilderness area.

The bushy-tailed woodrat, aka packrat, is a common pest of backcountry cabins. PHOTOGRAPH COURTESY OF THE NATIONAL PARK SERVICE.

The Wilderness Act allows the U.S. Forest Service to do what's required to administer the Bob with the use of the cabin network.

The workstations are great, but there's one issue that's always brewing under the surface at most of these cabins: the war between rangers and rodents. Fred is a four-star general in the wilderness war on vermin. He has developed key strategies and methods to take out packrats. Sometimes called mountain rats, these rodents can make life miserable around backcountry sheds, outhouses, and cabins.

The sledgehammer is a weapon of choice for Fred and other backcountry travelers. It is a little awkward but very effective. When used properly, it takes out the packrat with an air of finality. Only problem is, as Fred said, is that it's hard to hit a moving packrat with a sledgehammer. That's why he recommends using it in combination with a pitchfork.

Fred doesn't hate packrats generally, just when they get pesky in cabins, bring their filth with them, and pose a real threat of disease.

"Packrats are furry little animals, and if I'm riding down the trail and I saw a packrat hopping along, I'd say to him, "Have a nice day." But if he gets within a hundred yards of where I gotta roost, he's dead meat. He's on the no-go list."

The packrat, or more officially, "bushy-tailed woodrat," is a large rodent of the genus *Neotoma*, from the Greek *neo*, meaning "new," and *tomos,* meaning "cut." When named in 1858, it was a new kind of mammal with cutting teeth. A large male *Neotoma* can measure twenty inches long from nose to bushy tail and weigh a few pounds. In a confined area, a large male packrat can look as big as a young porcupine.

Packrats carry a deserved reputation as clever thieves of gear and food, and may be the foulest smelling creatures with the possible exception of skunks. The odor from packrats comes from their urine and body glands. They build gross nests or middens and can carry diseases. Experts say that packrat nests are swamped with urine and feces, and recommend removing nests with the aid of a professional. But it's not easy to find a professional pest remover twenty-five miles into the Bob.

Fred has an excuse for viewing packrats with disdain. At Granite Cabin in the Great Bear, he had to demolish and relocate a small barn in part because of a persistent packrat infestation.

Keeping ahead of packrats at the backcountry sites is a challenge. "One of the best ways I've found to get them is with a piece of stove pipe," said Fred. "Put a rat trap at each end facing outward and you got 'em. They love to run through stove pipe. Sometimes you don't have that opportunity and you have to improvise."

Packrats gravitate to backcountry cabins; everybody knows that. But that doesn't mean rangers have to take the invasion lying down. In one incident, old-time packer Gene Brash improvised a method to finally get a particularly slippery packrat, and Fred was present to see it and add the technique to his bag of tricks. At Black Bear Cabin one fall, a packrat took up residence in the woodpile on the station's small covered porch. "Gene tried and tried to trap him," said Fred, "but just couldn't get him, and he was too quick to catch. We knew that sooner or later that rat was going to get inside the cabin and if left in there, you knew what kind of mess you'd have." A resident packrat at Black Bear would be unacceptable given the heavy use by crews of this important station.

Then one evening, Gene got the idea to sprinkle a trail of grain from the woodpile to the cabin entrance, and left the door wide open. Gene waited for the clever rat to come inside the cabin, which it did, and then he slammed the door. "And then he had him," said Fred. "He chased the packrat down and killed him with a club. So that's thinking outside the box." Or, in this case, inside the cabin.

At Salmon Forks Cabin, about eight miles up the west-side South Fork trail from Black Bear, crews have been fighting a mostly losing battle with packrats for decades. On one occasion, Keith Granrud woke up in the middle of the night at the cabin. A bold and unrepentant packrat was running around the cabin at will, seemingly confident that people posed no threat to him. Crew members had just about given up trying to get him. Nothing had worked.

This night, the in-your-face packrat was up in the rafters, having a good old time. Keith shined a flashlight and held it on him and the rat made a fatal mistake: it froze. Keith grabbed his pistol and shot it out of the rafters, and the rat spun around and landed on one of the bunks.

"That did in the rat," said Fred, "but the roar [from the gunshot] just about did in the crew. They levitated out of their beds."

The Salmon Forks rat was bold, but he seemed meek compared with the crew of rats that had taken over the Granite Cabin barn in the Middle Fork's Great Bear Wilderness. On one work patrol, Fred rode the eighteen miles into Spruce Park and Granite with ranger Larry Brandell and a forestry trainee. The ranger had told Fred to take the trainee along for a wilderness experience. Soon the trainee would wonder if Fred and Larry should be looked at by somebody in the mental health field.

At Granite, the old shed or barn sat down by the river, and it had become rat infested and nasty. These rats didn't even have to work to get in, they could just walk through the cracks.

"Larry and I got off our horses and opened the door," said Fred, "and I don't know how many rats there were, but they were running all over the place. Larry and I went after the rats and the trainee stayed mounted, watching us react."

Fred and Larry were unprepared, so they improvised. Fred grabbed a little sledgehammer, but it was tough to hit the scurrying rats. "Finally, one of us grabbed a pitchfork and stuck the rat," said Fred, "then the other whacked him with the sledgehammer. We had closed the door. There was a lot of whooping and hollering involved. That night our trainee said, 'I thought you guys had just gone nuts and I was just about to turn around and head back to the trailhead.'"

Fred never did solve the rat problem at the old barn. At one point, he and a crew tried to disassemble it and move it to a new location, but that didn't work out, so they burned it.

Fred prefabricated a new barn at the Forest Service warehouse in Hungry Horse and packed it in with the help of Gene Brash. Ranger Kraig Lange and his dad, Knute, came in that fall to help rebuild it. They put the new barn up on the hillside and made it especially tight, even lining the inside with plywood. That solved most of the rat problem.

Deer mice were always a problem at cabins in the Bob, too; it seems that there was no way to keep them out. The deer mouse, *Peromyscus maniculatus,* is a gray-brown rodent seen commonly in habitats across the state and nation. It is one of the most widely distributed mammals in Montana. They are native, but because of their habits, they are not on anybody's favorite species list. Especially with backcountry rangers and trail crews.

Montana roller traps were the weapons of choice that most rangers employed to take out the little rodents. A stiff wire or piece of coat hanger was pushed through a small can, often a small parmesan cheese can, and the can was then spanned above a metal bucket half filled with water. Peanut butter was spread on the can and a board was propped against the bucket. The mice would climb the board, daintily tiptoe along the wire, and grab for the can; the can rolled and the mice would end up in the drink. Sometimes, a roller trap was mounted across a toilet seat in the outhouse, just to get back at the pesky deer mice.

"When the hantavirus scare came, mice became a big issue," said Fred. "We were directed to start taking careful precautions, using bleach water on surfaces and masks when you cleaned anything. If you trapped a mouse, you were supposed to wear protective gear and put the mouse and trap in a Ziploc double bag and bury it in a hole three feet deep." This, noted Fred, was impossible to do in the rocky soils of the Bob.

The threat of Hantavirus Pulmonary Syndrome is a serious concern for people who spend a lot of time at backcountry cabins. It's rare, but it can devastate the lungs, and severe cases can be fatal. Deer mice are the main carrier of the virus. Infections can begin if the virus is breathed in with dust, or if a person touches droppings or a nest and then touches their eyes, nose, or mouth. So backcountry crews have

Fred's son Al (left), Fred, and his granddaughter Teagan buck a log with a crosscut saw at Big Prairie. PHOTOGRAPH COURTESY OF FRED FLINT.

been doing the right thing: catching and killing as many mice as possible to reduce the threat.

These battles with vermin, including mice and rats, have been legion over the years. The rodents do really well in producing reinforcements for their casualties, and they are more than holding their own. As of now, the "feds-versus-rodents" competition stands at a draw.

When he started volunteering in the wilderness, Fred became an early member of the board of directors for the Bob Marshall Wilderness Foundation. Before he knew it, he'd served sixteen years. He was key in connecting the foundation to the practical side of helping out with the Bob. Term limits came along or Fred would still be serving; he still helps out. "I served on the board," said Fred, "because I just love the wilderness, and I wanted to give back."

Founded in 1996 to address citizen and agency concerns about lack of funding for trails, the Bob Marshall Wilderness Foundation lists three principles: keeping trails open in the Bob, supporting wilderness conservation, and inspiring youth and adult volunteers to build a land ethic. All these goals have been admirably met and exceeded. In its nearly twenty-five years, the foundation has churned out thousands of wilderness supporters. Its trail clearing and maintenance projects have totaled more than 5,000 miles of trails.

The foundation's group of leaders is deeply experienced in the Bob. Board members include a who's who of top-level, noted natural resource enthusiasts from around the Bob, including Don Scharfe, Pete Metzmaker, Greg Schatz, and longtime wilderness ranger Al Koss. Honorary members include such famous wilderness icons as Joel Holtrop, Dave Owen, and legendary outfitter Smoke Elser.

The foundation was set up to keep it practical and close to the land. At least one board member must have U.S. Forest Service ties, and one must be a member of the Back Country Horsemen.

One way that Fred has given back to the foundation is through his special skill with crosscut saws, which must be used when clearing trails in the wilderness. The foundation sent him to school to learn how to sharpen crosscuts, and he's become an expert at this dying art. Proper sharpening includes dealing with a tolerance of one-thousandth of an inch. All the saw teeth must be the same height, with the rakers slightly shorter. Fred sharpens all the foundation's saws, and some others as well, adding up to as many as 100 each year. He's sharpened 1,000 all told, and if you laid them all end to end, they'd stretch a mile.

Another facet of Fred's expertise is the art of backcountry food storage. Both the U.S. Forest Service and the foundation have stressed the need for wilderness travelers to accept and use good practices for keeping food out of reach of wildlife across the Bob. Fred watched the modern concept of proper backcountry food storage take shape over the decades and personally pioneered several improvements. In bygone days, the norm was "throw scraps over the bank, and feed the leftover veggies to the gophers." By the 1980s, things were changing rapidly for the better, but there were still many incidents of bears getting food rewards and hanging around camps. One incident with trail crews in the Great Bear portion of the wilderness convinced Fred to search for a better way.

A small black bear had been harassing Fred's trail crew working at Elk Lake, which sits in a stunning cirque about eight miles up the Devil

Forster Mountain frames the glassy waters of Elk Lake.
PHOTOGRAPH BY JOHN FRALEY.

Creek drainage in the Great Bear. The lake supports good numbers of westslope cutthroat trout, and it is relatively popular with anglers. Scattered subalpine fir and beargrass frame the beautiful camp area, and the view across the deep blue lake is bounded by the alpine slopes of Forster Mountain. The access trail, camp area, and the cirque also offer a huckleberry bonanza.

When the crew first set up camp, they noticed a "little know-nothing black bear" hanging around their camp. At first, they thought it was funny. But after a while it wasn't funny anymore. It got to the point where the bear came boldly into the camp and acted like he wanted to join them around the campfire and share their food. This bear displayed all the behaviors of food conditioning; he'd probably done this before with other parties camped there and succeeded in getting food rewards. Natural bear foods were everywhere, but the bear seemed focused on their food.

This invasion went on, and the bear continued to come in from time to time, regardless of the crew's attempt to haze him and secure their food. At one point, they hung their food in a bag more than twenty feet in the air and suspended away from the tree trunk, actually exceeding food storage standards that had yet to be established.

The trail crew felt pretty smug about their efforts, agreeing that it would now be impossible for the bear to access their food hung at that height. But as the crew watched in amazement one evening, the bear crawled up the tree, then leaped out and grabbed the food bag, and rode it down to the ground in kamikaze fashion, earning his nickname.

Fred asked a Montana Fish, Wildlife & Parks warden to go into Elk Lake and take care of the problem. The warden rode in a couple of times, but Kamikaze made himself scarce during these visits.

"Every time a warden rode in there to kill the bear, he wouldn't be there," said Fred. "Then later, he'd come back. He was clever, and very persistent. This bear showed that there is no truer saying, 'a fed bear is a dead bear.' He needed to be taken out, but we couldn't really get him."

Pestered by Kamikaze, Fred contacted the U.S. Forest Service's Equipment Development Center in Missoula and asked them to come up with a better way to secure food in the backcountry. This effort turned into probably the first bear-resistant boxes made in Region One. The center fashioned four prototype bear boxes. The boxes were aluminum, light for packing, and corrugated on the sides for strength. The size of Decker-style pack boxes, one could be loaded on each side of a horse. Fred told them what he wanted, and the center figured out a simple lid and a locking system to secure it. This design made it easy to open for the crews; it was quick and efficient, without a bunch of latches that would be tedious to open and close.

The bear boxes worked well, and even though Kamikaze still came into camp occasionally, he couldn't get into the boxes. Fred thinks a hunter probably solved the Kamikaze problem later that fall, or the clever bear just decided it wasn't worth his trouble since the boxes foiled his attempts to get at the food that he considered his.

Although this incident had inspired Fred to arrange for the development of bear-resistant boxes, he'd always done what he could to keep bears out of his camps. "Number one, I want to see bears at a distance," Fred said. "I don't want to socialize with them.

And number two, the bears need to be there; like the wolves, they belong in the wilderness."

But even the best efforts don't deter some bears, like the big grizzly that rearranged the Schafer Meadows cabin a number of years ago.

It was early in the season, before any crew was at Schafer. A private pilot had reported the break-in. Fred hopped a ride with a U.S. Forest Service pilot and flew in to assess the damage. Fred was dropped off at Schafer; the pilot had a few other observations to do and then he'd return to pick him up.

When Fred got to the station, he was amazed at the mess the bear had made. The grizzly had mangled the big door inside its metal doorframe, and shoved the whole works into the kitchen. Then he proceeded to rearrange everything in the cabin kitchen and office. The bear got into the salt, pepper, spices, sugar, flour—anything resembling food in the kitchen area. He crushed cans, and even defecated while he was at it. Everything was sticky and gooey, a huge mess. Fred decided that a small crew would have to be dispatched to the cabin for days to clean it up and repair and reinforce the doorframe.

"There was not much I could do," said Fred. "I was sitting in the office and it began to dawn on me that this had just happened, and I didn't have anything to defend myself with—this was before bear spray. I thought, 'If he comes back, I'll go upstairs, and close the trap door, or hide in the root cellar.'" Luckily, Fred heard the plane returning, so he vacated the cabin, skipped across the airstrip, and hopped into the plane's passenger seat. He never did have to face the big marauding griz alone.

During his Forest Service days, Fred loved the wilderness and packing so much that even when he was on vacation, he often rode right back into the Bob. On a classic high-elevation ride, Fred, his wife, Nancy, and his two sons, Jim and Al, enjoyed one of those always-remembered trips in the upper Middle Fork, with plenty of solitude, good fishing, and views that filled the mind and the soul. It was a trip for the ages, except for one snafu that highlighted a classic packing rule of thumb.

Al and Jim were practically born in the saddle and on the trail. On this trip, Al was five or six and old enough to ride, while Jim rode on the saddle in front of Fred. He wore a pair of overalls, so Fred could reach down and grab a strap to haul him up on the saddle. Joining the family on this trip were Fred's brother-in-law and sister-in-law, who were "no way horse people."

"We rode up the Spotted Bear River to Pentagon, and spent the first night there," said Fred. "Then next morning we rode on up to Switchback Pass, and got over the top." At this point, the riders had covered about twenty miles and had entered the Middle Fork of the Flathead drainage. For most of the first part of the trip, the trail cuts through the timber. But the last few miles offered some of the most, if not the most, spectacular scenery in the Bob Complex. At 8,873 feet, Pentagon Mountain dominates the skyline, and the ridge to the north joins 8,412-foot Kevan Mountain and a "triple divide" comprising the South Fork drainage, the Middle Fork drainage, and the actual Continental Divide as well. Switchback Pass forms a saddle between these mountains. It is an intriguing point of geography and geology, with odd and jumbled rock formations and so many great views it's unbelievable. To top it all off, it's lightly traveled compared to many Bob trails. The pass grips like a magnet, holding you to stay a few hours and drink in a place that most people will never see.

Once across the pass, the travelers headed along the high-country trail swinging along the Trilobite Range through country so pretty it's almost sad to travel through because you have to leave it behind. Dean Lake sits against Pentagon Mountain a few miles along the high trail, and it's hard to imagine a prettier cirque. This country, extending north to Chair Mountain, is the biggest piece of open expanse in the Great Bear. Add wildflowers and a clear sunny day, and a traveler just can't resist taking a lot of photos.

On Fred's family trip, the wildflowers were out in profusion: beargrass, paintbrush, columbine, glacier lilies, dozens of species in their glory, with a backdrop of some of the Bob's finest alpine scenery. It was like a siren, tempting Fred's brother-in-law to get off his horse.

"So, my brother-in-law decided he wanted to take some pictures of the wildflowers," said Fred. "Now, one of my basic rules in running pack animals is: don't stop unless you have to. A pack string in motion remains in motion, a pack string not in motion can make a disaster.

Fred Flint in the Middle Fork country, 2015.
PHOTOGRAPH COURTESY OF FRED FLINT.

Brother-in-law Jim asked me if we could stop so he could get off and take some photos. And I said, 'Well I guess.'"

Jim got off, checked his camera, and got set to take his pictures. He lined up the first memorable shot.

"About that time my sister-in-law's horse decided that it was time to lay down and roll," said Fred. "Not being a horse person, the sister-in-law freaked out and started screeching and hollering. That set off my wife's horse, and she was leading the string of three mules. Anyway, the lead rope got under her horse's tail, and he didn't care for that and started bucking around."

At that point, Nancy later told him, she "decided to get off." Fred said, "Yeah, I saw you make that decision; there was about three feet between you and the horse when you made that decision."

Things were getting worse, so Fred grabbed his son Jim by the overalls strap and dropped him in a brush pile where he'd be out of the way, then jumped off his horse and went over to help his sister-in-law get up and get squared away. In the meantime, the mules were bucking and the packs were coming loose. Then, and worse, the most dangerous thing happened.

"I had a crosscut saw tied over the top and it had come loose and was swinging around by one handle," said Fred. "Now I was worried. But we stood back and waited a minute and things settled down. Nobody got hurt, including the mule with the crosscut."

The crew got everything organized and repacked. The only thing that got broken was the brother-in-law's fishing pole, which snapped into three pieces. The lucky travelers rode along the range, below Trilobite Ridge, and down to Clack Meadows to camp for the night.

"And I said to my brother-in-law, 'You had a camera in your hands, did you get pictures of the wreck?' He said, 'No, the way you were swearing and carrying on I figured you would have whipped me on the spot.'"

"Maybe I would have," Fred returned. "But you should have taken some pictures anyway."

The next morning, the party continued their storybook tour through the upper Middle Fork, eventually going to Big River Meadows at the headwaters, Wapiti Park, then down to Schafer and out of the wilderness.

The rest of the trip went just fine, smooth and wreck-free. The mules calmed down and the riders got more comfortable with them. No one dared ask to stop the string again once it got underway.

Wilderness travelers have often debated the pros and cons of mules versus horses, both for packing and even for riding. Horse advocates might look down their noses at riding mules, but mule riding has its supporters. Some of the mule aficionados struck the backcountry crews as curiously eccentric.

A few times, Fred noted, parties from down South were seen traversing the Bob with a troop of small riding mules. These folks were convinced that there's nothing better in the hills than small Tennessee riding and packing mules. Mule supporters can be passionate. In fact, Columbia, Tennessee, is the epicenter of mule mania, and it's known as the mule capital of the world. There, on a weekend in late March or early April, a huge, annual event celebrates the advantages of riding mules. It includes thousands of mule riders, a Mule Day Parade, and the selection of a Mule Day Queen. Mule lovers walk around the grounds wearing T-shirts emblazoned with fun sayings like, "Who wants to be a Mule-ion-aire?"

One year at Schafer Meadows Ranger Station, a group of folks came through with little riding mules. They used a kind of McClellan saddle on them with pockets for their sawbucks. Some would ride, but most would pack the mules and hike with some of their gear. When they got to a place they wanted to stay, they'd unload and day-ride around from there.

This particular party was from the Kentucky-Tennessee region, and they were having a great time in Montana's big mountains, traversing the nation's premier wilderness. They had either trailered their mules up to Montana from the South or rented or borrowed them from a friend closer by. But one thing stood out with this party that had never been seen before by the Forest Service crew: they had decided that their mid-trip feast was going to be chicken, and they'd brought along a live rooster to fill that menu. They had named the rooster "Bob Marshall."

The mule party carried this rooster tethered to one of their pack mules. When they reached Schafer, the enthralled Forest Service crew gathered around to look at "Bob" and talk to the mulers. After all, how often do you see a live chicken in the Bob Marshall Wilderness?

The mule packers told the crew that they had become attached to this rooster, and there was a chance that their mascot might escape his planned fate. Everybody knows that it's pretty hard to kill and eat an animal once you've named it. When the time came, they would just have to take a vote.

So the mulers went on their merry way and were not heard of again on that trip; they were heading out to the east side of the Continental Divide over the Chinese Wall. Everyone was sort of hoping that things would go well for "Bob."

A couple of years later, Fred and another Forest Service ranger were patrolling down the South Fork in the Gordon Creek drainage and staying at Shaw Cabin. They rode up to Koessler Lake, which sits in a stunning, cliff-bound cirque, to check on any camp that might be set up there.

"There was a camp there," said Fred, "and as we walked in, I noticed quite a bunch of little mules, and tack similar to what had been described when the mule train passed by Schafer a year or two before. We walked in, said 'hi' to the camp, then the next thing out of my mouth was 'I have a question, what happened to Bob Marshall?' And they looked at me, like, 'How did you know about that?' Then they told me the story."

The story was tragic. Bob didn't make it. On that trip several years before, the mulers had gotten so attached to Bob that they designated him as their official trip mascot. The travelers started looking forward to Bob's loud crowing wake-up call each morning at dawn. They decided he'd be spared, make the whole trip, and then go home with them. Heck, he was slimming down with all the walking he was doing and wouldn't add up to much of a meal anyway. At times, Bob even walked along on his own, fitting in as part of the mule string, although he never wore a pack. He was well on his way to accomplishing something special—he'd be the only live chicken to ever traverse the Bob.

Having trekked through much of the west side of the Bob, the mulers crossed the pass and made it to a spot under the Chinese Wall, just over the east side. Several of the men decided they were going to hike above the trail to get a better look at the sweeping scenery. So they took Bob and tethered him to one of the mules, and he moved along with the pack string. The hikers started up the mountainside to gain a spectacular view, while one man stayed with Bob and the pack string.

The hikers got partway up the hillside and were looking around when they heard a commotion. They looked below them and saw that all Hades had broken loose. The trail-hardened rooster had decided to take off, maybe because he felt abandoned, no one knows. The rooster hit the end of the tether and went nuts, causing a ruckus. He flailed away and got up under a mule. The little mules reacted, started bucking, and it "wrecked the whole works." Some of the mules went off, jumped around below the trail, and threw their loads.

As they watched the scene below them, the men saw that their partner was having trouble trying to get control of the mules. He must have blamed Bob for the conflagration, because the man grasped Bob by the neck and dispatched him like a barnyard chicken. Bob's amazing trek through the Bob ended just after he crossed the Continental Divide. Sadly, he never got a chance to maybe meet a high-country ptarmigan or see the entire east side of the Chinese Wall. The mulers had Bob for dinner that night, although we don't know exactly how they cooked him.

SOURCES

Personal recorded interview by the author with Fred Flint, February 28, 2019, in Kalispell, MT. Several shorter informal interviews before and after.

Meanings of scientific names of wild and domesticated mammals of Arkansas. uam-web2.uamont.edu/facultyweb/huntj/meanings_of_scientific_names.htm.

Columbia, Tennessee, mule capital of the world. https://www.roadsideamerica.com/tip/7595.

Montana Department of Health and Human Services website, section on hantavirus: https://dphhs.mt.gov.

9

HEROES OF THE BOB

Backcountry Law

Teton County sheriff Big George Anderson heads into
the Bob to nab a tree-hugging fugitive (and other stories).

AROUND THE 400-MILE PERIMETER of the Bob Marshall Wilderness Complex, dozens of law enforcement officers stand ready to respond to backcountry emergencies and lawbreakers. These selfless officers serve the public trust and rank as true heroes of the Bob.

George O. Anderson had one of the longest runs as sheriff and coroner in Teton County history. As chief law enforcement officer, Big George served five terms: 1988 to 1990, 1991 to 1994, 1995 to 1998, 1999 to 2002, and 2003 to 2006. In every election but one, he was unopposed. In that one, he won by a margin of two to one. At six-foot four and 240 pounds, George was a big man with a reputation for being scrupulously fair. He was about as popular as a sheriff could be, given the nature of law enforcement. Like Dirty Harry, George carried a .44-caliber Smith and Wesson as his sidearm.

Counting his previous positions as sheriff's deputy and police officer, he served in Choteau law enforcement for well over thirty years. George enforced the law in one of the most scenic stretches of Big Sky Country, located as a major gateway to a vast wilderness backcountry. As he patrolled, he could gaze at the east face of the Rocky Mountain Front and the east side of the Bob Marshall Wilderness. He could look up at Ear Mountain and the country that A. B. Guthrie used as the backdrop of his classic novel, *The Big Sky*.

George Anderson served two tours of duty in Vietnam.
PHOTOGRAPH COURTESY OF GEORGE ANDERSON.

Over the years in Choteau, George saw it all—farm accidents and fires, fatalities, burglaries, drownings, and dozens of sheriff sales. Famously, in 2005, he was involved in an investigation that thwarted a dirtbag who was planning to kidnap television celebrity David Letterman's child from Letterman's 2,700-acre ranch near Choteau. On his show on March 21, and on CBS News on March 22, 2005, Letterman personally thanked two FBI agents, Teton County sheriff George Anderson, county attorney Joe Coble, and the people of Choteau. George had received a tip that the man was planning the abduction, and he immediately called a friend he knew in the FBI. They were able to nip the plot in the bud and apprehend the suspect. Luckily, George could arrest the man on a parole violation, so they could hold him for three days. They successfully charged him on the kidnap plot and various other charges, and put him away. At the Choteau sheriff's office, Letterman personally shook George's hand. "Katie Couric is still probably mad at me because I wouldn't take her calls," said George. "I was focusing on the case and wouldn't talk to any of those people."

This case's success resulted from George's emphasis on community policing, which encouraged the public to bolster law enforcement by providing tips and reporting problems early.

George spent his career responding to problems and helping people in distress. When you dig under the surface in any small town, you see a surprising number of violations and issues that have to be dealt with by local law enforcement, and Choteau is no exception. As reported in the local newspaper in just a two-week period one March, George and his deputies broke up a drug lab and responded to many medical emergencies, deer/car collisions, other car accidents, minors in possession, DUIs, suspicious persons, and theft. This one sheriff and Crimestoppers report featured more than twenty crimes and emergencies. For decades, George was crazy busy and definitely a hero to the east front residents. He wasn't drawn into the Bob very often, but when he was, he usually ended up with an epic story.

George was born in New Jersey but traveled all over the country because his father, George Sr., was in the military and served in World War II. In 1967, George Jr. enlisted in the U.S. Air Force and served as a military policeman. During two tours of Vietnam, he was a machine gunner on a defensive unit. He defended his base during the Tet Offensive. Back in the States, George served at Malmstrom Air Force Base in Great Falls as a senior security policeman. After his discharge from the Air Force in 1971, George moved to Choteau and was hired by the city police department. In 1973, the city police and the county sheriff's office merged, and George became a sheriff's deputy. Later, the offices split again, and George was the city police chief in Choteau for eleven years, then back with the sheriff's department. On September 21, 1988, George was appointed Teton County sheriff.

George and his wife, Florence, raised two boys, George and Lee, in Choteau. Both went on to become Montana state game wardens. Lee is the warden captain for Montana Fish, Wildlife & Parks in Kalispell.

During his career, George chased a few lawbreakers in the wilderness. In one odd case in the 1970s, the sheriff's office received a call in Choteau from some people up at Gibson Reservoir. This five-mile-long reservoir is formed by a dam on the Sun River. At its upper end, the North and South Forks of the Sun join. It is one of the major gateways to the Bob. The reporting parties were on an overlook at the lower end

George Anderson's son Lee is a game warden captain with the Montana Department of Fish, Wildlife & Parks. PHOTO COURTESY OF LEE ANDERSON.

of the reservoir. They had looked down and seen the roof of a vehicle, submerged in the reservoir near the boat ramp.

George and another deputy, Ray Price, drove up to Sun Canyon Road, took a right-hand turn at the bridge, and followed the road that goes all the way to the top of the overlook, right above the dam. At this overlook is a parking area and a pullout with some informational signs about the dam and reservoir. That point is probably about 500 to 600 vertical feet above the reservoir and affords a great view of the east front and the mountains and reefs of the Bob.

Based on the information they'd received, the two men and others looked down to the water where they could see the faint outlines of the hood of a vehicle beneath the surface. Within a short time, responders were able to get a cable attached to the vehicle, and it was pulled out. Then it really got interesting.

There was nobody in the car. The steering wheel and the gear shift lever were tied together.

"So, we thought, oh boy, this was a mafia hit or something and there's a dead body in the trunk," said George. "The trunk was popped and everyone held their breath, but there was nobody in it. Looked like they had put on the brake, tied the steering wheel and the gear shift together, then let go of the brake, and the vehicle went down fifty or one hundred feet, bounced, and flew out over the reservoir, hit the water and sank." It must have been pretty dramatic to watch.

A check of the vehicle showed who the owner was, and the owner and his family were contacted. Investigators found that they were two navy fellows, one who was driving the vehicle and the other who was a friend. Unfortunately, they were deserters.

"We backtracked and found that they had gone to a local outdoors store in Great Falls," said George, "equipped themselves with sleeping bags, backpacks, a rifle and a handgun each, and all kinds of stuff as if they were going to go into the mountains and stay awhile. Then they ditched the vehicle in the reservoir."

The two deserters hiked about four miles up the trail, snaking along the steep slopes of the reservoir to Scattering Springs, where they spent the first night. On the way, they passed Big George Creek, maybe named after a man they would soon meet. Soon, they thought, they would be past the head of the reservoir and heading into the Bob and the remote Sun River country, where they would simply disappear. But the fugitives' plans had a lot of holes. For instance, their feet were already sore at that point.

"The other goofy thing," George said, "was these knuckleheads had bought stiff cowboy boots and rubber overshoes, which aren't good for hiking in rocky terrain."

The men didn't seem to have much of a notion about secrecy either. At Scattering Springs, they shot their rifles and pistols with abandon, figuring they'd better get some target practice in. All the shooting was heard by folks at the K Bar L Ranch at the head of the reservoir. It must have sounded like a war, and way out of place for that time of year. Next day, the lodge folks sent a boat down, picked up George and Ray, and motored up the reservoir. They all got out and found the spot where the fugitives had camped.

"We found gun cleaning stuff and shell casings, and saw their footprints. The ranch folks said that they had seen two guys cross the bridge and hike up the South Fork of the Sun River, obviously the same men."

These guys were making every dumb-criminal mistake in the book.

In the meantime, the sheriff was in the process of lining up a helicopter to aid in the search. "We had a portable radio," said George, "but back in those days we didn't have service there so we couldn't communicate with them. But we had K Bar L tell them we were going to start up the South Fork Trail and into the wilderness. This was in the spring and some snow patches remained. We could see footprints and we were slowly tracking them."

George and Ray were hiking in the direction of Bear Lake. They kept hiking and reached the trail that headed up Bear Creek. But just past that junction they could see ahead of them a divot in the trail that went down toward the river.

"We looked down and saw a camp with all kinds of stuff," said George. "So we drew our weapons and started down to the camp, but when we got there, we saw lots of gear but nobody was there. So we decided we'd go back up and check out the trail. Ray was in front of me. Ray is a short guy and I'm a tall guy, so we were bent over walking up there and we looked up and here was this guy standing on the trail with a rifle."

It was one of the deserters.

"At that point we were up the Bear Creek trail maybe a half mile to three-quarters of a mile," said George. "We identified ourselves, and if he would have wanted to shoot, he might have got one shot off. But we disarmed him and took him back down to their camp. He told us that he and his partner were hunting for food; he said his partner was out there somewhere hunting."

At this point, George and Ray had one bird in hand and one in the bush, so they had to come up with a way to secure the man so they could go back out after the other perpetrator. George came up with an ingenious idea.

George figured that the camp was far enough down in that hole, with noise coming from the junction of the South Fork of the Sun River and the creek, so their first captor couldn't start hollering to try to warn his partner, and it would be hard for the other fugitive to come up behind them. "We brought him on down and tried to figure out what to do with him," George said. "Then I got the idea. I told him we were just going to handcuff him to a tree. 'What?' he said. 'What if a bear gets me?' stuff like that. And I said, 'Well that's too bad.' I put the handcuffs on him snug against a good-sized tree, so he just stood there, hugged the tree, and stared at the bark while we left to try and find his compatriot." George had found a tree that was just the right size. The captive's nose was right against the bark, so he couldn't turn his head to yell or tip off his partner.

George hiked up out of the bottom and waited in a spot above one side of the trail, while deputy Ray took up a position about fifty yards up on the other side.

"Then here come the other guy," said George, "and he looked like he was pretty darn nervous. He had his rifle at port arms and he was looking all around. I stepped up. I had my .30-06 rifle and I had my scope on him. I hollered at him, identified myself, and he saw me with a rifle. I said, 'My crosshairs are on your chest—drop your rifle.' He also had a western-style gun belt with a pistol in it and he dropped them both down. Ray came out, and I remember Ray stuck the end of his pistol right on the guy's nose. Then I walked up and we handcuffed him."

The deputies brought the second perpetrator back and reunited him with the tree-hugger. George made the captives pick up every piece of their camp and put it in their backpacks. The deserters' feet were killing them because of all the miles they had put in walking in the cowboy boots and rubber overshoes.

George told the men that they were going to pack it all out.

"They said, 'Can't we just leave it in here?' and I said, 'No, you're carrying it all out. We'll carry your rifles and your handguns.' So we started hiking back out, made communications with the office that we had captured them, and got in a boat at the K Bar L."

The deputies and their captives motored the five miles to the boat ramp. They escorted the deserters to the detention center in Choteau. Military officials came, picked them up, and took them away.

"I'm not sure what ever happened to them after that," said George. "All I know was that my sheriff was pissed—he didn't get to go on a helicopter ride to find them, because we'd caught them on foot."

When they nabbed the men, George said, the deserters knew that "their goose was cooked," and they admitted everything. They had planned on going back into the Bob Marshall Wilderness to spend the entire spring, summer, and fall and then pop out the other side and meld into society. They were heading into the mountains to disappear.

The saga of the tree-hugging fugitive was over. He and his partner never got to live off the land and hide out like mountain men in the Bob, thanks to the great police work of George and Ray.

In another incident, which also took place in the 1970s in the Bob Marshall, George went in to investigate what he called "the shootout at Cabin Creek." This time he and his crew rode in on a helicopter. In the face of the west wind roaring over the Front, it took three tries to get over 8,179-foot Sawtooth Ridge, and it wasn't pretty.

"We received a call that somebody had been shot but [we] didn't know any of the circumstances surrounding the incident," said George. "The sheriff arranged for a military helicopter to fly us in. The wind out of Augusta was blowing eighty miles an hour, it was just terrible."

The crew included Dr. Johnson, a local physician, George as EMT, and a crusty old game warden named Paul Mihalovich. The men were in a National Guard helicopter, bringing the Posse Comitatus Act into play; the act restricts the use of the U.S. Army for domestic law enforcement. So George was going in initially as an EMT to help Doc Johnson. In the gale-force wind, the determined, fearless chopper pilot tried to lift over the top of Sawtooth to head up the reservoir.

"The first time that the wind hit us," said George, "it knocked that helicopter down so fast that my cowboy hat popped off and stuck to the roof of the cabin of the chopper. We backed off, flew higher and tried again, and the wind spun us around about three 360s going backward. I was about ready to lose my cookies by then. It scared the bejesus out of me, I'll tell you."

The third try was the charm. "We got high enough above so that we moved forward, but it was like a roller coaster. When we finally topped that ridge, it was like a slingshot. We hit the open area and took off like a rocket up the reservoir." The crew then followed the North Fork of the Sun River past spectacular Sheep Reef and Arsenic Mountain and on to the Cabin Creek Cabin and camp area. According to the report George had received, there was some kind of dispute going on among outfitters and private parties that were camped near Cabin Creek.

George Anderson's law enforcement jurisdiction included the rugged North Fork of the Sun River west of Augusta.

"Three guys—Tom Troy and two others—got themselves half juiced-up and rode up from Gibson past that private party's camp. They never admitted this, but I believe they ripped the camp up. The owners rode up and saw this, and the son of one of the camp owners came riding up, guns were drawn, shots were fired, and one of the men with Troy was hit."

George and the crew got the wounded man in a sleeping bag. "The report was that he was shot in the arm, and we didn't know if by a hunting rifle or what. But if I remember it right, he was actually shot in his left wrist and the bullet went through the top and came out the back side of the wrist. We treated him and got him on the chopper. I threw my stuff out and stayed, and then hiked all over trying to figure out what had transpired."

George took statements from everyone involved who he could find, including Tom Troy. "Nobody was telling the truth in this entire thing," said George. "I'd never had so many people tell me so many lies. Troy said the other camp shot the guy and he and his guys weren't involved but just happened to be riding by when it happened."

As evening came on, Tom Troy and George rode out, pulling a string. They were headed out late, and it turned out to be a sketchy ride. In places, the trail narrows and skirts sheer drop-offs to the reservoir below.

"We rode the eighteen miles, much of it in the dark," said George. "That Gibson Lake trail can be scary during the day, let alone at night. And we were leading a pack string of about ten stock. On your way out on the left, you could barely make out a wall—dark strip on the trail, a little white strip of snow on the edge, then off into the abyss.

"We got out after midnight. It was a joy. I was leaning to the left with my foot out of my right stirrup, ready to bail if I had to. Tom Troy, a suspect in the shootout, was leading the way. But we made it around the reservoir and got picked up at the lodge."

The next day, George went over all the statements with the county attorney. After reading all the statements and getting George's report, the county attorney said, "I can't make head or tails out of this," so nobody was charged.

Later, George was subpoenaed into federal court in Great Falls, where the person who was shot sued the other parties. George gave his testimony, and then listened to everyone else testify about the shootout.

George remembered that the federal judge, in exasperation, said to the jury, "In all my years on the bench, I've never heard so many contradictory stories, and if you folks can figure this all out, good luck." The jury ended up deciding that both parties were equally culpable.

What ended up coming out of the trial, as George remembered it, was that the son of the camp owner, when he saw the camp's condition, pulled out a revolver and later claimed the shooting was accidental. His dad said that the reason they didn't tell George exactly what had happened was that they'd gotten into trouble before and lost some of their guns, and they didn't want to lose any more. That was a proverbial poor excuse.

Some of George's wilderness search and rescue operations ended in tragedy. On a mid-August day in 1976, Deputy Anderson received a call about a young hiker who fell off a ridge on Washboard Reef above Hidden Lake, also called Our Lake. The seventeen-year-old man, from Tennessee, was with a friend and the friend's adult brother. He had walked away down the ridge and didn't return. The two hiked out to the trailhead and notified authorities.

The sheriff at the time was Pete Howard, and he organized the sheriff's posse and placed Deputy Anderson in charge of the search and rescue party at the site.

"We brought horses and we got up there in late afternoon," said George. "We rode around the back side and were showed where this occurred, but it was getting dark. You have Our Lake sitting east to west, [a] little creek runs in, and the trail goes all the way over and there's a pass. There's a high ridge to the southwest, and we went up on that, but by that time it was getting dark [and] the wind was blowing.

"He had fallen on the west side of the ridge towards the Ray Creek drainage. We couldn't see him even though there was a good moon," George continued. "We were crawling around on these steep cliffs trying to find him. As I crawled along the edge, I heard this 'tink'—my badge had fallen off my coat and hit once on its way down the cliff. That's when I told the guys, this is too dangerous, we've got to go back."

The search party rode in the dark back down the Our Lake trail all the way back to the Headquarters Creek trailhead on the South Fork of the Teton River, arriving there about one o'clock in the morning. They came back to town, got a little sleep, then went back early in the morning.

"We rode all the way back up there and now we had plenty of light," said George. "I started climbing down and around that cliff and we found his body. You could see he had slid down the face of that cliff, and the back of his head had hit a pointed rock, causing a terrible head injury that resulted in instant death."

George continued, "What I believe happened was this. That ridge is so high you could see all the way back to the Chinese Wall. He had squatted down, on his haunches, and he was looking, maybe stayed down for a while, and at 8,000 feet when he stood up, he got dizzy, maybe slipped [or] lost his balance; you could see his trail sliding down that cliff."

George confirmed that the young man was dead, and the crew loaded him on a military stretcher. When he'd fallen, he had gone down the cliff and ended up all the way at the rockslides about half-way down the west side of the ridge.

"We couldn't bring him back over the top, it was just too steep," said George. "So we started trying to go downhill, but it created rock-slides, so we'd take rope tied to each side of the stretcher, and a couple guys on each side of the stretcher lowered him down a couple hundred yards. Then they would get out of the way so the guys above us could come on down, so if they kicked rocks loose, they wouldn't hit us. We leapfrogged all the way down."

The search party felt terrible for the young man, and everyone was in a somber mood. They did the best they could to reach the point where they planned to meet the horses to pack out the body. "We had about two miles to carry that stretcher, and it was really tough," said George. "You had six guys of different sizes and we had to go over steep, uneven ground and rocks. I was a young guy, but I thought a couple times we'd have to pack one of our own older guys out too." Because of the emergency nature of this incident, the search party ran low on water and food.

Meanwhile, George said that U.S. Forest Service packer Ray Mills (who had come along to Our Lake with the horses) took the horses and went all the way back out to the Headquarters Creek trailhead. Then he brought the horses all the way back in to the top of Headquarters Pass at 7,743 feet above sea level. The way George remembers it, Ray then brought the horses cross-country to the north along the headwaters of Ray Creek and met the crew on the west side. By that time, Ray had put in a total of about twelve miles with the horses. George called Ray an "absolute animal" in the mountains, and Ray went on to a stellar career with the agency.

When Mills and the horses arrived, the search party loaded the body on a horse. At one point, George led the horse carrying the body back down toward the trailhead. They met a few hikers coming in. "I wore my uniform coat with a replacement badge, so we got lots of looks from people," George remembered. "We rode down and met the coroner." Everyone felt sad about the young man. Luckily this was the only fatality within the Bob that George ever had to respond to.

As time went on and George became sheriff, the rescue and response process became more planned. In another incident in the Bob, a man named Doc Metzler rode up the trail from Cave Mountain, which is in the Teton River drainage. The next day, his horse showed up back at the Cave Mountain trailhead without him. Someone called the sheriff's office, and George activated the response team. The team brought a bus with all kinds of food and supplies to the trailhead, expecting a big effort to find a presumably injured man within the rugged high country of the Bob Marshall Wilderness.

"We thought sure we had a guy who was bucked off and badly injured," said George. "We looked for him for a day and found his tracks. But we ended up going back to the trailhead because it was getting dark and they were running into snowbanks." At the trailhead, George and a Forest Service officer ran into a young sergeant from Malmstrom Air Force Base who happened to be in the area and was connected with the helicopter squadron.

Because of the expanse of territory that stretches over the Divide and into the Route Creek drainage and the North Fork of the Sun, George asked the sergeant to arrange for a helicopter out of Great Falls to aid in the search. Next day, the searchers flew to the trailhead and picked up the Forest Service officer. They took off and flew over the top and into the Bob, searching for the lost man. They succeeded in finding him more quickly than expected.

This story had a happy but frustrating ending. George said that the man had ridden over the Divide at Route Creek Pass, into the Bob, and down the other side. But not very far. His horse had escaped him and trotted back to the trailhead.

"We found the man only about a mile or so over the top of the Divide. He had set up a tent and just sat there, waiting to be rescued, instead of walking back out. He wasn't even hurt." The lost man climbed aboard the chopper and they whisked him back to the trailhead.

"Here we had made extensive preparations, put in two days of effort, getting the military helicopter lined up and so on," said

George. "Everybody was worried for him. And that knucklehead could have easily walked back out to the trailhead. We were glad that he wasn't hurt, but I was mad, real mad. Anyway, we got him out. And his damn dog."

One odd and humorous case involving the Bob still makes George chuckle. "We'd received a call about a vehicle off the back side of the Teton Pass Road sitting in the top of the trees. I listened to the report and said, "Say what?""

George and a deputy drove up to the spot. "We got there and my jaw just dropped. Here was a car," said George, "twenty feet off the ground, upside down, in pine trees. So, I'm searching around there and worried about injured people. But nobody was around. So, we investigated and backtracked and found the owner of that car."

As the story goes, two young women were going to hike back into the Bob from the West Fork Teton trailhead. The access road is really twisty, and they missed a turn and slid off a fairly steep bank. Luckily, they ended with a soft landing upside down in the trees. They carefully gathered their gear, crawled out of the car, and climbed down.

Then they hiked up the road to the trailhead, went back into the Bob for a week, and never said a word to anyone.

"Well," said George, "we ended up having to get a tow truck to jerk that car out of the top of the trees. It wasn't drivable when they got done with it. The parents went up and waited for them. I turned the case over to the highway patrol."

The girls came out and made contact with their parents, who notified the authorities. Then the highway patrolman and George "had a visit with them." They told the girls that a simple note would have prevented a lot of effort and worry on the part of law enforcement and their parents.

"The girls told us, 'Well, we figured that we screwed up our trip and were in trouble anyway, so we're just going to go back into the wilderness.'"

The patrolman conducted the interview with the girls while George and a deputy stood nearby. "We were standing there," said George, "and I said to the deputy, 'You know, we've seen a lot of stuff, but in all my years this has to be one of the dumbest things I've ever seen.'" George can't remember what citations the girls received, if any. At

George Anderson proudly served as the Teton County sheriff until he retired in 2007. PHOTOGRAPH COURTESY OF GEORGE ANDERSON.

least this crazy story of the missing girls did have a happy ending—no one was injured.

George said that incidents like the Our Lake fatality, when young people died way before their time, weigh a lawman down and accumulate over the years. He had seen so much during his career: a crash scene of a neighbor boy, a ten-day-old baby brought in for an autopsy, a youngster killed at an intersection. Over the years, the sadness just accumulated. "I decided I just couldn't do it anymore," said George. "It was hard to do for so long. I was more hands-on, so I was involved in everything. I saw all the bad stuff. I had to deliver death messages for three kids whose parents were friends of mine."

George retired in 2007 after a lifetime of service to the public, in both the frontcountry and backcountry. He'd shrunk an inch from his previous height, and he asked his doctor why that happened. The doctor replied, "Age and gravity." George still lives in Choteau, and he left a strong legacy behind him. Before Big George retired, city and county officials named the new sheriff's office in Choteau after him.

People on the eastern stretch of the Bob Marshall were lucky to have a man like George protecting the public trust. He was always willing to respond when he was needed, no matter where or when. East to west, north to south, the Bob is surrounded by many such law enforcement heroes.

SOURCES

Recorded personal interview by the author with Teton County sheriff George Anderson (retired) via speaker phone, May 2, 2019. Follow-up conversations, spring 2019.

Various background articles in the *Choteau Acantha* newspaper, Choteau, MT, 1976–2007.

10

HEROES OF THE BOB

Packer Gal

*Colyne Hislop followed a circuitous route to become one
of the best young packers and trail crew leaders in the Bob.*

IT'S A LONG HIKE FROM THE MEADOW CREEK pack bridge to Big Prairie
Ranger Station, deep in the heart of the Bob Marshall Wilderness. The
pack bridge spans the cliff-bound Meadow Creek Gorge, where the
clear, bluish-green, rushing river, usually 100 yards wide, narrows to
about thirty feet. The currents boil through this extreme restriction;
many consider it the most unusual trailhead in the Bob.

One hot summer day, Colyne Hislop left the trailhead and hiked the
trail that parallels the South Fork of the Flathead River to the ranger
station, thirty-two miles upstream. Much of the way, the river is visible
but inaccessible without a lot of effort, and on hot days, it's tantalizing.

Colyne had been "outside" the Bob the previous week, attending
a friend's wedding. That was an unusual trip for her—she usually
wouldn't leave the wilderness until late in the fall. Now she was hiking
back into Big Prairie to resume her work with the U.S. Forest Service
as a packer and trail technician.

The heat was intense, and the wilderness was about to be shut
down to public access because of wildfires that were building. At mile
nineteen, feeling pretty good, Colyne reached Salmon Forks. "You get
to Salmon Forks," she said, "and you could stay here. But then you
think, I've got a great start, what am I going to do with myself the rest
of the day anyway, so you just keep hiking."

Colyne loads a heavy pack on Coconut.
PHOTOGRAPH COURTESY OF COLYNE HISLOP.

After twenty-four miles, the heat really got to her. "Once you get past the White River, that's when you suffer," said Colyne. "I was doing fine until after I crossed the White River. Then those last, dry seven miles with little shade to Big Prairie were the worst. It wasn't smoky yet and the wilderness wasn't shut down yet, but wow was it hot."

Colyne persevered, arrived at the ranger station, and fell right back into her work routine. There's no time to waste when you are serving the public in the backcountry, and there is much work to squeeze in during the short Montana summers.

Tall, strong, and dedicated, twenty-nine-year-old Colyne Hislop has earned her reputation as a trail crew leader, wrangler, and packer in the Bob. She can load an 80- to 100-pound pack on either side of a mule or horse and cinch it up with no trouble.

Her approach to stock is her own: a combination of firmness, empathy, and Zen. In the Bob Marshall backcountry, she is a leader of stock and a leader of people.

A believer in over-the-top care of horses, Colyne recently stood barefoot in the cobbly and cold South Fork of the Flathead River for an hour, holding a lead rope, to relieve the pain of a sore-legged horse.

Colyne Bernadette Hislop comes from a family of outfitters. Her father and namesake, Colin Barr Hislop, passed away before she was born in a tragic road accident. Colin was an outfitter and had camps in Bunker and Gorge Creeks. Colyne's mom made the name more feminine. "I have my dad's initials," said Colyne. "I definitely feel that it is a part of me." Colyne has two older sisters, Anne and Sarah, who like the outdoors, but not to the degree Colyne does.

"I've always loved the outdoors and I think it's part of who I am. I recognize it more and more as I spend time with the mules and packing in the wilderness. I remember our family photos of my mom riding a horse and my dad pulling a string."

Colyne's Hislop's father, Colin, was an outfitter. He passed away before Colyne was born. PHOTOGRAPH COURTESY OF COLYNE HISLOP.

Growing up, Colyne was a soccer star, which led her to a sports medicine degree. But she soon realized that the outdoors fit her better. "It's a great and useful degree, but I wanted to do something outdoors and wilderness focused."

Colyne got her start with the Montana Conservation Corps (MCC) in the Selway-Bitterroot and Frank Church Wildernesses during her college graduation summer, and she was hooked. She set her sights on the Bob, where she had spent time as a kid. She became an MCC crew leader and worked a summer at Big Prairie. After a brief stint with a physical therapy firm, she joined the U.S. Forest Service for the following summer at Big Prairie, working for Guy Zoellner.

"I did some trail work, river crew, whatever was needed," said Colyne. "I had done some packing with the MCC and I was interested in it, having grown up with stock. I built experience and by the summer of 2016, I was put into a crew leader position. We packed, cleared trail, worked with the crews. I love Big Prairie, it feels like home.

"I learned a lot about packing from Guy and from Bill Workman. They have different horsemanship styles, running from gentle to firm. One school of thought, for example, says that you show the stock love and they will show you love back."

Last summer, Colyne worked a lot with a horse named Saylavee (c'est la vie in French). He became her trusted trail horse, but he was very stubborn about taking a bit and had to be shown a lot of patience. With most horses, you can place your hand between their ears and gently slide in the bit. But Colyne learned that Saylavee was different—he didn't like his ears or head touched.

Colyne says that horses and mules pick up on the rider's emotions. If you are worried or angry, they can sense it, so you try not to get mad at them.

"Sometimes they know better," said Colyne. "But for the most part, once you put that halter on them, they are your responsibility. They get hungry, just like you get hungry. When it's a long day, we have to realize that they are working hard too, carrying 80 pounds a side. A big mule like Coconut can carry 100 pounds on a side. A small mule like Jake can't carry more than 80 pounds per side, but small mules are nimble and they will last longer."

Packers' rope work and mantying skills come second only to their expertise with stock. PHOTOGRAPH COURTESY OF COLYNE HISLOP.

Colyne believes that mules are loyal to the other stock, and they are smart but have tight memories and could be vindictive if they sense mistreatment. "Take Coconut, for example. I am very careful with that mule because she is cinchy. I wouldn't go up and just crank on any mule cinch, but on hers, I take extra care. If she thought you were being mean to her, she's the type of mule that would remember it. She would take a whack at you."

Colyne's horse savvy comes in part from a lifetime with stock. Her personal horse, Indian Joe, is twenty-three years old. She's had this smaller packhorse since she was a little girl. Sometimes, Colyne brings him into the wilderness and runs him with the string.

On one of Colyne's first hitches as a Forest Service crew leader, she and the crew were working in the Danaher drainage, out of Basin Cabin. Colyne was a little nervous being a crew leader, even though she had filled that role before. She wanted everything to go

Colyne (center) and co-workers (left to right) Madeline Rubida, Fischer Gangemi, Dana Bronkala, and Michael Reavis.

PHOTOGRAPH COURTESY OF MICHEAL REAVIS.

just right and wanted the crew to accomplish great work. She didn't want to disappoint anyone who had put confidence in her. Then it happened—they checked on the stock and found them gone. The electric fence was down.

"Oh no, the stock got out!" Colyne thought. "Every wrangler's nightmare." At the time it seemed like a disaster, even though it can happen pretty regularly in the backcountry. Pack stock tend to prefer being at their "home," in this case Big Prairie.

Colyne put all the halters in a pack. To avoid losing too much time, two of the crew kept clearing trail up toward Stadler Pass while Colyne hiked back twelve miles to Big Prairie to get the horses.

When Colyne got back to Big Prairie, she rounded up the horses, Tux and Indian Joe, and the mules, BT and Einstein. She had all their halters but no saddles, so she used breakaway twine, strung that around their necks to keep them together by their halters, and started leading them back to Basin Cabin.

"My boots were beginning to blow out and my feet were starting to hurt," said Colyne. "It was about 90 degrees out and I had twelve miles back to Basin. Then I thought, 'You know what, I've been riding bareback since I was a kid, so we're doing it.' Tux is a pretty tall horse, so I found a log, swung my leg up there, and away we went down the trail. I rode into Basin, and Fischer, one of the crew members, looked at me and chuckled. We crossed Basin Creek, put the stock back into the electric fence, and kept a good eye on them."

Inspired by Colyne's successful ride, the next morning Fischer tried to get up on Tux and ride him bareback. He was bouncing around on the horse's back, unbalanced.

"I just start laughing," said Colyne. "The mules are running around, and Joe gets free and starts running for Big Prairie, so I caught him. Fischer is not giving up. He gets a metal folding chair to get back up on Tux, but the chair collapses—he fell flat on his back right under Tux. Tux looked at him calmly, like 'What are you doing?'"

In recent years, Colyne and her crew have been challenged by big fires in the Youngs Creek drainage and other routes into the Bob. Some hitches extended from 80 hours to more like 100 hours, with ten- to twelve-hour days as they worked through burned areas and blowdowns. Sometimes trail workers were black with soot after a long day. Clearing these trails and then taking care of the stock each evening was tough for everyone. Colyne and her co-workers took pride in working hard and accomplishing as much as possible in a day. Wilderness travelers were quick to pass along their appreciation for keeping the wilderness trails accessible.

"When you are a crew leader, you come last," said Colyne. "Stock come first; they are working hard, they're carrying your gear. You have to drop their boxes, set up electric fence, remove saddles. They're hungry, and they need to eat; you do all that and basically put them to bed. Then you have to check on your crew, make sure everyone is all right. You can't just think of yourself. You are the last person to take your boots off at night."

*Colyne (center) and Aaron Klug inspect the fireproofed Sabido Cabin,
fall 2017. Grizzly bear management specialist Tim Manley is on the left.*
PHOTOGRAPH COURTESY OF TIM MANLEY.

Staying in the Bob into fall could be a near-spiritual experience.
In the fall of 2015, Colyne and co-worker Dana Bronkala went up
Youngs Creek to do hunter patrols. "We each rode a horse and we led
one mule," Colyne said. "We didn't see many hunters, but we were
able to see the drainage during a beautiful time of year. We rode up
to Leota Park and got to meet outfitter Jack Rich. We were camped
just below his camp. We were making a fire because the little camp
stove we had didn't work. We stayed up late around the fire telling
each other stories and listening to the coffeepot perking in all that dark
silence; the sky was so dark, and the stars were so clear.

"When we were setting up our camp, we noticed these large rocks
in a ring near our campsite. We talked to Jack Rich, and he told us that
they were actually tepee rings from the Salish Kootenai, who often

came in to hunt and fish there before World War II. I thought that was really cool. We met Jack's older sister, still riding in the Bob and enjoying it. She hugged us and gave us some snacks for the road. It was one of those special trips you have the privilege to enjoy and never forget."

Toward the end of 2017, the Spotted Bear trail foreman, Aaron Klug, needed a crew leader and Colyne volunteered to go for a couple of hitches. But fires blew up in the Middle Fork; the Scalp and Strawberry Fires were cooking along. A firefighter crew was wrapping the Sabido Cabin, but they weren't comfortable being there because of bear problems.

Some outfitters in the area reported that a grizzly had been coming into their camp, and at one point it managed to grab a sandwich, so it had nabbed a food reward. The outfitter had tried to scare it off and finally shot at it, possibly hitting it in the butt. At Spotted Bear, Colyne readied her fire pack and overnight pack and, within a few hours, she and the trail foreman rode a helicopter to Sabido to finish the job of fireproofing the cabin.

Sabido Cabin, named for the pioneering Sabidos family, perches on the edge of Big River Meadows, a remote spot at the head of Gateway Creek in the Middle Fork. Not far from the cabin, Gateway Creek plunges over the meadow's edge and hurries down to its junction with Strawberry Creek, upstream of the Middle Fork headwaters. The helicopter riders got an amazing tour and view of the Middle Fork and the fires as they flew over the landscape.

The helicopter landed in a meadow not far from the cabin. Colyne and the crew foreman, Aaron Klug, switched spots with the firefighters. The two went and talked to the outfitters and got an update on the bear. They let the outfitters know that grizzly bear specialist Tim Manley of Montana Fish, Wildlife & Parks and an assistant were coming in to set snares.

"We finished wrapping the cabin, and then one evening near dark we saw this little cinnamon-colored bear walking in," said Colyne. "We were looking at the bear, and looked at each other and said, 'That's a black bear, isn't it?' But then we started questioning ourselves. We thought that maybe it was a young grizzly that hadn't grown into its hump yet. We scared him off." Later, Aaron showed Tim Manley a cell phone picture of the bear, and Tim confirmed it as a black bear.

The next morning, not even 5 A.M. yet, the two workers were ready to get up. "We heard this chomp, chomp, chomp, kind of a clawing, chewing," said Colyne. "Then the realization hit us—he's chewing on the cabin." The bear was attracted to the shiny fire wrap on the cabin.

"So we both get our boots on and run around the cabin, and here's the little bear standing on his hind feet, reaching up toward the roof, and he's got his front paws on top and he's clawing and chewing on the cabin wrap. We yelled at him and clapped our hands and he just looked at us. We were really close, but he didn't care at all. We had bear spray but didn't use it." The bear moseyed away like it was no big deal.

Soon, Tim Manley of Montana Fish, Wildlife & Parks and his technician, Daniel Madel, helicoptered in to address the bear issue. Acting Spotted Bear ranger Gordon Ash had contacted Tim and asked him to go to Sabido to address the bear problem. Tim is considered one of the nation's foremost bear management experts, having handled about 300 grizzlies over the years. If anyone could catch this pesky bear, Tim and Daniel could.

The two experts reconnoitered the area and busily set some baited snares. After a few days, Daniel had to leave, so Rachel Manley, Tim's wife, was transported in to add expertise to the effort. Rachel has worked for the National Park Service, has worked extensively with bears, and now works in wildlife management for the U.S. Forest Service. The bear people were pulling out all the stops to try to capture this bear.

Tim is known as the best in the business. He always gets his bear.

But this bruin "Houdini" (he seemed like an escape artist), and any other bears that may have been living in the area, gave Tim and his co-workers the slip. The bear didn't show up again.

"I think they were there about a week," said Colyne. "It was fun having company and talking at night, but nothing happened. So Tim and Rachel flew back out."

The next night Houdini the bear showed up as if he knew that the bear experts had left. Colyne and Aaron were amazed. "We said, 'What?'"

The bear wandered around, visited the now-abandoned outfitter camp, and walked around the cabin. Colyne notified Spotted Bear.

Tim and yet another biologist, Jesse Coltrane, flew back in and set snares again. They helped wrap the cabin and put up electric fencing around the outfitter camp, but the bear didn't reappear. The thwarted biologists left after a few days because the fires were blowing up. The elusive bruin had simply vanished. Houdini had gone up against the best in the business, taken everything the biologists had thrown at him, yet managed to avoid capture.

"So we set lookout points, got sprinklers going, then we were flown out," said Colyne. "We were in there a total of twenty days." After the stint at Sabido, Colyne packed in to Schafer and Gooseberry, doing trail and fire rehab. Then she did some more trail maintenance in upper Youngs Creek to finish the season.

Like other backcountry workers, Colyne has had her own face-to-face battles with mice and packrats. It was nothing new around the cabins within the Bob. Over the decades, lots of energy has been expended in the clash between rodents and rangers. On a hitch to Basin Cabin to pack supplies and cut wood, Colyne and her co-worker Trent ran into one of the biggest packrats they'd ever seen.

Basin Cabin is notorious for critters, notably bats, mice, and pack-rats. It's always a competition between the "vermin" and the crews. And they both seemed to take special pleasure in winning.

"Seemed there was always a packrat living in the outhouse," said Colyne. "You could hear him crawling around in the walls; he would poke his nose out and look around. He'd pop out at you when you were going to the bathroom." This packrat was hard to get because people using the outhouse were focused on other matters and were usually caught off guard.

When Colyne and Trent opened up the cabin, they got a glimpse of their rival and worried about what might be in store for them. They could only hope that the rodent had not built a nest.

"We saw him and could smell him, and he was big," said Colyne. "He was a big packrat. We unloaded our boxes, put away the stock for the night in the corral across the creek. We spread our gear out on the porch. I had put an avocado in my leather nose bag along with my beanie and a few other things. The avocado had gotten squished onto my beanie. I also had an apple and a few other food items for lunch."

Colyne is as at home in the wilderness as she is "outside." Here on the South Fork of the Flathead River, near Big Prairie Ranger Station.
PHOTOGRAPH COURTESY OF COLYNE HISLOP.

"We were just relaxing," said Colyne, "getting settled, moving in and out of the cabin organizing things, and enjoying the night; we forgot all about the packrat. Trent walked outside the cabin and I heard him yell, 'Colyne, come out here, the packrat's got the apple!' He had grabbed the apple and ran off with it. He kept stealing the things we had spread out on the porch. Then he somehow stole the avocado . . . how's he grabbing that? We could see him munching on it, leave, then come back to eat more."

The monster packrat tried to take Colyne's favorite hat under the porch, but Trent grabbed it and saved it. That was the last straw.

"It then became our mission to try to get the packrat because he kept stealing our things," said Colyne. "We baited a rat trap with various things, but he kept evading it. We tried avocado, apple, and other things, but he was clever. Then we tried a piece of dried mango. We heard the trap go off one night and then I actually felt bad; Trent had to finish killing it while I watched. But I guess the packrat deserved it;

we got the monster. I had never had a packrat steal so many things. He stole the caps to the water cubies, you name it.

"Another time in Basin Cabin, we woke up and there was a big packrat running around. Somebody said, 'Get it!' So we all started chasing it around in the dark by headlamps, with tools, shovels, and a broom. We finally got that one with a Pulaski."

Mice are a problem at every backcountry cabin. Salmon Forks Cabin seems to harbor big numbers of them, running over the top of bunks and up and down the rafters and walls all night. Mice are small but still can elicit fear, even from tough backcountry workers.

"It was early in the morning at Salmon Forks," said Colyne, "and a mouse was running around, and I yelled, 'Get it, get it!' You could hear them all night. The mouse ran by Sydney and she lifted her feet and yelled 'EEK!' I had my Chaco's [sandals] on, so I stomped on him as he ran by.

"And at Danaher, last year at the end of the season, we had to spend a day cleaning the cabin. Mice had built nests. Mice chewed a hole in the food box and three mice were living in the bottom cabinet, and when you opened it they'd come at you and 'Aaah!' it would scare you. We got two of them, but one kept evading us and showing up in the bottom cabinet. We'd open it and he would charge out and startle us." As with other challenges, Colyne didn't let the rodents intimidate her. She just took it in stride.

Colyne's adventures in the Bob have been priceless. She has had the opportunity to spend many weeks on end without leaving the wilderness. No matter where her career eventually leads her, she can always cherish that Bob Marshall privilege. But every once in a while, even Colyne needed to leave the Bob for a short time.

In 2015, Colyne walked "outside" from Big Prairie to attend a friend's wedding. She headed up Youngs Creek to Hahn Cabin, where she met two "trail dogs" who were there for fire work and cabin protection and were ready to head out. The three young workers hiked to the head of Jenny Creek, over Youngs Pass, and down to the Lodgepole Creek trailhead, east of Seeley Lake. Colyne hiked a total distance of about thirty-two miles that day.

"My mom picked me up," said Colyne. "She remembered that trailhead; she used to pick up my dad at the same trailhead and bring him food and cold drinks. This day, Mom pulled up with a cooler of food and beer and did the same for me. She was ecstatic and excited to pick me up, saying, 'Oh, I remember this trailhead!' She was reliving memories, and we shared them together that day."

SOURCES

Personal interview by the author with Colyne Hislop, January 14, 2019, in Kalispell, MT. Several follow-up conversations.

Personal interview by the author with Tim Manley, Montana Fish, Wildlife & Parks, February 8, 2019.

Kids in the Bob

*Guy and Keagan Zoellner are raising a young
family deep in the Bob Marshall Wilderness.*

GUY AND KEAGAN ZOELLNER WERE RIDING TO BIG PRAIRIE, bound for a
summer of work and public service deep in the Bob. So far, they'd
ridden about twenty miles from the trailhead at Meadow Creek, and
they had twelve to go. But there was something unusual about these
two and their pack string of mules loaded with supplies: they were
also packing two little kids.

Rial, their son, two and a half years old, rode on a pillow on the
front of Guy's saddle. Greta was seven months old, and she rode with
Keagan in a front pack.

Everything was going great for this wilderness family on a beautiful
late spring day. As they rode through the old burn at Salmon Forks,
Simon, their border collie, was scuttling back and forth along the trail
up ahead.

"All of a sudden, Simon turned and jumped off the trail," said Guy.
"Right then Keagan saw two little bear cubs skirt up a tree. It all happened in an instant."

Guy whistled, and Simon turned and raced back toward the riders
with mama bear loping right behind him. The big black bear sow was
close, running three legged, trying to swat the frightened border collie. Keagan and Guy screamed and yelled, and right in front of them
Simon ducked under a log, but the bear couldn't fit because she was

Deep in the heart of the Bob Marshall Wilderness, Big Prairie Ranger Station is home to Guy and Keagan Zoellner and their two children, Rial and Greta. PHOTOGRAPH BY JOHN FRALEY.

too big, so she swatted at the log. The black bear was definitely trying to "neutralize" the border collie to protect her cubs. Simon slinked behind the crew, and the bear stopped ten feet away. Keagan yelled at the bear and she ran off.

"Phew, both Keagan and I were alarmed, excited, our hearts were beating fast," said Guy. "About thirty seconds later we started riding back up the trail again and it was quiet for a minute. Then Rial said, 'Can somebody tell me a story? I'm kind of bored.'"

Big Prairie Ranger Station, along the South Fork of the Flathead River, is the Bob's flagship station and center of trail maintenance and public service in the middle of the wilderness. This huge set of meadows and prairies is not a place accessed casually. To get to this most gorgeous of spots, the intrepid wilderness hiker or rider must trek about thirty miles from the nearest trailhead.

That's why many visitors are surprised and pleased when they see a couple of young kids running around, looking right at home, in this remote meadow and river. Rial and Greta Zoellner know Big Prairie—

the ranger station, ranger residence, bunkhouse, packer's cabin, meadows, frog pond, river—as well as anyone. They've spent a good piece of their lives there. They own the place.

Both kids have lived four or five months or so at Big Prairie each year since they were born. In fact, Greta spent about four months there *before* she was born.

Big Prairie ranger and trails manager Guy Zoellner and his wife, Keagan, both have stellar and well-respected histories and experience working for the U.S. Forest Service. They met at the University of Montana, where Guy majored in forestry and Keagan majored in outdoor recreation management. The couple married in 2009. Guy has worked at Big Prairie since 1998. Keagan has worked as a river ranger for years, and also served as executive director for the Bob Marshall Wilderness Foundation. Now, when she's out of the Bob in winter, she works as a ski patroller at Whitefish Mountain Resort.

When they decided to have children, they talked about the possibility of bringing them into Big Prairie. Of course, as a couple, they worried about the usual things that come to mind: shepherding very young children in and out safely, distance from a doctor or hospital, lack of medicines, and so on. And of course, they worried about what would happen if there were an accident, or a kid is allergic to peanuts or chokes on something. When most parents give their kids honey for the first time, they are twenty minutes from the emergency room. At Big Prairie it's a long way to town.

In the beginning, Guy didn't know if it would be practical to work his backcountry job and, at the same time, raise young children. The highest priority for the couple was the children, but they knew if they could pull it off it would be something unusual and special to share. "But my supervisor was all for it," said Guy. "I give Deb Mucklow a ton of credit that she let it happen. For her to do that in this day and age of sensitivity and litigation was huge, to let us take a six-month-old baby and ride with him back in the wilderness and then live in there all summer. Our eyes opened that we could do it, and then we just decided to make it part of our life and go all in."

Keagan visited a doctor and told him what they planned to do. They got the doctor's personal cell phone, the A.L.E.R.T. air ambulance phone number and "frequent flyer membership," and a satellite

Horses are part of life for Greta and Rial, here at Big Prairie.
PHOTOGRAPH BY MICHAEL REAVIS.

phone. Keagan was confident, and with all her wilderness training she was ready for anything.

One concern the couple had was the lack of normal socialization the kids would experience at Big Prairie. Guy checked with a friend who raised his kids at a wilderness station for the first seven years of their lives. The friend said that his son and daughter were connected together and close to nature. They both became environmental lawyers, and he was convinced that those years in the wilderness inspired their protective, conservation-minded attitude. After that, Guy was sold.

After a lot of reflection, they decided to try it, and as it turned out, Guy and Keagan discovered that it was somewhat easier and even more rewarding than they thought it would be. They found that, aside from the distance to a hospital, it was like second nature, and was a wonderful, unique opportunity for them and their kids. "You don't have to drive around," said Guy. "You can just be present with the kids, hang out with them. It's less complicated, and you spend more time together."

Guy and Keagan made the leap of faith when Rial was about six months old. "That first trip from the trailhead, there's a photo my mom took of us at Meadow Creek," said Guy. "Keagan is riding our little horse, Biscuit, and has six-month-old Rial in a front pack. I'm riding a Forest Service horse and I have the mules. The look on our faces is, 'We are going but I don't know.'"

Once they were at Big Prairie, the presence of their kids amazed visitors who walked, rode, or floated by the station. "I'd go to the station to greet visitors," said Keagan. "They'd see me with a baby monitor; I explained what it was, and they'd say, 'You have a *baby* in here?' Or people would see me and the kids down by the beach as they come floating by and exclaim, 'How did *they* get in here?'"

When Keagan was pregnant with Greta, she experienced the open arms and kindness of the backcountry community. All the "rough and tumble cowboys" would offer to help in any way—to bump a pack, check if she needed something—falling all over themselves to "roll out the red carpet."

"Some people might think we are kind of reckless, what we've done," said Keagan. "But we've had a lot of support. So far, only a

Greta enjoys a snack at Big Prairie. PHOTOGRAPH BY MICHAEL REAVIS.

few bumps and scrapes here and there, kids fell off their horses a time or two; knock on wood. Once I caught Greta in midair as she fell off her horse. She said, 'No problem, mommy catch you!'"

Keagan noted that with all the conveniences in town—carpet, central heating, a washing machine—you can relax a bit more. But in the wilderness, you can't take your eyes off the kids for a second. When Rial was a baby, Guy's mom picked them up at the trailhead. It was the first time Keagan relaxed and let her guard down in many weeks. Keagan buckled Rial in the car seat, and sat back to enjoy the drive. But she had pulled a rookie mom stunt and gave him a squeeze tube of pureed fruit. "I turned around," said Keagan, "and he was redecorating the entire back seat with pureed mango."

During their first season at Big Prairie, the couple didn't know what to expect. Keagan was concerned that Rial might not get adequate nutrition. So she pureed vegetables and dried them to pack in. And, of course, for several years, smelly diapers had to be handwashed, at one point eighteen diapers every four days. All the family's clothes had to be handwashed, which is a lot more work than it sounds.

Keagan said that when the kids were crawling, she lived in constant fear of choking objects and hantavirus. "They both survived crawling around in the backcountry," she said. "Big Prairie isn't bad. You can keep the ranger residence and station clean with bleach. But for the patrol cabins we had to carry a bleach spray bottle and be especially careful. You share the old cabins with a lot of rodent friends."

Keagan would fence off an area in the cabin with pack boxes and lay a manty tarp on the floor to keep the kids from wandering, and she watched them like a red-tailed hawk. The kids chewed on sticks and put rocks in their mouths. Their saddlebags were full of trail trinkets they picked up along the way.

The first year with Rial, few people even noticed that Guy and Keagan had a baby on the horse with them. Guy would wrap his coat around Rial, who rode in a front pack.

"That first year it was great," said Guy. "I could ride around on patrol, Keagan would ride with me, we would stop and talk to people. Rial stayed in every backcountry cabin in the South Fork with us. Keagan and I traded off carrying him. We had a station guard that took care of things at Big Prairie when we were on patrol."

Things didn't always roll along perfectly. The first autumn in the wilderness with Rial, they were checking camps on a trip over Pagoda Mountain into Brushy Park, a gorgeous and very remote place. On the ride in, the trail climbs up Helen Creek, then swings around to the south at an elevation of 7,500 feet where it skirts Pagoda Mountain. The view includes the stunning Damnation drainage, the high country around Pagoda, up and down the South Fork, the upper White River, Silvertip, and all the mountains to the east along the spine. The trail then plummets 2,000 feet down Pagoda Creek to reach Brushy Park. It's a rough trail to ride in and out. When they reached the park, Keagan, Guy, and Rial camped at the edge of a pretty meadow in a small wall tent with a little woodstove to keep it warm.

"Rial was ten months old, and I got up with him in the middle of the night," said Keagan. "I looked out the tent flap and there's not a horse to be seen—they've all run off. So we had a number of sleepless hours until first light.

"We got up," Keagan continued, "and Guy said, 'Well okay, I might be back today or maybe in two days. Do you want the radio or the satellite phone, the bear spray or the pistol?'"

Keagan took the satellite phone and the bear spray. She was worried because if the horses ran all the way back to Big Prairie, Guy would have to cover more than twenty miles on foot, then ride back the same distance. Plus, Keagan had only her cowboy boots, which are tough to hike in. "I thought, oh I really hope I don't have to hike all the way out of here carrying an infant and walking in cowboy boots."

Guy started after the horses and luckily caught up with them at a meadow with good grass known as "the football field," a few miles along the trail. The escaped stock were chowing down on grass. Guy rounded them up and was back at camp after only a few hours, a pleasant surprise for Keagan.

Taking things in stride seemed to work really well when potentially dangerous incidents happened while they were riding with the kids. Anyone who rides in the wilderness as much as Guy and Keagan will sometime or another get in a stock wreck, and that next year a memorable wreck in the Danaher drainage led to a family saying.

Keagan, Guy, and Rial were riding back toward Big Prairie after a resupply pack trip to Jumbo Lookout. They were riding down the trail between Basin and Big Prairie. Keagan was pregnant and riding Biscuit, the old gray horse, and Guy was riding Sam, the mule, while twenty-month-old Rial sat on a pillow in front of him. Guy was leading a string of five or six mules.

As they rode across the juniper sidehill, without warning the riders were swarmed by bees on the trail, causing an instant wreck. "Keagan got her horse across the bees," said Guy. "The mule I rode got across the bees, but then they swarmed up and they were stinging. In this kind of a classic wreck, everything loses its mind. Things are bucking, going crazy, so you have to just get out of there, so one option is you just run away from the bees. When you get into bees, mules just mentally shut down and run wherever.

"Packs were going all over, and I yelled, 'Just run!' So we were loping along the sidehill, with all these mules running along, bucking their packs off, and Rial was on my lap. I'm trying to watch the mules, and Rial's just 'Har har har'; he thinks it's fun and funny. He starts laughing, then starts screaming 'Der's a bear, der's a bear!' And I remember looking for it. The only thing that's going to make this wreck worse is if there was a bear in front of us. I looked forward and said, 'Where's the bear?' and he said, 'Right der!' Simon, our black dog, was having to crunch up and run like crazy to get away from us, and he did kind of look like a little bear running along."

When they got to the other side and things calmed down, Keagan told Guy he would have to go back through the bees, because their big camera case had fallen out of the baby bag during all the bucking. While Keagan held the string and watched Rial, Guy gallantly returned to the wreck site, dodging bees, and found the camera seventy-five yards directly down from the bee spot on the hillside. "I think Guy only got stung once," said Keagan.

The epic wreck coined a classic family saying: "Der's a bear, right der!" And, as usual, Simon the border collie was right in the middle of the action.

The toughest summer was probably when Keagan was pregnant and had a two-year-old kid to watch. That summer, the family stayed at Big Prairie until Halloween. Greta was born eleven days after they rode out, on November 6. She was three weeks early; if she'd arrived on schedule, she would have been born on Rial's birthday.

Keagan Zoellner with both kids on her horse.
PHOTOGRAPH COURTESY OF THE ZOELLNER FAMILY.

The next year, things got more complicated. Greta was seven months old, and Rial was two and a half years old.

"Used to be I could ride and handle the mules," said Guy. "Keagan could carry one kid on the horse. Now all of a sudden there was two of them, and each of us had to carry a kid."

Guy rode their big mule, Sam, all summer, with Greta in a front pack. Sam was calm, so it worked really well. Guy was always adjusting the order of the stock to see what worked best, aiming to have the fewest number of problems all day.

Guy Zoellner heads out on patrol from Big Prairie Ranger Station.
PHOTOGRAPH BY JOHN FRALEY.

"Once they were on the pillow, they got fun but exhausting," said Guy. "They constantly asked questions. In Rial's second year he was a talkative toddler. You were riding eight hours a day, and it forced you to be present in the wilderness with your kid, both on the same horse; there's no music, TV, other distractions. So you were a captive audience all day. 'What's that? Where are we going?'

"So we created a whole imaginative world. There's Clotter Blotter the Otter. His lodge is in the Middle Fork, and his best friend is Gawk the Hawk. Five years of stories, hundreds of these stories about the wilderness. If you asked Rial if Clotter Blotter is real, he'd say, 'Yeah, he lives in the Middle Fork.'"

The kids have spent much of their time at Big Prairie with Keagan, because it takes too much to bring them both along on patrols. But as Rial grew, he could ride his own horse, and that opened up more possibilities. He rode along on some of Guy's patrols to camps, where the folks always offered Guy coffee and Rial hot chocolate. Soon Greta will be there too. And Rial and Greta are favorites with the young men and women of the various trail crews that come and go on their work hitches, so there's often someone to visit with.

At Big Prairie, thirty-two miles into the wilderness, fires pose a real danger to a young family. Guy's mom once sent a letter asking about their safety when a fire was surging. But at Big Prairie, there's so much defensible area with all the prairie and meadows that Guy feels they are safer there than they might be with a fire in the town of Coram, which sits in a timbered area.

During the 2015 fire season, however, the whole wilderness was closed, so the Zoellners had to ride out. Rial and Greta viewed it as if they'd been kicked out of their home. "The kids know more than we think they do," said Guy. "They listen to the radio, what we talk about, and they know a lot of the guys working there. They'll say we had to leave because Jim Flint [U.S. Forest Service fire management officer] told us to. They called him a dirty scoundrel."

Because of the closure, the Zoellners left Big Prairie and rode up the South Fork trail, bound for Shaw Cabin, about fifteen miles upstream in the Gordon Creek drainage. Gordon Pass and the trailhead at Holland Lake would be their escape route. A fire had been spotted near Lena Lake, up a drainage only a few miles from Shaw Cabin. At 6:30 P.M. they were cutting through downed timber within a mile of the cabin, and they could see the plume from the fire. A Forest Service plane circled overhead.

"I could see the airplane circling above us and I asked Seth on the radio if we would be safe at Shaw, but there was silence. He finally said, 'I think you'll be okay for tonight, but get out of there first thing in the morning.'"

Reaching the cabin, Guy and Keagan felt worried and nervous. They had six miles, a bunch of switchbacks, and a few thousand feet in elevation gain to reach Gordon Pass, then nine more miles down to the trailhead at Holland Lake. They woke up the kids early, about 3 A.M., to get an early start.

"We headed over the pass in the dark," said Guy. "The stars were out, and Rial asked, 'Why are we going over the pass so early?' We didn't want to scare them, because they knew there was a fire, so

Even at an early age, Rial had mastered the art of telling fish tales.
PHOTOGRAPH COURTESY OF THE ZOELLNER FAMILY.

Keagan said, 'We just want to be on the pass to see the stars,' and both kids said, 'Oh, that's cool,' so we looked up at the big sky and the stars."

Now that Rial is getting older, his only option to go along on Guy's patrols is to ride a horse; he's too big to carry, and he's not big enough to walk fifteen miles in a day. "We have to let him go," said Guy. "You take your hands off the horse and you have to trust a young boy and the horse. For lots of ranch kids it's second nature, and hopefully it will be that way with them."

At Big Prairie, the family lives along one of the best fishing rivers in the state, and much of the time they have the river all to themselves. As they have grown, Rial and Greta have become exceptional anglers for their age. Rial can tie his own fly, tie it on the leader, catch his own fish, drag it up on the bank, and club it. The only thing Guy needs to do is split the belly. Then they pull out the guts, clean the fish, and take it back and cook it. "They understand where food comes from," said Guy.

Trail crew members and other employees at Big Prairie during the summer are lucky. They live only a short walk from the river. On many rivers, you might catch a fish, or you might not. But on the South Fork catching a fish is pretty much guaranteed. And they have Rial and Greta for fishing guides.

Jason Robinson, a station guard who grew up in the Flathead but never really fished very much, wanted to learn. So one day Jason, Guy, and the kids went down to the river to fish. The kids dispersed to catch bugs or frogs, and Guy gave Jason a tutorial on how to cast the fly and what to do if a fish strikes. About ten casts in, Jason yelled, "I got a fish!"

As soon as he said that, Rial and Greta charged out of "opposing bushes." They yelled at him to back up and instructed him on how to pull the westslope cutthroat trout out of the water. The fish flopped on the bank and Rial jumped on it. Greta grabbed a branch and Rial held the fish out, and they said, "Thank you for your flesh and fun," and told Jason to say the same thing and he did, and then Greta whacked it. Jason got out his knife and opened up the fish, then the kids taught Jason how to gut it.

Rial has shown great promise as a top fisherman since he was four. He started catching fish on his own that year. The remote, upper White River at Brushy Park is chock-full of little westslope cutthroat; stretches of the stream go dry late in the summer, and where the water bubbles back up the fish are crowded and hungry.

"We finally reached our camp spot," said Keagan. "I was setting up our wall tent and stove when Rial ran up to me and said, 'Mom, where's my fly rod?' So I gave him his rod and continued setting up camp. Greta was puttering around by my feet as I got the woodstove going."

Rial was quiet as a deer mouse down the bank by the creek. Keagan had not heard a peep from his direction for a half hour. She kept an eye on him by watching his blond head bobbing around as he moved up and down a little stretch of the stream. Suddenly, Keagan heard him shout, "Mommy, Mommy!"

Keagan ran down to the stream and asked Rial if he'd caught a fish. He said, "Yeah I caught a lot!" He gestured with his head and

Keagan looked over. "Rial had caught, bonked, and was preparing to eat a few little tiny fish," said Keagan. "He smiled and looked at me and said, 'Mommy, me and 'Deta, we're going to eat good tonight!'"

Keagan cleaned the fish. At that age, she didn't allow Rial to use a knife. A bad cut in the backcountry might mean they would have to get their A.L.E.R.T. frequent flyer card out. Keagan is adept at EMT and health issues and could handle most emergencies, but risks loom larger when you're in a remote spot.

There have been a few times when Guy and Keagan thought about flying one of the kids out. Once, when he was four, they thought Rial had giardiasis, a diarrheal disease caused by the waterborne parasite *Giardia lamblia*. He was lying around, couldn't eat, couldn't sleep, and had all the symptoms. He had gotten really sick in the tent at Little Salmon Creek, about halfway between Big Prairie and the trailhead at Meadow Creek.

Keagan called the doctor on the satellite phone and described Rial's symptoms. The doctor thought it sounded like giardiasis, so Keagan arranged for some medicine to be transported in.

"It turned into this epic story," said Guy. "My dad picked up the prescription, took it to Hungry Horse, and then Pat Van Eimeren [a Forest Service fish biologist] drove it up the reservoir road that night, got it to packer Mike Reavis, who would be on his way from Black Bear to Big Prairie. The medicine would arrive at Big Prairie in about eight hours."

All told, by that point Rial had been sick for about twelve days. The couple was worried. But that morning Rial woke up, and for the first time in twelve days he looked good. He stretched and said, "Anybody going to make me some pancakes?" He had kicked the bug, whatever it was, and Guy and Keagan never gave him the medicine.

Another time, Rial badly cut his finger on the lid of a peach can. Keagan was worried about it but decided it would heal. A trip to town for stitches would've been stressful and taken up about a week, so she kept Rial at Big Prairie and doctored it. Keagan kept it covered and managed it; it took about a month, but it finally healed completely.

When you sum it up, the Zoellner family lives in the wilderness from June to Halloween, four or five months each year. That means a third of the kids' lives have been spent in the wilderness. Rial has been

What better place than Big Prairie to fly a kite. PHOTOGRAPH BY JOHN FRALEY.

in there seven seasons; he's already spent more than two years of his life in the Bob. In this day and age, that is almost unheard of.

"I am exceptionally glad we've had them back there," said Guy. "What's really cool is the understanding that they have about public land, what that means. The kids have grown up not only recreating on it but living on it. They get to live at Big Prairie, but they realize they don't own it. Home shifts back and forth. It's crazy how comfortable they are in both places. When they get back to Big Prairie, they are right back home. And sometimes we realize that we are living like people in the old days with all the time we spend together. We are like the Peter Pan family."

They have been waiting to see if at some point the kids won't want to go into Big Prairie for the entire season. But so far, they both want

Armed with a net and curiosity, Rial, Greta, and Keagan turn Big Prairie into a learning laboratory. PHOTOGRAPH BY JOHN FRALEY.

to go. They have their town friends, but they are really excited to go to Big Prairie, and they talk about it when they are out. Guy and Keagan didn't think they would be in the wilderness with the kids this long, but it has worked out.

"So we'll just keep going," said Guy. "There's no reason to not do it at this point. Maybe in four or five years it will be harder. They are their own best friends. They have a million and a half acres to run around in and relatively few rules." Keagan's rule is: once the kids eat breakfast and the sun hits the prairie, they are free to roam. With some supervision and checking in, of course.

A challenging thing about raising kids at Big Prairie is coming back to town. Town has appointments and school, driving, and social media. Lights and cars bug the kids at first when they leave the wilderness. Once, right after they got out to Augusta, Greta was startled when she and Keagan went into a restaurant bathroom and Keagan turned on a light. "She hit the floor and said, 'What's that up in the sky?'" said Keagan. "And I told her, 'It's just a lightbulb, honey.'"

"When we get out, we say, 'Phew, we made it another year with no one getting hurt,'" said Guy. "No A.L.E.R.T. helicopter. And we realize we were a little intense in the summer back there; you can't drop your guard. Last year we got out on a Tuesday night, then we dropped Rial off to school the next day and off he goes. The school sends in material and Keagan takes them through the lesson plans at Big Prairie; they don't miss a beat. West Glacier school is great. Kids are malleable that way," he said. Adults? Guy replied, "Keagan and I need a week."

Keagan and Guy have made the wilderness lifestyle work for their family. They've had to maintain a certain risk tolerance to live with kids in such an isolated setting. When Guy is away on patrol, Keagan might be the only adult for twenty miles around, so she must have confidence in her ability to keep the youngsters safe. "Once we saw fresh mountain lion tracks in the mud," said Keagan. "Simon was barking, and we went over to look around and saw a fresh, intact deer liver on the ground. Probably left by a mountain lion with a kill cached somewhere. So the kids and I made a lot more noise. We kept Simon nice and tight and continued along, but it does make your hair stand on end going along with two little pieces of cougar bait you are carrying, not to mention the dog."

As they have gotten older, the two kids have developed their own identities. Rial's favorite thing to do is chasing frogs and bugs, while Greta really likes riding the horses, with Guy or Keagan leading her. To play outdoors, most parents have to put their kids in a car and go someplace, but Rial and Greta live there. Rial has learned to snorkel and goes down to the river each day. He has a little farmer john wetsuit to insulate him from the 50-degree waters of the South Fork. He hops in, laps the run, and then floats it again, seeing whitefish, cutthroat, and bull trout.

"I can see the appreciation for nature developing in the kids, especially Rial; the interest is there," said Guy. "The bugs, the fish, the outdoors, the way things work in the environment."

As the river flows dropped last fall, some long-nosed suckers got stranded in the remnants of the frog pond and slough off the South

*For Rial and Greta Zoellner, Big Prairie is home but also school
and playground.* PHOTOGRAPH BY JOHN FRALEY.

Fork, just down from the ranger residence. All that was left was a shallow little wet spot just a few feet in diameter; everything else was dry.

"I can't believe those suckers survived," said Guy. "They were lying on their sides, struggling to work their gills."

The struggling fish included about a dozen four- or five-inchers, and fifty smaller ones about an inch long, probably fry of the year. The kids filled an apricot bag with water and took the fish back to the ranger residence, put them in a glass jar, and revived them. About half the big ones died, but all the little ones lived. The next day, the family took the excited suckers down to the South Fork and had a release party. The suckers gilled in the cold, oxygenated water, and darted off into the current.

"I'm sure the bull trout were pleased," said Guy.

After many wilderness seasons with the kids, Keagan and Guy know Rial and Greta on a level that very few people can experience.

Every parent shares fun and special things with their kids, but few share so many special moments in the wilderness.

Last fall, Rial wanted to ride his horse to the top of a mountain and spend the night. So, the family rode down to Salmon Forks to check some camps and stayed a night there. "The next day, we rode up to Mud Lake Lookout, because we needed to check out the trail," said Keagan. "We packed food, water, horse feed, gear, and electric fencing. We reached the top, set up the electric fence, put the stock in the little corral, and fed them some hay. We got to do a little grouse hunt in the evening. We woke up to a fresh coating of snow the next morning, the first of the season. Rial was excited, he was on cloud nine. He looked at me and said, 'Mom, this has been the best day of the year!'"

Already an enthusiastic naturalist, Rial Zoellner enjoys catching frogs.
PHOTOGRAPH BY JOHN FRALEY.

From left to right, Greta, Rial, Keagan, and Guy, with Simon the dog, at home at Big Prairie Ranger Station. PHOTOGRAPH BY JOHN FRALEY.

SOURCES

Personal recorded interview by the author with Guy Zoellner, January 30, 2019. Follow-up conversations, spring 2019.

Personal recorded interview by the author with Keagan Zoellner, February 11, 2019.

12

HEROES OF THE BOB

Griz in the Bob:
Cooney's Lost Journals

*Unearthing the journals of pioneering wildlife biologist
Bob Cooney, who did the first comprehensive grizzly
bear surveys in the Bob Marshall Wilderness.*

WHEN YOU THINK OF ICONIC SYMBOLS of the Bob Marshall Wilderness, the grizzly bear rises to the top in most people's minds. The Bob would just not be the same without the great bear, and we are so lucky that this big carnivore is thriving across the wilderness and beyond.

For the current strong population status of the grizzly in the Bob today, to a large extent we can thank a young state biologist. Eight decades ago, as Montana's first professional biologist, he surveyed the entire wilderness to document the bear's presence, food habits, and habitat. Then he went on to have a long career championing the protection of the wilderness and the grizzly bear.

Robert F. "Bob" Cooney was born in Canyon Ferry, Montana, in 1909, to Fanny and Fred Cooney. Fanny went on to become Montana's most famous cartoonist. Bob's early education was of the "pioneer type" at the family ranch near Townsend, where he was the middle child of three. He later attended high school in Helena. From the beginning, his parents could see that he loved the outdoors.

Bob entered the University of Montana in the mid-1930s, and in the winter of 1934–1935 he lucked out and got on with a study of elk

Bob Cooney at Carmichael Cabin in 1938. PHOTOGRAPH COURTESY
OF MONTANA FISH, WILDLIFE & PARKS.

winter range in the upper Sun River under the direction of the U.S.
Forest Service. It was one of the earliest biological surveys in the primitive areas that would become the Bob Marshall Wilderness. (Luckily,
a portion of the area had been designated as the Sun River Game
Preserve in 1913.) Bob continued his studies and graduated, then went
to work for the Forest Service in 1937.

The U.S. Congress passed the Pittman-Robertson Act that same year,
and federal matching funds became available for state wildlife management across the nation. Bob was hired by the Montana Fish and Game
Department in 1940 as its first professional wildlife biologist. He was
designated head of the wildlife restoration program. For his first big
assignment, he conducted a survey of grizzly and black bears, mountain
goats, and other wildlife spanning the east side of the Bob Marshall
Wilderness, then spilling over to the entire west side as well.

Bob would have gone into military service and the war effort, but
reportedly he was held back for a purpose. If the United States was
invaded, it was thought that game populations might be important
for feeding the civilian population. It was deemed critical that experts

document, manage, and restore wildlife across Montana and the Bob Marshall.

From July 12 through October 3, 1941, Bob Cooney, assisted by Ray Gibler, traveled about 2,000 miles on horseback and foot to survey grizzly bears, mountain goats, and other wildlife in the Bob. At that time, Cooney noted, this was the only area in the United States outside of national parks that supported the great bear. Many of Bob's surveys focused on the east side of the wilderness, along the entire Chinese Wall, south to north, down its drainages, and out to the Rocky Mountain Front. But he also surveyed large areas of the west side, including the upper South Fork of the Flathead from Meadow to Danaher Creeks, and pretty much the entire Middle Fork of the Flathead. By the time they were done, they had covered much of the newly designated Bob and most of what later became the Great Bear Wilderness.

The epic survey began on a sunny day, July 12, 1941. Bob and Ray left the Gibler Ranch and rode forty miles that day along the east front of the Bob in the Deep Creek, Green Gulch, and Sheep Gulch areas. Bob reported seeing four mountain goats and two bears, including one large brown female and a cub. Most of the time, the men documented bear presence using bear sign. On this trip, Bob saw lots of tracks, and signs of feeding, typically bears turning over rocks and logs. He estimated one grizzly and eight black bears used the area.

Right from the start, the study documented the fact that the grizzlies and black bears of the Bob were mostly herbivorous. Bob noted that bears, based on droppings, were eating mostly grasses and beargrass leaves, along with a few Columbian ground squirrels and ants. In one grizzly scat, they found mostly vegetation, with fifty percent beargrass leaves, forty percent grasses and other vegetation, and the remains of one Columbian ground squirrel. Another griz scat had 100 percent spruce buds. They were confirming that bears eat mostly vegetable matter, especially in early summer. Bob also observed seventy elk, five mule deer, and two coyotes that day.

Two days later, Bob noted that he saw seventeen goats above Hidden Lake. Also observed were one black bear and a blue grouse with chicks.

In one encounter that documented what has become a rare species in the wilderness, Bob saw "one ptarmigan and three chicks on the

For camouflage, a ptarmigan's plumage changes from white in winter to grayish-brown in summer, with a mottled look between seasons.
PHOTOGRAPH BY JIM WILLIAMS.

divide of Hidden Lake at 7,700 feet, feeding along the edge of a rock-slide. The young were about twenty percent grown. The old hen was about the color of a sharptailed grouse. Had a little yellow strip over the eyes. The little fellows had little wing feathers; may have been able to fly but didn't attempt to. Were fairly tame. I got to within fifteen feet of old and young."

In another ptarmigan sighting a few weeks later, Bob noted a male and female pair high above the drainage of the West Fork of the Sun River. "A male & female ptarmigan (mature) on Prairie Reef near the lookout . . . they were apparently a pair as they moved about together. (Probably their young or eggs have been destroyed by snow or hail.) They were very tame and I got within eight feet of them for a picture. The male had considerable white on tail, wings, and lower breast. The rest was a mottled brown and gray. A red area showed above his eyes when he moved about. When sitting still it did not show. He would fluff up when the female came near. They were both feeding on dryad and other alpine plants."

In Montana, white-tailed ptarmigan are rarely seen outside Glacier Park. Bob was documenting a relic species confined to the highest and most remote places. Bob Cooney's "dream survey" was off to a great start.

As the biologists penetrated deeper into the wilderness in later July, their bear observations and wildlife sightings picked up. It seemed that the Chinese Wall country between Indian Point, Prairie Reef, and the Moose Creek drainage was particularly productive. The habitat stretching along the base of the wall attracted grizzly use like a magnet.

On July 26, Bob had a fascinating view of grizzly behavior in what he termed a "life history note" in his journal. He was able to watch a large grizzly sow and two yearlings do what grizzlies do best. Along with Bob, about seventy head of elk watched them too. It was better than TV.

"I had crossed through the head of Pine Creek Basin when I heard a long coarse bawling beneath me," he wrote. "I rode quickly back, noticed seventy-three elk on the side hill just below me. The elk were

A sow grizzly with two yearlings. PHOTOGRAPH COURTESY OF MONTANA FISH, WILDLIFE & PARKS.

looking down into the basin below more curious than afraid. I looked down into the scattered brown fir remains before I made out a large grizzly female with 2 yearlings. They were heavily digging under a large log. Apparently, she unearthed the chipmunk or ground squirrel as there was a great deal of bawling from the yearlings. They crawled around the big bear. One of the yearlings got the tidbit and dashed

A page from Bob Cooney's field journal notes "two grizzly bear droppings showing important use of White Bark Pine seeds."

PHOTOGRAPH COURTESY OF DR. HAROLD PICTON.

about 50 feet away to eat it. The old female was a large bear. Her predominant color was brown. The cubs were black on the back and shoulders light brown. All had the characteristic grizzly hump. As the mother moved up through the basin one of the yearlings remained close to her; the other stayed away a little bit but would come galloping back." Bob snapped a few photos of the feeding griz trio.

The next day Bob and Ray rode forty-four miles following separate routes from the head of Moose Creek under the Chinese Wall and down Rock Creek to Gates Park. This remote swath, a big portion within the large 1919 burn, held an encouraging abundance of wildlife. Bob noted that he saw three goats and ten bull elk near Larch Hill Pass, then forty-seven cow elk and twelve more bulls, and five mule deer, as they rode down the Moose and Rock Creek drainages. Abundant sign of grizzlies included six sets of tracks, torn-up anthills and logs, turned-over rocks, and droppings. The grizzly scat analysis again showed much vegetation but also plenty of ants. Bob noted that when grizzlies ate ants, they shoveled them in with abandon, also gulping "sticks, bits of wood, rock, and dirt." The scats showed plenty of huckleberries and nannyberries, now ripening in season, older whitebark pine nut cases from a squirrel cache, and hair and bones of a hoary marmot.

Along the Chinese Wall trail at Rock Creek that day, Bob noted a peculiar find: a dead cow elk in good condition that was still warm with no apparent cause of death. In his necropsy of the elk, Bob noted, "Several gallons of fluid (water apparently) in body cavity. Animal was not in the least bloated. Intestines appeared normal also liver, stomach, lungs and heart. (Still a bit of food internal of stomach and intestine.) I concluded that possibly the elk had eaten a poisonous plant. Either Camas or water hemlock."

The survey was yielding solid results. Bob was documenting wildlife numbers and especially grizzly bear habits in the only remaining piece of country in the northern Continental Divide area outside Glacier that supported the great icon. Confirming the use of whitebark pine nuts and the herbivorous diet of grizzlies was particularly valuable, as was documenting their opportunistic reliance on insects. They noted that the bears dug the roots of cow parsnip and other plants. Again, Moose Creek and the country along the base of the Chinese

Wall emerged as a griz hot spot. The naturalist in Bob was reveling in the joys of the high country, from Hoadley Creek to Scapegoat Mountain, and to Halfmoon Peak, Ahorn Basin, and the South Fork of the Sun River.

Even though the bulk of grizzly and black bear diets appeared to be vegetation, these opportunistic bruins looked for elk calves or any other big pieces of protein that they might be able to grab. Earlier in the month at Indian Point, a ranger had noted that a bear whacked an elk calf and dragged it over underneath a big fir tree, where it sat with its back against the tree and devoured the calf.

For the rest of July, Bob covered some of the most spectacular high country in the West, and it teemed with wildlife, kind of like the Montana Serengeti. Bob and Ray rode the east side of the Bob Marshall from the southern end of the Chinese Wall to the northern end, riding along and up and down the drainages from Pretty Prairie and Indian Creek, to Wrong Creek and Gates Park, to Moonlight Peak to the Open Fork and Lake Levale, to Headquarters Creek to Teton Pass to Larch Hill Pass, all the way noting bear and sign, elk, and large numbers of "fool hens" or Franklin's grouse (widely called spruce grouse today). The last day of July was epic—they rode fifty-eight miles of survey route from Gates Park up to the Wall trail, Lick Creek, Red Shale Creek, Larch Hill, and Moose Creek. They noted nine bull elk, sixteen cow and calf elk, eight mountain goats, six mature bighorn sheep rams, brown bears (species undetermined), and three grizzly bears. They covered 201 miles in the last week of July. Bob Cooney had himself a dream job, and he was excelling in the game counts for this vast, largely unsurveyed gem of wilderness.

Lucky Bob Cooney was enveloped in mind-stunning country throughout his survey, and he wondered at the topography. His study area and the geology behind it were aptly described a decade later by Montana State University geology professor Dr. Charles Deiss:

> The rugged and spectacular limestone area, between the West Fork of the Sun River on the east, the Spotted Bear River on the north, and Danaher Creek on the south is called by geologists the Silvertip Syncline (a downfold) or the White River Basin, because Silver Tip Mountain and White River lie

in the central part of this mass of limestone. Within the region most of the imposing cliffs are formed entirely of Cambrian Rocks. Perhaps the most sublime and widely known of these features is the Chinese Wall and its continuations southward nearly to Camp Creek Pass, and northward beyond Larch Hill on the west side of Wall Creek.

Bob and Ray were riding through this spectacular country and loving every minute of it.

After a brief visit to Helena to check in and resupply, Bob and Ray returned to the backcountry. They assembled a small pack string, planning on being in the mountains for several weeks. The riders would enter from the east front, then ride up the Teton drainage and over the Continental Divide for an extensive survey of the Middle Fork of the Flathead, an area that would eventually become part of the Bob Marshall Wilderness Complex.

On August 10, the men with their pack string entered from the east side, starting out in the upper Teton drainage, and working their way to the top of Mount Wright on the wilderness edge. They spotted two mature grizzlies in the Bruce Creek basin, and three more "brown bears" in the same basin. While on top, the man occupying the fire lookout informed Bob that he'd seen three female ptarmigan along with ten young that were all fledged. He also saw a solitary male ptarmigan. It seemed that Mount Wright, at 8,850 feet, offered good habitat for the birds, which before long would start making the transition to their white winter plumage.

As Bob and Ray entered the Middle Fork drainage on August 12, they were not able to observe as much wildlife, in part because of the more timbered and brushy nature of the drainages. On Bowl and Trail Creeks they reported light use of elk. On August 13, they rode more than thirty miles, from their camp at Basin Creek to its headwaters, back over the Divide, over Switchback Pass, past Dean Lake into the head of Clack Creek, past Gooseberry Park, and up the Middle Fork and Bowl Creek back to their camp. Amazingly, through all that country, they observed only three goats, along the cliffs of spectacular Trilobite Ridge, which Bob generally compared to the Chinese Wall. Bob noted sign of five black bears and two grizzlies.

Pentagon Mountain looms over Dean Lake. PHOTOGRAPH BY JOHN FRALEY.

The next day, Bob and Ray split up and covered Trilobite, Gateway Creek, Gooseberry, and upper Birch Creek over the Divide, riding a total of thirty-six miles. They saw no game, and only sign of a few black bears.

The following morning, Ray took the outfit downriver to Schafer Meadows Ranger Station. Bob rode thirty-four miles and hit pay dirt with bear sign. He rode up Strawberry Creek to the headwaters, and down from the head of Cox Creek past Beaver Lake and through Wapiti Park to the main river trail, then on to Schafer. He noted thirteen individual areas of black bear sign and three sets of griz sign. Scats all contained mostly huckleberries and huckleberry leaves. He noted, "The bear now seem to be searching for huckleberry patches. When possible are using these fruits exclusive of other foods." The bears were into the "hyperphagia stage," piling on the sugar calories to build fat for winter denning. The extensive fields of huckleberries in the Middle Fork impressed the surveyors. Everything fed on them.

Bob even documented "fool hens" or Franklin's grouse, very abundant in the Middle Fork, concentrating on these purple fruits.

On August 16, Bob and Ray left the ranger station and crossed the Middle Fork. It was a notable day—exactly one year before, regional forester Evan Kelley and Secretary of Agriculture Henry Wallace had administratively combined three primitive areas and designated the 950,000-acre backcountry gem as the Bob Marshall Wilderness Area, named in honor of Robert Marshall, who had passed away in 1939 at the age of thirty-eight.

Bob Cooney and Ray rode up Dolly Varden Creek to the Argosy Creek junction that day. Bob hiked up Argosy and down Roaring Creek, a steep and remote trek. He noted five elk and one large brown bear at the head of Argosy Creek in a huckleberry patch. He also found ten sign and tracks of black bear and two of grizzly. One interesting way Bob could tell the difference was the apparent bluntness of the claw marks on logs that were being torn up. Black bear claws were

Grizzly bear sign includes "diggings" like this. PHOTOGRAPH BY JOHN FRALEY.

Whitebark pine grows at the upper limit of tree line, as seen in the Great Bear portion of the Bob. PHOTOGRAPH BY JOHN FRALEY.

sharp, while grizzlies' claws were blunt due to their digging habits. Scat analysis showed they contained ninety percent huckleberries and ten percent huckleberry leaves.

Bob and Ray continued to explore the Middle Fork country. They rode up the remote drainages of Calbick Creek, Miner Creek, Scott Lake, and the Flotilla Lake basin along the South Fork divide. Bob carefully wrote descriptions of each drainage and its forage availability, and documented much wildlife sign. When they found bear scat, they analyzed it and recorded the relative amount of each food item. In late August, they were finding predominantly huckleberries in the scat. Bears of both species were in hyperphagia mode, gobbling up the high-sugar food, piling on the calories. They were amazingly efficient in their berry uptake: consistently, Bob recorded around eighty to ninety percent of the scat was berries, and only ten to twenty percent incidentally consumed leaves.

They rode down the Middle Fork drainage all the way to Spruce Park and penetrated the seldom-visited drainages of Dryad and Bradley Creeks, where they saw one of the biggest black bears of the survey. Bob was careful to document habitat and wildlife in every corner of what would become the Great Bear. They didn't visually observe as many bears here as in the more open areas of the Bob Marshall, but they documented and analyzed extensive bear sign. Back then (as it is today), the brush and timber of the Middle Fork made it tough to see wildlife.

Bob rode many miles through the central Middle Fork and described the major drainages of Granite, Morrison, Puzzle, and Lodgepole Creeks. The last three streams join the river across from Miner Creek, and that junction is known as Three Forks.

Along with Granite Creek, these reaches represented bull trout spawning heaven. The two surveyors were floored by the size of the big chars, ranging up to twenty pounds. Bob mentioned taking "moving pictures of Ray catching a Dolly Varden trout on river just below Three Forks cabin." At this point, these big bulls had migrated upstream more than 100 miles from Flathead Lake to reach their spawning grounds. Bob took a photo of Ray with a nine-and-three-quarter-pound bull trout. They fished in Flotilla Lake for cutthroat trout that averaged fourteen inches. Fishing was super, a great fringe

A young grizzly bear feeds on berries, a favored food toward the end of summer. PHOTOGRAPH COURTESY OF MONTANA FISH, WILDLIFE, AND PARKS.

benefit, and it supplied fresh food. It also served as a break from the intense concentration required of the day-after-day survey.

During those twelve days on this Middle Fork survey, Bob and Ray covered 322 miles, making loops through almost the entire drainage. This distance and volume of survey work in just twelve days is astounding, a tribute to Cooney's dedication to documenting the status of wildlife all across the Bob Marshall.

Bob never mentions much about his stock, but they must have been good. The riders were traveling big miles through the highest elevations of the wilderness. During the next ten days, Bob and Ray covered 250 miles of the north and east portion of the Middle Fork and beyond, up Twenty-five Mile Creek, to Challenge Creek, then over the Continental Divide and through the Badger–Two Medicine and Birch Creek drainages. They swung south and east through the wilderness into the Sun River drainage, over Corrugate Ridge, through Bruce Creek, on past Mount Wright, and out to the east front. On the route they observed six grizzlies. On one day, Bob noted sixteen major grizzly and black bear sign items, ranging from good tracks to scat concentrations to feeding sites. At one point at the head of Bruce Creek, Bob was surrounded by griz sign and torn-up alpine meadows. He noted, "Considerable signs of grizzly bear. This is one of the best grizzly bear ranges we've seen. White Bark pine."

Bob made specific notes documenting the grizzly's high-country food habits, again confirming the poorly understood and complex relationship of whitebark pine nuts, squirrels, and grizzlies. On August 27, he noted:

> Today we noticed two grizzly bear [scat] showing important use of White Bark pine nuts. One was made up entirely of this food and the other half. There is little doubt but that the grizzly bear are searching for the nuts in squirrel caches and this takes place at high elevations where the white barked pine is found. The nuts would be strong in fats and oils so they would be important at this time when the bear are trying to put on much fat as possible preparing for hibernation. Huckleberry is still the most important food. Some little use of grass yet but this has fallen off a great deal soon as the fruit crops become ripe.

Bob and Ray rode out of the wilderness on August 29. Bob returned to Helena to prepare for the next round. They started back in from the east side on September 6 and rode up the Teton drainage, over to Wrong Creek, and down to Gates Park to set up camp. Bull elk serenaded Bob with enthusiastic bugling. At the head of Wrong Creek, the elk surrounded him. "The bulls were bugling continuously as I rode through there during late afternoon. No doubt grizzly are working through the head of Wrong Creek. . . ." Bob enjoyed another idyllic day alone in the wilderness high country.

Over the next few days, they camped at Our (or Hidden) Lake. Bob surveyed Red Shale Creek, Lookout Mountain, Spotted Bear Pass, and all along the Continental Divide. They were racking up big numbers of goats, and elk numbers were through the roof. Bear sign was everywhere. Bob noted that grizzlies were up high, tearing up the landscape, looking for whitebark pine caches. "They are very successful in this judging from their droppings," he noted. "Black bears in this area may be doing this too but we have no definite information on this." He noted, "Huckleberry is pretty well out of the picture now."

Bob noted that a grizzly with yearlings above Our Lake was living entirely on whitebark pine nuts. He wrote that this was "extremely notable." He found seven major droppings sites where grizzlies were feeding 100 percent on pine nuts. Bob noted that a very large grizzly was plowing up the ground and digging squirrel caches 100 yards east of Spotted Bear Pass. He noted that the grizzlies were piled up in the "white bark zone" in alpine habitat.

Bob surveyed along the Wall Creek Cliffs, Pentagon Mountain, and Hart Lake basin, some of the most beautiful high country in the entire Bob Marshall. He continued to run into more sign of grizzlies tearing up the ground for nut caches in these higher elevations. When they dropped in elevation around Pentagon Cabin, they noted huckleberry still present in the bear scats.

On the summit of Table Mountain, Bob ran into a covey of five ptarmigan, a species he was beginning to appreciate. He noted that the trusting birds were "not very wild." Now into mid-September, their breasts and the undersides of their wings had already turned a snowy white.

On September 11, Bob and Ray rode down the Spotted Bear River and checked over Dean Creek and Pot Mountain, noting lots of bear sign, including tracks and feeding. The next day, Bob rode up Silvertip Creek and returned. Bear sign was common, and the silvertip bruins were eating pine nuts or huckleberries depending on the habitat zone.

On September 14, the surveyors rode down the Spotted Bear River and checked the Bruce and Bunker Creek drainages, and then on up to Meadow Creek. Bear sign was heavy, and they analyzed nine different groups of scats; in these elevations on the west side of the Divide, the scat contained 100 percent huckleberries. In all their surveys on the west side, it seemed that Franklin's (spruce) grouse was king of the birds. Over the coming days, the men moved up the South Fork of the Flathead past Mid Creek and Black Bear Creek, and then set up headquarters at Salmon Forks, where Big Salmon Creek spills into the South Fork.

From this point, Bob checked out the Helen Creek and Damnation Creek drainages, Pagoda Mountain, the upper White River, and Little

Salmon Creek. They rode up to four-mile-long Big Salmon Lake and beyond to Tango Point, then to Upper Holland Lake in the Swan drainage. From there, Bob rode over spectacular Gordon Pass, where the strata above Lick Lake arches above the cirque, and down to Shaw Cabin on Gordon Creek. Ray rode from upper Big Salmon past Lena Lake and down Shaw Creek to meet Bob at the cabin. The two men were covering about thirty miles a day, riding through some of the best country the west side of the wilderness had to offer. Every day must have felt like Christmas morning because it was new country to them.

The next day, Ray rode with the outfit about sixteen miles to Big Prairie Ranger Station. Bob rode an amazing thirty-four-mile route over the high-country ridges, taking the long and beautiful way around to Big Prairie. He noted his ride in a matter-of-fact way, writing, "I rode up the Cardinal Creek trail to the divide between Gordon Creek and Babcock Creek then down the ridge past Kid Mountain, thence over Gordon Peak and Pilot Peak and on down the ridge to the South Fork River and on down to Big Prairie Ranger Station." Bob was made for this wilderness griz survey—not everyone would have the energy and moxie for such a ride over high, rough country, climbing and descending many thousands of feet, navigating 8,200-foot peaks. For his trouble, Bob saw three bull elk, and one bull with a harem of cows. He noted four significant groups of bear sign, including two distinct, separate sets of griz tracks in the snow. He noted good grizzly habitat, with stands of whitebark pine. It started storming about 11 A.M., and snow accumulated to three inches all along the high ridges and peaks. He didn't mention if it was dark before he reached Big Prairie and joined Ray. The next day Bob and Ray rested. While at the Big Prairie station, Ray and Bob visited with Ranger Leif Anderson. Leif shared seven grizzly bear sightings he'd made over the summer and fall.

On September 22, Bob and Ray got an early start and covered forty-six miles. They rode up Bartlett and Holbrook Creeks. Later that day, Bob hiked up to Tillson Lookout, over to the Flathead Alps, down Brownstone Creek, and back to Big Prairie. Bob Cooney was starting to walk like Bob Marshall, the recent namesake of the wilderness. In all those miles, Bob Cooney saw only one male goat and a handful of whitebark pine bear scats in the Flathead Alps.

The next day, the surveyors rode up the Youngs Creek drainage, past Hole-in-the-Wall to Hahn Creek, then on to the Jenny Creek Cabin near the headwaters. They saw three mountain goats on the side of Flatiron Mountain. They noted two sets of fresh griz tracks and six sites of bears feeding. After overnighting it, they rode back to Big Prairie. A few days later, Bob and Ray rode downriver to the White River, then upstream to Brushy Park where they camped. From there to the Divide they recorded numerous grizzly sign.

On a rainy September 27, the two men rode from Big Prairie to the Danaher Ranger Station. Over the next several days, they explored the upper Danaher, seeing little game in cool, foggy conditions. Bob jumped a griz near Rapid Creek, and the big bruin dashed through the snow, leaving its very large set of prints, including a nine-inch-long rear footprint.

On the last day of September, Bob and Ray gathered up the stock and they rode up Camp Creek, over the Continental Divide through Pearl Basin, down Ahorn Creek to the West Fork and then to the South Fork of the Sun River, and out to Benchmark, for a total of thirty-two trail miles. On the way, the men saw elk, goats, and a bunch of grizzly tracks in the snow from Basin Creek to Ahorn. Bob was able to identify them as belonging to eight different grizzlies. One of the tracks measured about six by ten inches, sobering to look at perfectly imprinted in the snow, especially since the claws projected out another three inches. It was almost as if the griz were giving Bob and Ray a show on their last day on the Bob Marshall Wilderness griz survey.

As they passed through the gorgeous Pearl Basin, Bob described the scene: "We noted in the fresh snow in Pearl Basin that the female grizzly and her two yearlings were hunting for white bark pine nuts in squirrel caches. Were digging under logs etc. This type of feeding is still very important (from our observations, the most important food at this time)."

Clearly a biologist deep at heart, Bob had ended his survey notes in his last field notebook with another mention of one of his most important findings—the ecological dance between whitebark pine, red squirrels, and *Ursus*.

During the last month of this pioneering survey, Bob had ridden 657 miles through the Bob Marshall. He closed it out on September 30 but probably wished it would never end.

As the years went by, Bob Cooney was always proud of the groundbreaking, extremely ambitious grizzly bear study he designed and conducted. What a wonderful opportunity it was, right out of the gate as a thirty-one-year-old biologist. The study had encompassed pretty much all the major drainages in the Bob and Great Bear, covering a huge wilderness area from Spruce Park and Schafer Meadows to Gooseberry Park and Trilobite Ridge in the Middle Fork's northwest portion, to the entire South Fork of the Flathead drainage from Spotted Bear to Bunker Creek past Big Prairie to the head of Youngs and Danaher Creeks, across the Divide to the Sun River country with the Chinese Wall and Ahorn Basin, and beyond to the southeast and the edge of today's Scapegoat Wilderness. All told, this effort still stands as the most comprehensive on-the-ground wildlife survey ever undertaken in what is now the Bob Marshall Wilderness Complex.

In the pioneering survey, Bob and Ray covered 1,803 miles on horseback alone, over a total of more than seventy survey days. Including surveys on foot, Cooney estimated that they covered 2,017 miles of active survey route. Bob visually observed and positively documented twenty-two grizzlies, meticulously recorded hundreds of tracks and sign points, including log and rock feeding areas, and analyzed food habits via sign and detailed analysis of scat. He also recorded dozens of other grizzly sightings provided by U.S. Forest Service rangers and others.

Very importantly, Bob confirmed the surprising extensive use of whitebark pine seeds that grizzlies lifted from squirrel and possibly Clark's nutcracker caches. This unique ecological tie between the trees, the squirrels, and the grizzlies had been suspected, but Bob confirmed it by documenting a large number of feeding areas and scats.

Their count of goats totaled 159, and they carefully recorded their sex, age, and location. Goats were widespread across the breadth of the Bob, but the Chinese Wall area definitely stood out for its goat numbers. This was the first comprehensive count of goats across the Bob Marshall, and it indicated sufficient numbers to be a source of goats that managers could use to extend their range. Adding to the goats observed by the biologists, Bob recorded reliable sightings of many more goats seen by lookouts and others. Bob also recorded about 1,000 elk sightings from his observations and others.

Bob carefully recorded sightings of white-tailed ptarmigan, an enigmatic species at the southern end of its range that was relatively rare in the Bob Marshall Wilderness even then. The ptarmigan records from this survey told biologists where the birds lived and a little about their behavior eight decades ago, before their numbers dwindled to nearly zero.

Bob's wildlife surveys were among the first. His detailed look at numbers and food habits of the great bear was the first comprehensive study of *Ursus arctos horribilus* across the wilderness. Happily, this icon is much more numerous now than it was when Cooney documented its use of the Bob eight decades ago. His study helped give fodder to the notion that the Bob should be saved as a bastion of this magnificent carnivore, which since 1983 has been Montana's state animal.

As his career unfolded, Bob Cooney pioneered the capture and relocation of wildlife species across the state, and he excelled as a leader in wildlife restoration. He won numerous awards from national groups and the University of Montana distinguished Alumnus Award. He later had a special assignment working with the national Wilderness Society to promote the value of wildlife in wilderness area protection. In 1994, the Montana Wilderness Association gave Bob a special award for his work in promoting the connection between wildlife and wilderness.

In a national popular article from the 1950s, Cooney wrote eloquently about the Bob Marshall and the future of the grizzly: "This mountainous region covers approximately a million acres. . . . Accessible only by trails, it represents the most important single requirement for the maintenance of the largest grizzly bear population left in the United States."

He continued, "We must, in fairness to the animal and to the economy of the West, consider the grizzly as a wilderness species. And it is upon the preservation of these wilderness areas that the future of the grizzly in the United States will depend." In his view of grizzlies, Bob Cooney was decades ahead of his time.

In fact, Bob testified before the U.S. Senate Committee on Interior and Insular Affairs, in 1958, during hearings for the National Wilderness Preservation Act. Representing the Montana Fish and

Game Commission, Cooney stated, "The grizzly bear population has reached a critical low in the United States. It has been found that the grizzly shuns areas dominated by man's activities. The chief hope, therefore, for the survival of this highly prized game species lies in the preservation of a reasonable amount of wilderness range."

During the time of Bob Cooney's survey, public attitudes toward the grizzly bear were negative, summed up by one wildlife manager as "kill them, kill them all." In fact, the "game surveys" conducted by the U.S. Forest Service in the South Fork in the 1920s and 1930s included all-out predator hunts. Mountain lions and coyotes were targeted, along with any grizzlies that happened to have emerged from dens. Bob's griz survey helped put in perspective the reality about grizzlies and their place in the ecosystem.

Bob Cooney was a lifelong champion of the Bob Marshall Wilderness and its iconic symbol, the grizzly. During the three months he spent surveying the great bears as a young biologist, the wilderness captured his heart, and he was ever willing to buck the naysayers and swim upstream to preserve the country and the bears.

Bob's personal life was as rich as his professional endeavors. He and his wife, Carol, raised two children and were married for seventy-one years. The old wilderness advocate passed away in 2007 at ninety-seven years of age, maybe at the end thinking of those wonderful, pioneering days riding across the Bob Marshall.

By all measures, Bob Cooney was a unique and stellar hero of the Bob Marshall Wilderness.

Special Note

Much thanks to Dr. Harold Picton, Wildlife Professor Emeritus at Montana State University, Bozeman. Along with Terry Lonner, Dr. Picton was a co-author of *Montana's Wildlife Legacy: Decimation to Restoration* (2008) and an accompanying film, *Back from the Brink*, documenting Montana's wildlife recovery. Dr. Picton carefully transcribed Bob Cooney's never-before-published, handwritten notes from the 1941 survey and, as arranged by Jim Williams, graciously allowed me to use them. In the 1950s, Dr. Picton conducted his groundbreaking master's thesis research on elk in the Sun River area and wrote extensively about it. I am proud to say that Dr. Picton was my Wildlife

Management professor at MSU in the mid-1970s. Jim Williams of FWP was a co-producer of the film and book, and he generously advised me in telling this story. Jim discovered Bob Cooney's original, handwritten, unpublished journals in a long-forgotten box, making this story possible. Dr. Picton kindly reviewed this chapter and made important suggestions.

SOURCES

Robert Cooney obituary, *Great Falls Tribune,* January 5, 2007.

Bob Cooney field notebooks 1–6, July 12, 1941, to October 3, 1941. "Grizzly Bear and Mountain Goat Study—Bob Marshall Complex," handwritten but transcribed in 2008 by Dr. Harold Picton, wildlife professor at Montana State University, retired. Dr. Picton also included notes on the status of grizzlies and grizzly management, attached to the above transcribed notes. This information is on file at the Montana Fish, Wildlife & Parks Region One office in Kalispell.

Information and guidance supplied by Jim Williams, April and May, 2019.

Cooney, Robert F. Compilation of grizzly bear track measurements and methods of survey. Progress report. Montana Fish and Game Department, Helena, 1941.

Guide to the Bob Marshall Wilderness. U.S. Forest Service, Northern Region, Missoula, MT, March 1958.

Picton, Harold D. "Use of Vegetative Types, Migration, and Hunter Harvest of the Sun River Elk Herd, Montana." Master's Thesis, Montana State College, Bozeman, 1959.

Cooney, Robert F. "The Grizzly Bear." Popular magazine article from the 1950s, prior to the Endangered Species Act, in which Cooney warns that the griz is headed to extinction, with wilderness preservation its only chance to avoid it.

Robert F. Cooney testimony before the 85th Congress, U.S. Senate Committee on Interior and Insular Affairs, regarding the National Wilderness Preservation Act, S. 4028, November 1958.

13
HEROES OF THE BOB

Master Storyteller, Great Teacher

*Legendary outfitter Smoke Elser has inspired
thousands with his love of the Bob.*

SMOKE ELSER HAS PACKED IN THE BOB longer than most people have
been alive, and he's still at it. Also known for his classes on wilderness
packing, Smoke has taught three generations of wilderness enthusiasts
the art of packing in the backcountry with horses and mules. When
he started teaching his classes, Lyndon Johnson had just been elected
president of the United States.

Smoke literally wrote the book on packing. His 1980 title, *Packin'
in on Mules and Horses,* is still a best seller. The book, written with
Bill Brown, serves as the text for his packing classes. Smoke is known
by his thousands of students for his entertaining and creative teaching
of key techniques, including horse and mule lore, setting up camps,
and a host of complicated knots and ways of mantying loads.

In promoting Montana's wilderness lands, Smoke has always been
there. From the 1964 Wilderness Act and original legal designation
of the Bob, through the establishment of the Scapegoat (1972) and
Great Bear (1978) Wildernesses and, more recently, the Blackfoot-
Clearwater Stewardship Act, Smoke, along with other outfitters, has
been a key champion.

Smoke is probably the best-known outfitter-packer in Montana. And much of his home range has been in the Bob Marshall country. His wife, Thelma, has been with him all the way. For a time, Thelma and Smoke led parallel ·pack trips into the Bob, sometimes coming together thirty-plus miles into the backcountry with their separate strings. The couple became known for their ability to describe and interpret the Bob, and make it come alive for their guests.

For more than sixty years now, Smoke has led pack trips, spending thousands of nights in the Bob Marshall country. To all those guests, he has given his soul. A charismatic teacher, his goal has been to entertain, but more importantly, to inspire his guests about the wilderness. In his eighties, he still packs and teaches with unmatched vigor.

The future packing legend was born in New Waterford, Ohio, about sixty miles south of Cleveland. Smoke was born in the middle of a cold winter on January 22, 1934. "My mother told me my bottle froze under the pillow," said Smoke. His family moved to Columbiana, where his grandfather raised draft horses, which he used to build roads in summer and plow snow in winter. A small building insulated with cork housed 100-pound ice blocks. As a youngster, Smoke and his dad delivered coal in the winter, cleaned the truck thoroughly, then delivered crushed ice in burlap bags to bars and stores in the summer.

Smoke did not excel in high school, but he graduated in 1955. He played football. "I'd hate to go back and look at my report cards," he said. He was very good at shop and building things. His shop teacher had been a Civilian Conservation Corps worker in Montana and knew a crew leader there. Smoke told him he wanted to work in the woods and become a forest ranger.

His teacher wrote Bill Fallis in Montana, and sure enough, he hired Smoke to serve on the Hogback Lookout near Helena that summer. After a few weeks of training, he spent the rest of the summer at high elevation in the Belt Mountains, just east of the Sleeping Giant and Missouri River. When Bill came to pick him up in early fall, Smoke asked if other work was available. He was hired on to stack brush in the Trout Creek area west of Thompson Falls. He and another worker stayed in a cabin that he later learned his future wife, Thelma, had lived in. Around Thanksgiving, after the work ran out, Smoke hopped a Greyhound bus and returned to Ohio. He had saved his checks and invested his earnings in improvements for his mom's house.

Smoke stayed in touch with the U.S. Forest Service, and the next spring he returned to Montana to work on a trail crew under a leader named Cloycie in the Trout Creek area all that summer. Then came the assignment that led to Smoke's packing future. He was assigned the job of taking care of Seabiscuit, the forest supervisor's horse (not the famous racehorse). To catch him, the men would have to run him into the corral. Once he was caught, he was okay, and generally safe. Cloycie assigned Seabiscuit's care to Smoke, telling him to figure out a good way to catch him.

"So I'd go out in the corral and sit in a chair," said Smoke. "I'd put a little pan of grain under the chair and patiently read a book. I'd watch and wait and I'd read. Seabiscuit wouldn't even come close, at first, but eventually I got so I could catch him. It took me half of the summer, but I finally mastered it."

Smoke's job, when not working on trails, was to load Seabiscuit and another horse in the old International stock truck and take them to the trailhead when the supervisor, Doug Moyer, and his assistant, John Milodragovich, were set to ride into the backcountry, which they did quite a lot. Once, Smoke dropped them at the Benchmark trailhead and then drove to Beaver Creek out of Lincoln to pick them up at an agreed-upon time at the end of the trip.

"While I was waiting," said Smoke, "outfitter Tom Edwards and another man came riding out of the hills leading a big pack string of mules and horses. Boy, I was fascinated with that."

The string included a group of about twelve important people known as the Helena Wilderness Riders. Smoke started talking to Tom and asked him a fateful question. "Hey, how about a job?" Smoke said. "I won't be working for the Forest Service forever, and I'd like to ride horses and pack, that's my dream. And Tom said to me, 'Well, I don't know, sonny. Come up and see me; I live in Ovando. Just ask somebody where the White Tail Ranch is.'"

Smoke started school at the University of Montana that winter, 1957, and he drove up to Ovando to see Tom. The snow was so deep at the ranch that it was like driving through long tunnels. Smoke talked to Tom and his wife, Helen. Tom told him that he didn't know him or what he knew about horses. Smoke would have to work two weeks for free, but they would feed him and give him a place to live. So that spring Smoke went to work for Tom, doing anything that needed to be done, and Tom taught Smoke how to pack. Smoke proved himself and packed for Tom that summer.

At the same time, Smoke met Thelma in Helena while on a supply run for the White Tail Ranch. Someone had arranged a blind date for the pair, and they went to a movie at the Marlow Theatre downtown. That winter he moved to Helena and worked for the state nursery. It took "a coupla three months" for Smoke to be certain that Thelma was the gal for him. (Later, in the fall of 1958, they married.)

During the summer of 1957, Smoke worked for Tom, mostly in the Bob Marshall. They packed into Meadow Creek Lake, in what would become the Scapegoat portion of the Bob, riding right from the ranch and through Alpine Park to where Meadow Creek joins Arrastra Creek. Smoke remembers working with the packhorses Troubles and Lonesome; Tom preferred horses over mules for packing. For his saddle horse, Smoke rode Chief, a pinto. On the first trip, they rode up into the Meadow Creek country, which held a beautiful, grassy lake in the East Fork of the Blackfoot drainage. The packers set up a big, comfortable fishing camp, which was allowed back in those days. They erected a fourteen-by-sixteen-foot cooking tent and built tables with stashed lumber. They set up three wall tents, put cots in them, and built a wooden toilet. The camp was known for its convenience, comfort, great fishing, and stunning scenery.

Tom had noticed that Meadow Creek Lake (really just a wide spot in the creek drainage) was getting shallower, and he was worried it might dry up one day. So the men packed in about ten steel fence posts and drove them in at intervals across the lake's narrow outlet. Across the outlet they strung two rolls of chicken wire fencing that they'd packed in. Then Smoke and Tom poled a log raft out into the lake and stirred up the vegetation. It floated down and built up on the fence they'd built to raise the water level of the lake a few feet.

Someone had brought milk cans of rainbow trout in to stock the lake, and these produced hybrids known as cutbows. Smoke and Tom brought in guests and they fished the entire area, the lake and the streams. The guests could fish from rafts built of lodgepole, which enabled them to get out to the deeper holes and springs that held the bigger trout. They maintained the makeshift dam for years.

In Smoke's first full year, 1958, on the fifth of July, Tom led a group of clients up the North Fork of the Blackfoot, above the falls and on up to the Dry Fork. They fished below and above the falls. Helen was sick, so she stayed back at the ranch. Smoke was the official expedition cook, as well as the main packer. They rode on into the Danaher, stopping at Bar Creek, Howard Copenhaver's old camp. Tom told Smoke he was going to take the guests for a ride and asked if he wanted to go. Smoke said sure. They rode four or five miles down to the mouth of Fool Hen Creek, then switchbacked up the hill to Sentinel Lookout. The crew and guests were about to witness a piece of wilderness history.

A U.S. Forest Service ranger was pouring kerosene all around the lookout; the structure was no longer sound, and officials had ordered it burned rather than rehabbed. Tom asked if they could have anything that was in the lookout, and the ranger said sure. So they climbed into the lookout—everything was there, the cots, chairs, and an Osborne Fire Finder and other devices. Smoke took a coffeepot, saucer and cup, and other keepsakes that he still displays in his barn. The Forest Service torched the lookout, and it "looked like a big candle on top of that mountain," just after the Fourth of July. Their guests were fascinated with the whole scene. Right then, Smoke started getting the idea that interpreting the wilderness and its history would be a special addition to pack trips. Smoke, Tom, and their guests watched the lookout burn, and then Smoke recalled that "[I] stuffed the coffee pot, saucer, and cup in my saddlebags and we rode back to camp."

They all sat around the campfire, and Tom played his mandolin and told the story of Sentinel Mountain, where the Blackfeet would have scouts sitting at the high point to block the Salish from going over the Continental Divide and east to buffalo country. Tom told them that the two tribes had skirmishes down on the flats near Basin Creek in the later 1800s. The Salish figured out that they could get into the Danaher, formerly Willow Creek, and go east to buffalo country that way.

On Smoke's free day in the area, he began learning from Tom Edwards the rich history of this wide, willowy drainage at the headwaters of the South Fork of the Flathead. Twenty-three-year-old Smoke was building the base of knowledge and stories he would use to become the Bob's best interpreter of the land. He explored around Bar Creek and found structures, posts in the ground, and slats. Tom told Smoke that the Salish would come in and catch fish, then dry them on those racks. He also saw the remnants of an elk trap built by Merle Rongrud, an early biologist for the state. As years went on, the Forest Service tore it down, but the remnants can still be seen.

Next, Smoke hiked up to a big meadow and noted lots of ditches and a dam; these were the remnants of the irrigation system that old homesteader Tom Danaher built to flood his hay land at the turn of the century. Danaher, a giant in the history of the Blackfoot and South Fork drainages, diverted Bar Creek to flow right by his place. He lived in there with his two daughters, who were born there, for their first seven years. The daughters both eventually became schoolteachers. To get the hay down to his cabin, Danaher loaded it with a pitchfork onto a sled and slid it to the homestead.

Danaher came in with the railroad, Smoke later learned. He built a hotel in Lincoln, then sold it and went into the valley that came to be known as the Danaher, then came out and bought the hotel again. Originally, Danaher went into the Bob, up Willow Creek to trap beaver, and came out at Coram. He had the idea to homestead the big, wide drainage at the head of the South Fork, so he would go into the bars and find non-English-speaking patrons who had worked on the railroad. He invited them and their families into the Danaher. He told them he'd pay $24 a month, and each would get 160 acres through homestead claims. Some of the folks worked for Tom, putting up hay and feeding cattle, but the area proved too rough and too far in to get the cattle to market, and way too much snow buried the land in winter. At one point, Danaher had to shoot some cattle because he ran out of hay to feed them. Some of the men built homesteads—the Foxes, Holopeters, and Wilhelms. Tom bought out a few of the homesteaders, and eventually all the homesteads failed, transferred from owner to owner, and then the U.S. Forest Service acquired the land, which is now such a big part of the Bob. Smoke learned to interpret this fascinating history to the guests.

"All the time, Tom [Edwards] was teaching me," said Smoke. "And I told him I wanted to be an outfitter. I wanted to tell stories about the land and the people."

During Smoke's second year, they went into business with Howard Copenhaver, who owned a nearby ranch. Howard liked mules, so brought them into the business, and they tripled the number of guests they hosted. Smoke started working more for Howard, because he could pack and cook and move from camp to camp. They began expanding their area and introducing guests to more history. On one trip, they rode down to Big Prairie where crews were still putting up hay in the smokejumper barn and had Allis-Chalmers tractors. Then they swung around up Youngs Creek and came out Monture Creek. Eventually the business began taking bigger parties, up to twenty guests. Howard was really good with stock, and Tom was really good with people. "It could be raining day and night, and the guests would still have a great time," said Smoke. "His mandolin and stories kept the visitors entertained." Smoke was soaking it all in and becoming adept at packing. Luckily, from the beginning, people just liked this earnest young man, and he in turn simply loved people.

Smoke stayed with Tom and Howard, packing in the same areas, until about 1960–1961. The Danaher at that time was not producing many elk. So they moved the hunting operation to the Bitterroot for a few years, then came back. Tom and Howard got along fine, but their wives didn't, so they split up their businesses. Smoke stayed with them on their fishing trips in the Bob.

The winter of 1963, Howard called Smoke and invited him to come up for Thanksgiving dinner. He told Smoke to drive his old 1950 Chevy stock truck because there was lots of snow and it would get around better. Thelma and Smoke drove up to Howard's ranch and enjoyed Thanksgiving dinner with Howard and Margaret.

Howard and Smoke went down to the pack shed, where Howard showed him the packsaddles he'd bought and traded for. In the corral were four mules. As Smoke remembers, "[Howard] said, 'I'm going to give you these mules. If you're going to get started in the outfitting business, you're going to need stock.'" He charged $50 apiece, which was a steal. And they were mules that Smoke had handled—Mose, Roany, Sal, and Buck. Smoke and Thelma drove home with the mules, but Smoke was living in a trailer court; he didn't have any pasture. His miraculous luck persisted. He went to talk to the owner of the trailer court, who said, "You're in luck. I just bought a piece of land adjacent

Smoke Elser leads a pack string across a river in the Bob Marshall Wilderness. PHOTOGRAPH COURTESY OF SMOKE ELSER.

to the court and there's a piece of pasture there." Smoke said, "We turned the mules out on the pasture, and that's how we got started in our own business."

That same year, Smoke bought out a packing business in Ovando. They had planned on a sheriff sale, but the packer told Smoke that if he had $2,000, he would sell it to him, to avoid the sale. The outfit included about thirteen horses, plus saddles and a bunch of odds and ends. Smoke didn't have the money.

"We came home and I was working for a guy to train a few colts," said Smoke. "I told him I had a chance to buy this outfit but had no money to do it. We were sitting there eating lunch, and he said, 'Instead of working on those colts today, let's go downtown.' We went to the First National Bank and signed a loan for $2,000 for me to buy the outfit."

In the meantime, in 1964 Smoke graduated from University of Montana in forestry. He and Thelma had acquired their outfitter license. As Smoke tells it, "At the time all you had to do was go down to the Montana Fish, Wildlife & Parks office, pay $10, and you were an outfitter." Eventually, Smoke and Thelma acquired land and a barn up the Rattlesnake for their business, a home base that still serves them well today.

At first, the young couple struggled to get enough clients to make their business solvent. Finally, Smoke struck pay dirt. The head of the University of Montana Foundation, Tom Collins, contacted Smoke (who was now a UM alumnus) to ask him about packing into the Bob. He wanted to take the university president, Robert Johns, and other important folks connected to the university, on a fishing and packing trip. He was looking for a fun, inspiring retreat where they could enjoy nature and build comradery.

Tom surprised Smoke when he told him that they didn't want to ride horses into the wilderness, they wanted to fly in instead. So they chose Schafer Meadows, a beautiful flat in the heart of the Middle Fork of the Flathead country, as their base camp. From there they could fish the Middle Fork and three mountain lakes downstream, Bradley, Scott, and Flotilla, known for good fishing in a beautiful, remote setting.

Tom contracted two small planes to fly the guests in. The Schafer airstrip had been grandfathered in when the Wilderness Act was passed in 1964, so Tom and his party could land there. The plan was for Smoke to ride in with a pack train to haul in all their gear and move the party around to the various fishing spots.

Tom brought all the gear and food to Smoke's barn so he could pack it up. It turned out to be a huge pile. He'd brought three cases of Highlander beer, which was brewed right in Missoula, and enough food to feed a hungry trail crew.

Smoke needed help for the pack trip. Tom knew of a boy from Ohio, just out of high school, whose dad wanted him to "become a man." Dave Ritz was inexperienced and had epilepsy, but Smoke hired him and Tom helped pay his wages. Smoke was to pack in and meet the party at the airstrip on the arranged day, and then take them to a camp he would establish nearby along the river. After they flew in, Tom and the guests would fish the river and the three lakes over a five-day stretch.

Smoke loaded up the horses and mules in the old stock truck, and Dave drove the old pickup with the gear, and they headed for Spotted Bear, a gateway into the wilderness. For the trip, Smoke had eight head: four mules, two packhorses, and two riding horses. They drove into a ranch on the edge of the wilderness and unloaded the stock. The next day, they drove the old truck and the pickup a few miles to the trailhead up the Spotted Bear River. They unloaded the trucks and packed up all the gear. It was late June, and Smoke could see that there was still lots of snow. That's when he started to get the inkling that the plan might not go all that well.

Smoke and Dave rode out from the trailhead early, but they had to repack some of the loads because Dave was not experienced. After about a four-mile trek along the trail, they topped the range and reached the slopes near Gunsight Mountain.

"That whole north slope was full of snow," said Smoke. "I said, 'Geez we can't even get there.'"

Smoke led one stock at a time down the slope. It took several hours to finally get through the snow-covered sidehills. "A couple of the stock fell down in the snow and slid way down the slope," said Smoke, "and I only had one, inexperienced helper, but anyway we finally got through the slope and we headed for the Middle Fork." The snow slowed their progress, but they had one thing going for them: lots of hours of daylight in late June.

Meanwhile, back at Schafer, Tom and the group had flown into the airstrip, and they told the Forest Service ranger stationed there that a packer was bringing in all their stuff. Much to their chagrin, the ranger told them that a packer could not get in because all the passes were snowed shut. Tom, disappointed, asked the ranger to call the aviation company in Kalispell and ask that the planes fly back in that evening and pick them up. With the long day length, the ranger scheduled the pick-up for eight thirty that evening.

Smoke and Dave rode out of the snow and continued down the Miner Creek trail past the junction to Scott and Flotilla Lakes and reached the Middle Fork of the Flathead River. Smoke knew that after crossing the river they would only have about four miles of trail to Schafer Meadows. But looking across the rushing river, Smoke's enthusiasm fell—early in the season and with all the snowmelt, crossing the swollen, boulder-strewn river wasn't going to be easy.

"There were stumps and logs floating down the river, and it was very high," said Smoke. "I could see that the horses would have to swim some of it."

Smoke got across the ford, leading the two big horses and a mule. The current pushed hard against the stock, but they were able to mostly keep their feet. He motioned to Dave to start across.

Dave rode into the river and started across, doing well at first. The horses had crossed many rivers, and they confidently clopped into the current and aimed at the other side where Smoke waited. Then, when he was about two-thirds of the way across, Dave had an epileptic seizure and nearly fell off his horse. Smoke knew of Dave's condition but not that it was so precarious.

"I rode my horse back out into the river," said Smoke, "caught the reins, and grabbed Dave by his shirt. We made it to shore, but oh boy were we wet, just soaked." The packs turned out to be fine since they were mantied and rode high on the backs of the horses and mules.

After shaking off as much water as they could, the packers crossed Morrison Creek and rode up to join the Big River trail. They continued along the wide, lodgepole-lined avenue and on into Schafer, arriving in the early evening. Against the odds, Smoke and Dave had negotiated twenty tough miles and made it in safely with all the food and gear.

Smoke rode up the beautiful meadows at the airstrip and past the scattered lodgepole around the ranger station. He saw the ranger standing by the station. When the ranger saw Smoke and Dave with the pack string, his jaw dropped. He said, "How did you make it in here? I told your guys that it would be impossible for you to get through the pass, and I arranged a couple of planes to fly them out, should be here in a couple hours. Your guys are out fishing right now."

"Call the planes off," said Smoke, "we've got all their gear and we're going to stay."

The ranger pointed out a great place to camp, about a half mile downriver on a nice little bench just below the airstrip. The spot perched on the river's edge and offered some pasture for the horses. Smoke and Dave rode the short distance to the campsite and got to work.

"I told Dave to brush down the stock, picket a couple of them, turn them loose, and put bells on 'em," said Smoke. "And in the meantime, I set up a kitchen fly and a wood stove. I set up three tents, tepee tents with four pegs, so that was easy. I took eight or ten cans of beer down to the river so they'd be cold. I had started supper, had their sleeping bags and pads in their tents, built a nice fire, and by about seven we were all ready."

Smoke heard talking and splashing down by the river, so he walked down the little trail and listened.

"I heard them say, 'Hey, somebody left some beer here. Let's get some beer. It's Highlander, it's good beer.'"

The men were standing there by the river with their waders on; they'd been fishing their way downstream. They'd just popped open their beer cans, when Smoke walked out of the brush.

"They couldn't believe it," said Smoke. "They said, 'Smoke, where in the hell have you been? How did you make it in here?' They thought they were going to get back to the airstrip and fly out at eight thirty. I told them, 'Hell I canceled the airplanes, we've got everything here.'" The party walked up the little trail and into the fully set-up camp and enjoyed a hearty supper.

The rest is history. That serendipitous meeting changed everything, and Smoke's long legend began its upward swing right there with Tom Collins, President Johns, and the other dignitaries associated with the university who were on that trip. The initial idea for the annual Montana Grizzly Riders trip by the University of Montana Foundation was born.

The next day, the party broke camp and went down to Three Forks, where Smoke and Dave had crossed the river, and they set up camp in a little meadow in a beautiful flat near the abandoned ranger station. The riders were ferried across the river, and they fished the Middle Fork and Scott, Bradley, and Flotilla Lakes, and had a great fish-filled time. Scott Lake is shallow, but the lake and the outlet hold surprisingly large cutthroat trout. At Flotilla, located a few miles above Scott in an alpine cirque, the riders caught cutthroat on nearly every cast amid sweeping alpine scenery.

On that trip they discussed fundraising. Around the campfire one night, President Johns said, "We need to figure out how to get some money in, Tom; we're only bringing in a few thousand dollars a year for the foundation." They all agreed that if they took donors on a trip like this, it would be a great way to raise lots of money.

The party camped for four exciting and relaxing days at Three Forks. On the fifth day, Tom and the officials traveled the four miles back up to the airstrip to meet their planes for the flight back to Missoula. Smoke and Dave re-crossed the Middle Fork and rode the fourteen or so miles back up Miner Creek, across the divide into the Spotted Bear, and back out to the trailhead where they'd left the trucks. The return trip was a little easier for the horses because of the lighter packs and already broken trail, and because a lot of the snow had melted during the warm, sunny days while they were at Schafer.

That winter, Tom Collins called Smoke into his office at the university, and they talked about bringing some fishing parties into the wilderness to help raise money for the foundation. Smoke suggested that they plan one large annual trip. They decided to officially call it the "Grizzly Riders." Tom decided that each year they would invite twenty alumni who had made money in their careers and ask each to bring one friend.

"The idea," said Smoke, "was to corral them in the hills for five days where they couldn't talk to anyone else, and they had to talk to the people who run the university." The Grizzly Riders has now passed its fifty-third year, has its own flag, and has raised many millions of dollars for the foundation. And Smoke is still tied in. The organizers put together a nice brochure to advertise each trip.

The next year, at Smoke's suggestion, the Grizzly Riders rode about twenty miles into Meadow Creek and up to Alpine Park, Tom Edwards' and Smoke's old stomping grounds in the Scapegoat portion of the Bob. To accommodate the growing number of riders, Smoke borrowed horses from Howard Copenhaver and others, amassing around 110 head of stock. It was a monumental effort with challenging logistics, but Smoke made it work. His reputation spread among entrepreneurs and successful University of Montana alumni. On the trip, guests fished Meadow Creek Lake and the fish-filled streams and lakes in the area, enjoying a five-day break from their hectic schedules. The trip was a big success, the foundation collected a lot of money, and Smoke's reputation continued to grow.

The next year, the Grizzly Riders trip did not work out well. Smoke said that another outfitter took the group in to the high-elevation country in the Gallatin, and they were not as prepared. The outfitter just dropped the gear and the riders had to set up their own camps, do their own cooking, and chop their own wood. Amazingly, two of the participants died of heart attacks. It would seem that this would have been the end of the Riders, but Smoke rescued the program the next year.

Tom Collins called Smoke in again, and they decided to return to a lower-elevation site where the guests could be flown in, because they really weren't in the condition required to ride or walk very far. They chose Schafer Meadows for the third Grizzly Riders trip in 1968, returning to the successful site that hosted the inaugural event.

Tom made arrangements to fly into Schafer the twenty or so participants in larger Douglas DC-2s (fourteen-seaters) and one other plane. Smoke rode in with a large pack string and several helpers to set up camp and ferry people around. When the guests landed at Schafer, Smoke had them mount up and ride the four miles from the airstrip to the Three Forks camp along the Middle Fork. Smoke said that some of the guests flew their own airplane in. The event was much easier on the office-bound dignitaries and proved to be very successful.

To pack in the gear, Smoke loaded up, drove to U.S. Highway 2 just west of Marias Pass, and took Skyland Road to the Morrison Creek trailhead. It was an easy pack down Morrison and Lodgepole Creeks to the nice flat along the Middle Fork. Smoke loaded and packed elaborate meals to the camp. "We packed in lots of beer," said Smoke. "And I had two complete mule loads of magnum bottles of champagne."

Smoke packed in a fourteen-foot-long table to serve the guests in the middle of the wilderness. He'd built the table in his barn. He connected a long piece of canvas with lathe nailed in and rolled it up for packing. Then at the camp, he rolled it out and stretched it between two posts at either end. Add a tablecloth, camp chairs, and log rounds to sit on, and it felt just like a frontcountry picnic.

The ranger at Schafer told Smoke to go ahead and build a corral, so he built a nice one attached to trees along the trail. It was a great time, as all the guests sat around the campfire, listened to Smoke's stories, and shared their own. Smoke's storytelling became a major attraction. Montana Fish, Wildlife & Parks and U.S. Forest Service officials would also ride in to give the guests talks about the wilderness. The event was a huge success in terms of fundraising, and Smoke went on to host the Grizzly Riders at the Schafer and Three Forks location for the next nine years.

The lathe-and-canvas table proved to be an inspiration. "On that table on about the fourth day they would write checks," said Smoke. "We had several that were made out for $500,000, and in those days that was a helluva chunk of money, a lot of money. And they gave 'em to Tom Collins for the foundation. We had officials of Boeing, Lamont Gloves, Gore-Tex, Northern Pacific Railway, a large Buick car dealership, many important people." Smoke said that the guests over the years contributed to the halting of logging plans in areas of what would become the Great Bear Wilderness. In particular, the 1969 trip and news articles written by Dale Burk were key in putting the kibosh on plans to road this magnificent area. The alumni from those trips became great supporters of wilderness.

The Grizzly Riders changed Smoke's business. The entrepreneurs would tell all their rich friends to go on a pack trip with Smoke, a fun guy, great cook, competent packer, and a great interpreter of the land. He was able to expand his business and buy new trucks and more stock.

"I took them for a long time," said Smoke. "But now they've gotten too old, and they go to the E Bar L Dude Ranch and stay there. I still go every time."

Smoke worked hard to make sure each trip he led was unusual and special. He had learned the outfitting business from Tom Edwards and Howard Copenhaver. They were very good, and passed on so much of value to Smoke, but he wanted to take it to another level. He and Thelma decided to view themselves as special hosts to the guests, and they focused on inspiring them.

"Thelma and I wanted to do something different," said Smoke. "I decided that I didn't want to be exactly like Tom and Howard, I wanted to interpret the country to our guests. Because I think they needed added value. Fishing and hunting is great; it's lots of fun to get an elk and a dozen fish and that's fine. But we wanted to give them

Smoke and Thelma Elser. PHOTOGRAPH COURTESY OF SMOKE ELSER.

something different; what we tried to do is to interpret the land and inspire them about wilderness."

Smoke and Thelma learned all the plants and animals, all the history they could find out about the backcountry, and the location of all the old cabins. He spent any free time he had in the wilderness exploring and gaining knowledge. Smoke began gathering it all in his mind from his first trip with Tom and went on to perfect his dream. Guests found that there was something special in a Smoke Elser trip. When they rode out after a trip with him in the Bob, they felt inspired, and they knew wilderness on a different level. Smoke had a special way with people and captivated them with his movie narrator voice and the cadence of a master storyteller. Their operation became a family affair—Smoke and Thelma did the leading and cooking, while their oldest daughter, Tammy, packed and wrangled horses. Their youngest daughter, Vickie, ran the home ranch and trained some of the mule colts to ride and pack.

On one classic trip about thirty years ago, Smoke and Thelma squired separate parties into opposite sides of the Bob. As she often did, Thelma booked the parties and organized the food, even pre-preparing some dishes at their place, freezing the food, and bringing it in. She was known for her homemade gourmet spaghetti sauce. Thelma booked a party of eight for herself, and a party of ten for Smoke.

Thelma's party of eight would ride in at Benchmark, cross the Continental Divide at White River Pass, and come out at Holland Lake. Smoke's party wanted mostly to fish, and didn't want to go over the high country, so he led them up Monture Creek and into Youngs Creek and the South Fork, for great fishing in the rivers.

Thelma, her wranglers, and her guests rode from Benchmark up the West Fork of the Sun River to Indian Creek and over White River Pass, one of the most scenic and spectacular points in the Bob. The guests could gaze over Haystack Mountain and see part of the Chinese Wall. After crossing the pass, they dropped down Molly Creek to the upper Whiter River drainage and followed the trail down to the forks of the White River, where they camped on a bench above the river. This site offered a nice spring for drinking water and great fishing nearby; they planned to spend three days there.

They set up the camp in a favorite spot on one side of the trail and kept the horses in some meadows back in the timber. Thelma had cooked breakfast and everyone was done eating; the guests were spread up and down the White River, fishing its clear waters for the abundant westslope cutthroat trout. In the open-ended cook tent, Thelma had just drained the bacon grease into the stove and tossed in the food scraps and extra hotcakes to burn. She looked up and froze—walking down the trail not forty feet away was a huge grizzly, and it was wearing a big collar. The bear walked to within about thirty

Smoke Elser at the Chinese Wall. PHOTOGRAPH COURTESY OF SMOKE ELSER.

feet of the camp, swung its head back and forth, looked around, then just walked on down the trail. Maybe he didn't like what Thelma was cooking.

Several days before, Smoke had started his trip from Monture Creek. They camped the first night at Bear Park, a favorite and beautiful site. The next day, Smoke led his party down Hahn Creek and on to Youngs Creek at Hole-in-the-Wall. At this beautiful, wide stretch of stream, the guests fanned out and enjoyed fast fishing for large cutthroat trout in the meandering part of the creek and in the big, deep holes downstream in the canyon. The group enjoyed the beautiful evening with good food, fresh trout, and great stories around the campfire.

The next day Smoke and his ten guests rode past Big Prairie and down the South Fork trail to the mouth of the White River, a total distance of about seventeen miles. This was a good distance for the guests; they were getting saddle-tough. Smoke and his wrangler set up a comfortable camp in this very spacious setting. The White River flows through a broad floodplain, and ponderosa parklands offer great campsites. The site offered Smoke an opportunity to tell the story of old Joe Murphy and Murphy Flat, just across the river from camp.

Thelma was camped a few miles up the White River, but the two parties couldn't camp together because of Forest Service party size limits. Smoke rode up the trail a few miles to Thelma's camp to talk about their adventures so far, which had gone smoothly. This was the day before she had seen the bear.

The next day, Thelma and her party rode down the White River, stopped at Smoke's camp, and told the group about seeing the bear that morning. There were a couple of ladies in Smoke's camp who were concerned. Smoke didn't carry a gun, and pepper spray was not in general use yet. Smoke had noticed a set of grizzly tracks that went right past his camp and then on down the South Fork trail. Both parties considered themselves lucky that the griz had just passed on through.

As it turned out, the Forest Service trail crew down the trail about five miles wasn't so lucky. The crew was building corduroy across some swampy areas and was camped near Mud Lake.

"The bear stopped there," said Smoke, "tore up their camp, ran everybody up trees, and really raised hell." The next day, Smoke packed up and the party started down the South Fork trail. They met

Smoke and Thelma in the kitchen at the White River camp.
PHOTOGRAPH COURTESY OF SMOKE ELSER.

a Forest Service ranger and state game warden who had been sent to kill the bear because it was so conditioned to human food. The bear was wearing a collar in the first place because it had gotten into trouble, and the state biologists had relocated it in the backcountry in hopes it would change its ways. But they were learning that once a bear was food conditioned, it probably needed to be removed rather than relocated.

On his thousands of nights in the Bob, Smoke never carried a firearm specifically for bear protection, and he had well-thought-out reasons for it.

"I never carried a firearm for bears, never, neither one of us," he said. "For one thing, if you are going to run into bear problems it probably is going to be at night. And with a pistol in the dark you are not going to be very accurate. And you are probably not going to shoot a rifle at night. So, we just never carried."

Instead, Smoke insisted that all his camps be very clean. They didn't carry horse pellets because they were made with molasses. He carried grain—rolled oats—and bears didn't seem to bother that. Smoke was involved in the early stages of the "leave no trace" ethic, and it paid off for him and his guests.

Smoke's theory of bear avoidance sure worked over the years—they never had a bear problem. In the Mud Lake example, the collared, food-conditioned bear had walked right on by Thelma's and Smoke's camps, then plodded downriver and nailed the Forest Service camp five miles downstream.

After the stay at the White River, Thelma led her crew of eight guests across the South Fork to ponderosa-lined Murphy Flat. The group rode up Holbrook Creek to its head to reach Lena Lake, where they camped. At the time, the beautiful little foot-shaped lake held rainbow trout that had been planted there, rather than the native cutthroats. Because they were rainbows, they surprised the guests by jumping out of the water several times each as they were played and brought in.

Smoke took his crew of ten guests and rode down the river trail, crossed at Salmon Forks, and trekked on up along Big Salmon Lake. Within a few days, both pack trains rode over Pendant Pass and exited the Bob at Holland Lake. Smoke had arranged to use a corral there

A young Smoke Elser leads a pack string across Big Salmon Creek deep in the Bob. PHOTOGRAPH COURTESY OF SMOKE ELSER.

at Owl Creek Packer Camp. All the stock were reunited and readied for the trip home.

The guests enjoyed this amazing wilderness couple who interpreted the land for them. They had stunning scenery, with cold water as clear as can be hurrying over rocks of green, white, red, and yellow. The fishing was unreal, and the meals tasted even better, flavored by the sauce of wilderness, and to top it off, they experienced a little excitement with the passing grizzly. It was a perfect Elser trip.

On fall trips, Smoke has guided many inexperienced hunters over the years, but one stands out for his oddness and lack of preparation. On a fine fall day, Smoke led a hunting trip to Camp Pass and Canyon Creek, a favorite hunting area where he had a nice high-elevation camp that was a relatively short ten- or twelve-mile ride from the Monture Creek trailhead. The hunters rode past the falls and on up Falls Creek to the camp, situated on the edge of the Scapegoat portion of the Bob. From the camp, they could hunt the entire upper drainage and over into Canyon Creek in the upper North Fork of the Blackfoot.

Along on the trip were five hunters to be squired by Smoke and his guide, Robin; an additional hunter missed the start because of a plane delay in Detroit. Smoke would have to ride out of the wilderness and

Smoke Elser and guests take a break from the saddles.
PHOTOGRAPH COURTESY OF SMOKE ELSER.

pick him up a little later. The party reached the welcoming site among the subalpine fir and meadows and set up camp. They enjoyed great campfire talk and then turned in early, excited for the next day's hunt in a fine, wilderness setting.

At dawn the next morning, Smoke rode back out to pick up the sixth hunter, going the extra mile to make sure the guest had his opportunity for a wilderness hunt. After the hunter's plane arrived in Missoula, Smoke met him and drove the sixty miles or so back to the Monture trailhead. Smoke got the client set up on a riding horse, loaded his gear on a mule, and led the happy hunter up Falls Creek and back to camp.

"We got into camp just at dark and the other hunters were just coming in," said Smoke. "They'd just finished hunting their first day. They had seen elk and deer but hadn't got a shot. So I unloaded his gear and he started taking everything into the tent. It dawned on me just then: 'Where in the heck is your rifle?' And he said, 'Oh I've got it.' And I said, 'Where in the hell is it, then?'

"He walked into the fourteen-by-sixteen-foot fly area where we did the cooking, and he says, 'Here's my rifle.' It was still in a cardboard box. And I said, 'Jeepers criminy!' And we opened it up."

It was still in grease, wrapped in the brown paper that they used in those days. He told Smoke that he had a scope, too. He went into the tent and brought that out, and it was also still in its box.

"So there we sat," said Smoke. "I said, 'And you are going to go hunting tomorrow and you've never fired this rifle?'"

"No," said the man, "I bought it on the way out here. For this trip, I just went down to the store and bought a brand-new rifle."

So the men sat around camp with their Leathermans and a screwdriver putting the rifle together. They had to put the stock on, align the barrel, basically put it together from the bottom up. Smoke got it all assembled and then tried to bore-sight it.

"You know," said Smoke, "if you take a spoon and shine a flashlight through the barrel and center the light on the spoon, you can bore-sight it reasonable, not as good as if you had all the equipment. And we bore-sighted it with open sights, then mounted the scope, but we had all kinds of trouble. With those little screws you needed eyeglass screwdrivers to really be able to do it. But we got everything on."

Smoke and Robin got up at about four o'clock the next morning and cooked breakfast; their goal was to get out of camp and up on the hill by about five thirty. The hunter was excited to use his newly assembled rifle, and he was anxious to get out hunting. It was time for the men to eat a quick breakfast. He joined the other hunters in the cook tent.

The man looked like he'd just walked out of a Halloween costume store. "He had bought bright orange coveralls, and they were just out of the wrappings," said Smoke. "He was orange from head to toe. I mean, he even had a stocking cap that was orange. It was almost blinding. And I thought, boy, this is going to be tough."

They saddled up the horses and were all ready to get the hunters out on a crisp fall day in the high country. The orange hunter got on his horse and the party rode up the ridge. Smoke guided him to several good overlooks. They watched over the country and didn't see much—a few elk. Smoke saw something way over in Conger Basin in the Scapegoat, but that was too far to go. Smoke suggested that the hunter take a shot with the rifle to check on its accuracy after their efforts to bore-sight it. He told him that since they'd already hunted this area and would move to a different spot down the creek tomorrow, the shot wouldn't scare anything.

By that time the men had dropped more than 1,000 feet off the divide and down into Camp Lake. Smoke said, "See that white snag over on the other side of the lake, and he said, 'Yeah I see it.' Lay right down and take a real good shot at that."

Smoke had checked the hunter's ammo, because he didn't trust the hunter to use the right caliber. When the hunter came in for breakfast that morning, he had three different boxes of shells: .30-06, .270, and .30-30 shells. His rifle was .30-06 caliber. He had asked Smoke, "Which one of these shells do I use?" Because of this, Smoke was careful to load the correct shells, because otherwise the barrel could explode. The hunter took a knee and fired at the snag, and the crack of the shot echoed across Camp Lake. Unfortunately, the bullet hit a tree about fifty yards to the right of the snag. So Smoke tried "adjusting and monkeying with" the scope, but they couldn't dial it in to Smoke's satisfaction.

The orange hunter insisted on carrying the heavy, inaccurate rifle during the entire trip. Finally, by the last day of the hunt, Smoke convinced him to borrow a rifle, and he made a good shot on a nice mule deer buck—he finally bagged his animal and he was thrilled. The hunter was happy to get anything after all the problems with his rifle. Smoke had pulled off another successful hunt, even ensuring a good result for one of the most unusual and eccentric hunters he'd ever guided.

The orange hunter proved to be challenging, but on another hunt in the same area, Smoke and Robin almost lost a hunter. Smoke and his guests had hunted all the way down to Camp Lake, came around the bottom, and headed back to camp to have lunch. Then Smoke realized that he was missing one of his hunters. Robin went to the lake again, and Smoke went up on top, but they couldn't find the hunter.

"We looked all over, fired a couple of shots even," said Smoke. "Geez it was getting towards dark and we were really worried because he couldn't walk real well. We thought he understood that he was to just hunt down till he hit the trail, and then wait and we'd pick him up."

Smoke and Robin looked for four or five hours, and it was starting to get dark. It also started to rain—damp early October weather had set in. Robin and Smoke went to the top of the hill at Camp Pass. They built a big fire, hoping the hunter would see it, and the two men needed to warm up too.

"Then we heard one single shot," said Smoke. "The shot came from Conger Basin. I fired a pistol, Robin fired a shot, not another shot came from the hunter. I looked at Robin, Robin looked at me, and we agreed that somebody is going to have to go down in that canyon and find him."

Just about then they heard the most awful scream they'd ever heard. "It made the hair stand up on the back of my neck," said Smoke. "Real loud scream. There was a lion on that slope."

The hunter was Smoke's charge, so he drew the lot to go after him. The brush was high, and the sidehill was steep. Smoke slid downhill and climbed through the brush, using a single flashlight. By the time he got down into the canyon, the flashlight was fading and Smoke didn't have extra batteries, so he couldn't see much of anything.

"There I am standing in the dark," said Smoke. "I looked around and hollered and crossed Conger Creek, then stopped for a minute. And I thought geez, where is that hunter? The shot came from right about here. I yelled again at the top of my voice, then just off to my side, the hunter calmly said, 'Hello Smoke.' Geez, he was standing right there just soaked and wet."

Smoke asked the hunter why he only shot once. He explained that he didn't have any more rounds; he brought only three for the elk and that was all. Smoke led him back up the ridge to a large rock, a landmark that Smoke knew. They continued, picking their way along in the dark. Smoke led them across Bugle Basin. He knew of a shortcut down a little creek to the trail from there.

"It was black as coal," said Smoke. "I started down the little creek and we'd gone sixty or seventy yards, and by golly here comes Robin up the trail with a lantern and another one of our hunters out looking for us. Robin had guessed right about where we'd be."

After their improbable meeting, the men were happy and relieved, and they headed back to camp. The lost hunter's brother was waiting back in camp for them to arrive.

"We got into camp, and the hunter's brother was sitting at the corner of the table, and he said, matter of factly, 'How was the hunting?' and here we were soaking wet, it was midnight, and Robin had just found us on a sidehill in the coal-black dark. It should have been obvious how the hunting was." On this close call, the lost hunter benefited from the knowledge and skill of Smoke and his excellent guide, and he was grateful to be safe.

Another challenge that Smoke faced on some trips was unexpected cold, wet weather, which would make it harder for the guests to enjoy themselves, especially on a summer trip. On one trip into Youngs Creek, Smoke and his guests were inspired by a young boy who took everything the weather could dish out, yet remained as happy as could be.

The trip began from the Monture Creek trailhead. They camped the first night at Bear Park, about fourteen miles in, on their way to the South Fork. The weather was clear, and the guests enjoyed the sunshine and warm temperatures. The next morning, the party rode over the top and down into Youngs Creek. They camped at the beautiful campsite below Hole-in-the-Wall in the flat across Youngs Creek. Another beautiful day inspired the guests, and they fished up and down the creek. They had good success on large westslope cutthroat trout in this big tributary, especially downstream into the canyon where the stream rushes to meet Danaher Creek to form the South Fork of the Flathead River. After a starry night around the campfire, the next morning again held nice and sunny; the great fishing continued.

But that afternoon, threatening clouds built to the west, so Smoke and his guides tied down and resecured the rain flys above the tents and cook area. That evening, the guests returned from fishing soaking wet. The sunshine and warmth of the last few days were now just a memory, and the guests' spirits fell.

"It rained all night and the next day," said Smoke, "just rained and rained. I built a big fire, and everybody huddled under the fly and tried to stay warm. There was no fishing going on; every once in a while, somebody would go out and try, but it was too miserable, wet, and windy."

Just before everyone was ready to turn in that night, Smoke thought he heard something up around the horses' picket area, so he and the wrangler went into the inky blackness and checked on the picketed horses and they were fine; they could hear the bells on the horses on the hill above camp. They thought everything was okay.

"We came back into camp," said Smoke, "and I told the guests that maybe we better hit the sack, because it's probably going to rain all night too. Everybody got up and stretched, and got ready to go to their sleeping bags, which were probably wet. And out of the brush came a horse, a packhorse, and a little kid riding bareback on his horse. And I mean the little kid was about twelve, maybe not even that old, and he was wearing tennis shoes. His dad was mounted and leading a packhorse."

It seemed almost supernatural how the boy and his dad just appeared out of the darkness with no sound.

The travelers had been riding in the rain, and they were soaked, really wet. They had no raincoats and very little gear; they'd been cooking meals of fish over a fire. They had ridden down over Pyramid Pass to the river and spent a few days fishing when the weather was nice. Now the rain was driving them out.

When they rode into camp, Smoke urged them to get under the fly and around the fire, have some coffee and warm up. In spite of the wet and cold, the boy gushed excitedly about the great time they were having: great fishing, riding, going way back into the wilderness. Everyone was impressed with the boy's bright attitude and toughness—it cheered up the whole crew. After a while around the fire, they surprised everyone when they got ready to leave. Smoke urged them to stay around the fire; it was too dark, cold, and wet to ride off. But no, they were headed out over Pyramid Pass and on to the town of Seeley Lake that night. In the dark.

"My gosh," said Smoke, "it's a long way, more than twenty miles to the trailhead. How do you expect to make it in the dark? You might as well set up here; you can sleep under the fly."

The riders would have to cover about eighteen miles on a rocky trail with creek crossings and climb several thousand feet of elevation to reach the pass, then drop about four miles on switchbacks down the other side of the Swan Range to reach the trailhead.

"Well," the dad said, "we didn't bring a tent. And we've been wet for a couple of days and we just got to get out. Our sleeping bags are soaked."

Smoke tried again to convince the man to not try to ride out that night. He told him that they were welcome to stay in camp and curl up under the fire tarp. "No," the dad said, "we gotta get out of here." The night was black. "How are you even going to find the trail?" asked Smoke. The dad said, "Oh, my old horse knows how to get to Seeley Lake." Smoke's impression was that he meant to ride all the way to Seeley. From the Pyramid Pass trailhead, the access road runs another eight miles to Seeley, making the total trip, in the dark, about thirty-two miles.

"So they mounted their horses and turned them around right in front of the fly," said Smoke. "They thanked us for the nice stay around the fire. I had tried everything to talk them out of going. The boy was riding bareback, no saddle, sitting on the back of the horse, holding on to its mane. The dad had a saddle, and the packhorse, you could tell they were just farm horses, they weren't used to being in the hills. And as they rode off in the dark, we heard the kid yell, 'Woohoo! Ain't we got fun, Dad!'"

Smoke never heard how they did, and he never saw the dad or the amazing young boy again. He thought that they lived in Seeley Lake. But the boy had left a big impression on Smoke, and he always wondered about him.

Besides experiencing the joy of leading many youngsters into the wilderness, Smoke has been lucky to squire several people with disabilities into the Bob. Smoke introduced one lady, Joyce, who used a wheelchair, to riding horses around his place. He fashioned a special saddle for her. Then, on a special trip, Smoke led her into Camp Pass. At camp, Smoke set up a special toilet for her to use and other accommodations.

"She just liked to ride," said Smoke. "She couldn't walk, and the wheelchair couldn't negotiate rough ground, so the horse gave her the mobility to get around. At first, she might have thought it would be impossible to get into the wilderness. But she did it."

She told Smoke, "Now I can ride over and look at that rock, or I can ride across the creek and look at those trees. Normally there's no way I could do that."

Smoke packed another lady, Marietta, who used a wheelchair, all the way into the Danaher, twenty-four miles one way. He felt great

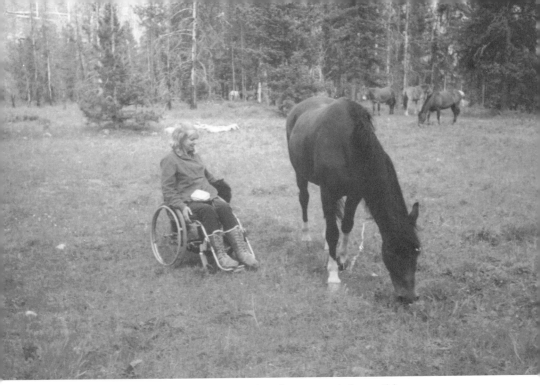

On at least two occasions, Smoke Elser proved that wilderness can be accessible to everyone. PHOTOGRAPH COURTESY OF SMOKE ELSER.

pleasure in being able to give these ladies the wilderness experience that he loved. It might seem impossible to pull off, but Smoke did it.

Sometimes on a hunting trip in the wilderness, you lose a friend. When Smoke was still working for the White Tail Ranch, he and Howard Copenhaver set up a hunting camp in the heart of the Danaher. That fall, they'd run a series of guided hunts, eight to ten days each, with six or eight guests each time. The camp was at Bar Creek, a tributary of Danaher Creek, about a twenty-mile ride from the North Fork of the Blackfoot trailhead. The season had turned out to be a good one, with many of the guests bagging elk.

On the last hunt of the year, the two men led only two hunters, but they had strung along enough mules to pack out the whole camp. Along with Smoke and Howard was an Airedale dog by the name of Cheese. Cheese helped Howard hunt mountain lions in the winter. Cheese was a big, tough dog. He stood three feet high and was known to chase lions from Kleinschmidt Flats, over the ridge to Arrastra Creek, and back out into the valley. Over the years on the wilderness trips, Cheese always stayed with Smoke and Howard. He guarded the Bar Creek camp when they were out with guests. Cheese would stay in camp. Howard would say, "Cheese, stay here. Stay." And Cheese would lie down by the stove, and there he'd stay.

By the time of this hunt, Cheese was getting pretty old. The guides led the hunters on long day hunts from camp, and one of the hunters got a nice elk. They packed the elk into camp and hung up the quarters. Around the campfire, Smoke talked about the history of the Danaher like only he could; the group was having a special wilderness experience.

The next-to-last morning, Howard asked Smoke to start tearing down the camp that had served them so well for the hunting season, while he took out the hunters for the day. Smoke broke down everything that he could, but he left the kitchen tent to sleep in that night; they would tear it down the next morning. After a fun evening, and with snow starting to fall, the guides and their guests spread out their bedrolls under the cook tent and went to sleep.

The next morning after breakfast, the men tidied up the camp for the coming winter. They took down and packed the last tent. They had built a little tree house between three trees, and they stowed stovepipes and other things in that. Everyone was ready to head up the trail, and Cheese was jumping up and down, ready to get going. He always followed the mule string, and all was well as they started out from camp.

"We had everything loaded, the tents and the whole camp," said Smoke. "I was leading four mules, Howard was leading four. And the hunters were just ahead of me. We got out about a mile from camp and Howard yelled up to me, 'Do you see Cheese up there?' And I said nope, so Howard yelled, 'Hey Cheese!' and called him two or three times, but Cheese never came. So Howard tied up his mules around Limestone Creek and rode back to see if he could find him."

Howard rode back and found Cheese sitting in camp, and said, "What's going on, Cheese?" The dog seemed fine, so Howard rode back out of camp and Cheese followed him for a bit but then went right back to the camp site. Cheese again just sat in the area where the last tent had been, in the tent's outline in the snow. Howard put a rope around Cheese's neck and led him all the way to Limestone Creek. Cheese was dragging. He just didn't want to go. Howard said to Smoke, "I don't know what's wrong with him." Howard tried to put him up on the saddle, but Cheese was too big to put on a horse or mule.

"It was snowing to beat heck, and we had to get our guests out," said Smoke. "Howard said, 'I'm just going to turn him loose, he will just have to follow our mules.' As we rode, Howard called him, just called and called and whistled. We rode to Dwight Creek, about another two or three miles, heading for the Dry Fork divide, Whiskey Ridge, and the North Fork of the Blackfoot. When we got to Dwight Creek, we realized that Cheese was not going to follow."

Howard rode back again, and Smoke could hear him whistling and hollering. Howard returned and told Smoke to ride on with the guests while he rode back to try one more time. Howard rode back a ways, but he couldn't find his beloved dog.

"So, we ended up riding out through the light snow," said Smoke. "Cheese stayed in camp and we never saw the dog again. It was our saddest trip. I think Cheese was of age, about twelve, and he'd decided that was it, and he would just stay in the wilderness. He came on every trip we went on and followed me around all the time. We were really attached to him, and it was really sad. He was a good dog, though, [a] great dog."

Smoke spent many trips in the Youngs Creek drainage over the years, often camping at Hole-in-the-Wall. The prominent cave there has always attracted attention and wonder. It was rumored to go way back into the mountain, or to hold treasure from a train robbery.

One legend about the cave has persisted for more than a hundred years. Old-timer Doris Huffine noted in her journal from the 1930s that "Mr. White let some men have his mule to go looking for $144,000 that is hidden up the South Fork by Hole-in-the-Wall. The money was hidden by bandits who robbed a train [she was referring to the 1893 Great Northern train robbery near old McCarthyville]. Most of them were shot at Coram, but a few escaped and it is thought that they hid their money up the South Fork. They have found an old camp up there with some old shells just like they used in those days so they are going to do some digging to see if they can't find the money. Mr. White is to get a share of it for the use of his mule."

On one trip to Hole-in-the-Wall with a few guests, Smoke's packer Tom Flowers and his wife Lisa were determined to get into the cave using climbing gear. Smoke had met the young couple at a spring outfitter meeting at the White Tail Ranch, where they were working. Tom said he would like to guide and outfit in the hills, so Smoke hired the engaging, hardworking couple to work in his outfitting business. One of Smoke's main camps that he brought guests into was in the little meadow across Youngs Creek, right below the Hole-in-the-Wall cliff.

"We often camped at Hole-in-the-Wall," said Smoke. "Like everybody else, we were always wondering what was in that cave. Several people I knew, including Gordon Ash, had tried to get into that cave but couldn't do it. But Tom and Lisa were determined. Tom was a mountain climber—I didn't know that. He and Lisa had climbed a lot of mountains in the Missions. On this particular trip, we had a small party and Tom asked if he could bring his climbing gear, said he would rappel down from the top to enter the cave."

Smoke was skeptical and a little worried about the young couple, but Tom and Lisa decided they were going to do it and brought all their climbing gear on the trip. They had a mule-load of gear, including all their climbing ropes, helmets, and tools. A young man, Steve Nichol, came along with the climbers. On the trip, the crew had a layover day at the camp below the cave, and Smoke told Tom that if he was going to climb it, this was the day.

The climbers got going early in the morning, went up the draw, and got above the Hole-in-the-Wall cave. Everyone watched from below. "They rigged up all their ropes and got their helmets on," said Smoke. "He had a little pick of some sort to dig into the rock. So here he came over the edge of the mountain, dropped down to the level of the Hole-in-the-Wall, but he couldn't get into it, so he had to swing, finally far enough to dig in his pick, and he got into the cave."

Soon, Lisa and Steve rappelled down and joined Tom in the cave, and they explored its nooks and crannies.

"But the cave didn't really go anywhere," said Smoke. "It just went back a little way into the mountain. The spelunkers used headlamps and explored the dark corners, but there was nothing unusual—no signs of occupation or hidden treasure. Tom said you could tell it was just all full of rocks." According to this exploration anyway, the legends of Hole-in-the-Wall cave have been shattered.

The Hole-in-the-Wall cave rests high on a cliff face above Youngs Creek.
PHOTOGRAPH BY JOHN FRALEY.

But another legend about the Bob that was kept hush-hush was confirmed. Smoke said that there were many temporary lookouts sprinkled across the Bob during World War II. One mostly unreported lookout in the Bob perched on top of the Chinese Wall. Smoke said that there was a "lookout station" on Haystack Mountain along the Chinese Wall that was occupied in the 1940s.

Signs still remain on top of the wall where the man had set up camp, right on top of Haystack, just to the left of the trail, including the grounding wires that attached to the tent to divert lightning strikes. For a "garbage can," the lookout used a big crack in the cliff rocks where he threw bottles, cans, and other junk. Even today, if you lie down and shine a flashlight, the junk can be seen 100 feet down in the crack.

This lookout had a special assignment, as did others, during the war. The lookout watched for fires, but he also watched for incendiary

Tom Flowers stands at the entrance to Hole-in-the-Wall.

balloons set afloat in the jet stream by the Japanese. These "Fu-Go" or fire balloon bombs were launched from submarines operating in the Pacific, or from Japan itself, and at the time were the longest-range attacks in the history of warfare.

The balloons, which the Japanese also called "Windship Weapons," were designed to start fires and burn forests, requiring manpower to control the fires. Some of the balloons were equipped with "anti-personnel" bombs. The lookout's job was to shoot down balloons he observed floating in across the Continental Divide. It's not known if this lookout observed any, but Smoke knows of one balloon remnant found by an outfitter in the Danaher. The government kept the whole subject hush-hush, to prevent citizens from becoming worried that the Japanese could penetrate so far into the U.S. mainland.

The Japanese fashioned the balloons from paper, silk, and light wood, and they were kept aloft by hydrogen or helium. Each contained from one to five incendiary bombs suspended around the outside edge. The Imperial Japanese Navy launched more than 9,000 of these unorthodox weapons from the Pacific, and many reached the U.S. mainland. They were designed to instill fear, confusion, and panic. Six people, five of them children, were killed when a balloon detonated on May 5, 1945, in Oregon.

Thirty-two of these balloons reached Montana. There was a mandatory news blackout about the balloons so the Japanese could not learn the results of their launches. One balloon was found near Kalispell by woodcutters, but its discovery was suppressed. One was found hanging in a tree in 1947 near Basin, north of Butte. Outfitter Howard Copenhaver told Smoke that he found remnants of one of the old balloons suspended in a tree in the Danaher. This is the kind of story that Smoke was known for, the kind of story that captivated his guests and enriched their experience.

All told, Smoke has been so lucky to discover his passion in such a wonderful place as the Bob. For many who know him, Smoke and the wilderness are inseparable.

"I feel like I've lived my life in the Bob Marshall," said Smoke, "and I love to see young folks discover it. I got a letter one time about twenty or more years ago. And it was from a young boy, who addressed the letter to 'Bob Marshall, Missoula, Montana.' For some reason or another, they put it in our mailbox. The letter read, 'Dear Bob. I want to come to your wilderness. And I want to bring my sister and my dad and mother. How do I do that?' I framed it. The teacher gave him the assignment to write the letter. I wrote him back several times." The boy's letter was music to his ears. This was another chance to introduce a new generation to his special place.

Smoke's long history in the Bob has become an epic story. It's his home, his church, and his spirit place. Guests say that Smoke makes each of them feel important and special. He loves people, and has inspired his guests, one at a time, to connect to wilderness, each in their own way.

An icon to anyone who loves wilderness, Smoke has shaped the Bob by sharing its legacy and by inspiring so many. And, in turn, the Bob has shaped him. "Wilderness keeps me young in my head and my heart," said Smoke. "When I'm riding a horse in the Bob, I just feel real good inside. The Bob is home. I love it there."

Smoke Elser is happiest on a horse in the wilderness.

PHOTOGRAPH COURTESY OF SMOKE ELSER.

SOURCES

Personal recorded interview by the author with Smoke Elser at his historic barn, February 22, 2019.

Additional interview by the author with Smoke Elser at his barn, April 16, 2019. Many follow-up phone conversations.

Firefly project, Japanese balloons in 1945. California Department of Conservation, online resource. Wikipedia information on Japanese incendiary balloons, online resource.

Doris Huffine diaries, 1930s, regarding Hole-in-the-Wall cave legend, from the Huffine Collection.

14

HEROES OF THE BOB

Spirits

AFTER YOU'VE READ OR EXPERIENCED STORIES traced out on the landscape, you view the land in a different way. When you hike along a stream, through the timber, or over a pass where so much has happened over the years, things feel different—your sense of place changes, maybe you hear whispers of travelers from the past.

Old-timers have left their DNA behind, and their elements cycle through the landscape. Is it that much of a stretch to believe that something of their spirits lingers too?

In late September of 1973, at nineteen years old, I skipped a day of school at the University of Montana and spent a few days in the Bob Marshall Wilderness. Carrying my cheap backpack, I hiked with a friend up the switchbacks to Upper Holland Lake, a quiet tarn about six miles by trail and a few thousand feet up from the trailhead along Holland Lake. We camped for the night. I caught a few nice cutthroat trout that I baked in aluminum foil over coals in the fire. My area of study at UM was Wildlife Biology, Aquatic Option, so of course I was really interested in these high-country trout.

The next morning, I left my friend camped at the lake and, following the trail most traveled, hiked the switchbacks a mile and a half up and over Pendant Pass at about 7,000 feet. Atop this alpine pass stood a tall, rustic sign with a lot of character, marking the entry point into the Bob Marshall Wilderness. I found this really exciting, because I'd

Gordon Pass. PHOTOGRAPH BY JOHN FRALEY.

been reading about Bob Marshall. And the new 1973 wilderness map that I carried featured Bob's picture and a nice writeup about his passion and his exploits.

I sped past Pendant Lake and down into the Big Salmon Creek drainage. Although I would travel this route many times in the future, on this trip it was all new country to me. But, strangely, it felt like I'd traveled through it for years. The alpine benches, shallow lakes, and rivulets just had a familiar feel.

As I neared Pendant Cabin, about four miles down from the pass, my eye caught a big shape walking up to the edge of the trail ahead of me. A huge bull elk in the wilderness is an impressive thing, especially when it's only about thirty yards away. The bull sized me up, just standing there, then spun and slowly trotted off across a little meadow and into the timber. Wow, I thought, I hope I have an encounter like this during big game season.

I swung southeast at the Big Salmon trail junction and strolled along for six miles past the Lena Lake trail and down Shaw Creek to its mouth on Gordon Creek. Nearby, on a flat bench, sits the Shaw Creek Cabin. Gordon Creek is what I like to call a "Cadillac stream." Its waters teem with westslope cutthroat trout, and lower down it's a spawning area for big migratory bull trout. Gordon is a large tributary that feeds a vital flow of water into the upper South Fork of the Flathead.

I dropped a ways below the Shaw Creek Cabin and set up my camp at Shirttail Park, which features a pretty little meadow surrounded by conifers right on the stream bank. The next morning, I fished downstream on Gordon Creek and caught some of the biggest cutts of my life, up to sixteen inches and a couple of pounds. I kept a couple to pack out and took some photos of them near my fly rod along the stream's shore. I was simply in heaven.

The next morning, I pulled camp and hiked the six miles up Gordon Creek and over Gordon Pass. I felt like I could have walked all day and night, I was so excited. A spectacular place, I thought. I made up my mind to do a study of all these waters someday, and I eventually did.

Striding down from Gordon Pass, I again reached Upper Holland Lake and closed the loop.

And that's when the spookiness began.

I ran into an old Forest Service ranger who said he was staying in an old cabin at the upper end of the lake, and we chatted for quite a while. He could see that I loved covering ground in the backcountry. I told him about the cutthroats I caught and the pre–hunting season bull elk I'd seen, right on the trail, and he seemed interested. He had something to say about the elk.

"Well, kid, hunting season's open in this district right now," he said. "In fact, it began a few weeks ago, on September 15."

I was crestfallen. It would have been a slam-dunk shot, and I just let that bull walk away. I could have carried my trusty 6mm Remington and gotten myself a nice bull elk. Of course, it would have been a challenge to bone it and pack it out the ten miles, piece by piece, to the trailhead. But I was young, a runner and a wrestler, and I sure thought I could have done it.

The old hand told me that he would share a secret, only with me. He told me of a pass south of here out of Seeley Lake on the boundary of the Bob, where the wilderness hunting district is only about a five-mile hike in. He said it was great elk country, and most people, who are being outfitted, ride on by, headed farther into the wilderness. He told me to try that spot. I thanked him and hiked around Upper Holland and back down the switchbacks to the trailhead. I had already begun to plan my hunt for a week or so down the line.

But here's the funny thing: I later checked on who that old-timer might have been, but I was told that there wasn't any Forest Service ranger stationed at Upper Holland Lake.

A week or so later, about the second week of October, I was following that hot tip, heading back to the Bob in my good friend's old truck. Terry McCoy was a terrestrial wildlife student at the University of Montana. The previous year, we had lived in the same dorm and shared maybe a dozen backcountry ski trips and hiking trips in the Scapegoat, Bob, Salmon River Mountains, and Bitterroots. We both loved the backcountry. Terry was a work-study student who flew and located elk via radio telemetry for Dr. Bob Ream, who was conducting an elk-logging study in the Sapphire Mountain Range. So, I figured, Terry must know a lot about elk. It turned out that he did, but not in a conventional way.

We reached the trailhead late that evening and began hiking up the switchbacks. At the wilderness boundary, we walked into a big mule deer buck; I had him in my scope, but there just wasn't quite enough light. We continued over the South Fork divide and down the other side to an alpine lake to camp for the night, wildly excited for what the next day might bring.

The next morning, we climbed out of our sleeping bags before dawn. We had planned on starting a fire before going out hunting, but a mysterious elk bugle cut our plans short. As soon as Terry was up, he said, "Did you hear that elk bugle? Come on, let's get going before he moves." I had to admit that I hadn't heard the call. In fact, I thought Terry just imagined he'd heard it. I was skeptical, but I was willing to take his word for it.

We quickly got our packs together and started hiking up the shelf-like alpine benches as dawn broke. "There it is again," Terry said, as we climbed. "It's coming from the other side of that ridge." I'd never had hearing problems, but I couldn't hear that elk bugling. That's great, I thought—Terry was so enthusiastic. But we were not going to top that ridge and see a big bull just standing there, bugling away.

We went over another bench and got up to the ridge where Terry insisted the call of the monarch was coming from. We sneaked up to the crest and looked across a little alpine basin. There, about 150 yards away, stood a big bull elk, head down, feeding on the beargrass slope.

I was astonished. First off, I'd never heard a thing. Second, not only had Terry "heard" the bugle a number of times, but he seemed to know exactly where it came from and led us right to the spot, over the benches and little cliffs, through country in which neither of us had ever set foot.

From a kneeling position, Terry took aim at the bull through his scope and pulled the trigger on his Winchester bolt action .308. Snap, the firing pin did not set off the primer. He levered in another shell—same thing. At this point I was thinking that I should take the shot, then "boom!" his rifle fired on the third attempt.

The bull seemed as surprised as I was. He backed down the slope a few steps, swung around, and stood there, wobbly. Terry fired again and the bull went down. Terry McCoy had bagged himself a six-point bull elk that had bugled a tune only he could hear.

The rest of that day we pieced up the elk and packed it down to our camp near the alpine lake. We boned out one rear leg. We planned to pack out that meat and the loose meat we'd cut off the carcass the next day. On subalpine firs around our camp, we hung the three remaining legs and some loose meat in bags. Terry used his hatchet to remove the skullcap and the nice set of six-point antlers.

On our way back to Missoula after we got out with our backpack loads, we stopped at Clearwater Junction to get gas. Several people complimented Terry on the elk rack, which he had in the back of his pickup. Terry gave me all the meat I packed out that day.

The next day, Terry, with Bob and Cathy Ream, went back up the trail with a couple of horses and packed out the rest of the meat. Cathy hiked up to the carcass and carved more meat off the neck and ribs, so nothing was wasted. Packing out his elk inspired Terry to learn more about packing, and that winter, I remember that he took Smoke

Elser's packing class at Smoke's barn, not far from the Reams' house up the Rattlesnake in Missoula.

Then and now, I've never quite figured out the whole hunt. I'm sure that I didn't hear any elk bugle, and I couldn't figure out any way Terry could have known where that elk was feeding. Maybe someone put that elk there just for him.

Less than a year later, Terry was dead, killed on August 31, 1974, in a small plane crash on Cleveland Mountain while charting elk locations using radio telemetry. Originally, I was to go along on the flight, but the evening before they had to switch planes, so he and a contract pilot flew in a smaller, two-seater aircraft. Terry and I had planned to leave on a backpack trip into Big Salmon Lake later that day when he returned from the flight. I slept in his trailer the night before and heard him grab an apple on his way out the door. I was supposed to meet him after his flight at the Forestry Building on the UM campus. I waited in my little Volkswagen Beetle with our backpacks, but Terry didn't show up at 11 A.M. as planned.

It took several days to find the plane on the heavily timbered mountain ridge in the Sapphire Mountains. I joined the massive ground and air search in the Welcome Creek drainage, but it had turned up nothing. Ream finally spotted a trace of the crash from a helicopter. Four smokejumpers were dropped into the steep, thickly timbered terrain, and they floated down to land in the lodgepole at the crash site. I was at the smokejumper center at the Missoula airport when the jumpers reached the plane. Over the radio, I heard, "No joy on the ground."

I've never felt at peace about Terry's short life, and its influence on my wilderness life. That was almost a half century ago. I've spent a career—a lifetime—enjoying the wilderness that Terry only got to experience for a fleeting few years. Terry was headed for a great career as a wildlife biologist, and his passion for wilderness would have carried him across the Bob and beyond many times.

Terry never got back to that alpine slope in the Bob where he shot the elk meant only for him. Or maybe he did. In fact, I'm pretty sure he did. But that's another part of the overall story that I've been chasing for decades, and I'm saving it for my next book.

Index

Author on Kevan Mountain near Switchback Pass.
PHOTOGRAPH BY KEVIN FRALEY.

About the Author

John Fraley came to Montana as a teenager to attend the University of Montana, where he received a B.S. in Wildlife Biology. He continued his education at Montana State University and received an M.S. in Fish and Wildlife Management. John worked for the state wildlife agency for nearly forty years, mostly in the forks of the Flathead; he retired in 2017. For thirty-four years he has served as an adjunct instructor at Flathead Valley Community College where he teaches wildlife conservation and other courses. John has written three previous books on Flathead pioneers within Glacier National Park and the Bob Marshall Wilderness: *Wild River Pioneers,* in 2008; *Rangers, Trappers, and Trailblazers,* in 2018; and *A Woman's Way West,* rereleased in 2019 by Farcountry Press. Over the years, he has written numerous magazine articles on the history of the Flathead. John's wife, Dana, and children, Kevin, Heather, and Troy, continue to share with him a love of wandering around the backcountry of the three forks of the Flathead.

THE BOB MARSHALL WILDERNESS FOUNDATION connects Americans with their wilderness heritage by providing access to and stewardship of one of the world's most spectacular places—Montana's 1.5-million-acre Bob Marshall Wilderness Complex.

As wilderness icon Robert Marshall wrote in 1928, "…the enjoyment of solitude, complete independence, and the beauty of undefiled panoramas is absolutely essential to happiness." The Foundation helps make these values accessible to all through trail projects and habitat restoration. Each year, hundreds of volunteers learn the value of a land ethic and giving back to the wilderness.

When you purchase a copy of this book, a portion of the proceeds goes directly into the Foundation's work as stewards of this wonderful place we call the "Bob."

Thank you for your support of America's flagship wilderness!

BOB MARSHALL
WILDERNESS
FOUNDATION